A
Complete
INTRODUCTION
to the Bible

Christopher Gilbert

Paulist Press
New York/ Mahwah, NJ

Cover and book design by Lynn Else

Library of Congress Cataloging-in-Publication Data

Gilbert, Christopher P.
  A complete introduction to the Bible / Christopher Gilbert.
    p. cm.
  Includes bibliographical references and index.
  ISBN 978-0-8091-4552-2 (alk. paper)
  1. Bible—Introductions. I. Title.
  BS475.3.G55 2009
  220.6′1—dc22

                                                    2008030907

Published by Paulist Press
997 Macarthur Boulevard
Mahwah, New Jersey 07430

www.paulistpress.com

Printed and bound in the
United States of America

Contents

Contents

And he said, "Go forth, and stand upon the mount before the LORD." And behold, the LORD passed by, and a great and strong wind rent the mountains, and broke in pieces the rocks before the LORD, but the LORD was not in the wind; and after the wind an earthquake, but the LORD was not in the earthquake; and after the earthquake a fire, but the LORD was not in the fire; and after the fire a still small voice. And when Elijah heard it, he wrapped his face in his mantle.

1 Kings 19:11–13 (RSV)

Preface

As is the case with any great work of literature, the extent to which one can appreciate the Bible is linked to the extent to which one understands it. Like many other ancient books, the Bible can be tremendously difficult to understand, especially to one reading it for the first time. Scholars have found that it is easier to understand the Bible when one reads it with an eye toward the historical contexts in which the Bible developed. For this reason, a great deal of scholarship has been devoted to understanding and explaining those historical contexts. Unfortunately, the works of biblical scholars can be daunting to the average reader; there are many such works, those works are often very long, and—since most scholars write for an audience of their fellow scholars—those works often contain academic language and a level of detail that can be overwhelming to nonspecialists.

The purpose of this work is to provide a literary and historical introduction to the Bible for readers who have no previous training in theology, literary analysis, or ancient history. This book is not intended to be comprehensive; some topics are discussed more thoroughly than others, but no topics have been covered exhaustively, and many have been passed over altogether. Instead, this book is intended to serve as a springboard. It is my hope that readers who are interested in learning more about a particular topic will pursue further study of that topic—perhaps by reading some of the works listed in the bibliography.

The ideas presented here represent the cumulative work of biblical scholars spanning the last two centuries. In the course of writing this book, I have thus borrowed ideas from many different scholarly works, all of which are listed in the bibliography.

Whenever I borrowed a specific idea from one author in particular, or depended heavily on a given author's treatment of a subject in writing my own, I have cited that author's work in the endnotes. Unless otherwise noted, all biblical quotations are from the New Revised Standard Version Bible.

Acknowledgments

Without the help of my very talented friends and colleagues, this book would never have come to be. First and foremost, I wish to thank Lenore Erickson, Emerita Instructor of Philosophy at Cuesta College, for giving me thoughtful feedback on early drafts of every part of this work. I am also greatly indebted to Jeff Siker and Thomas Rausch, SJ, both of Loyola Marymount University, for patiently reading and commenting on large portions of the manuscript.

There are many people at Cuesta College whose help I have greatly appreciated. Vice President of Student Learning Harry Schade, Social Sciences Division Chair Randy Gold, and my colleague Peter Dill have all given me invaluable encouragement and support. Kent Brudney and Mark Weber helped me to prepare my book proposal and advised me in my search for a publisher. Jennifer Correa, of the Cuesta College library, obtained countless books and journal articles for me and was thus a tremendous help in my research. Vicki Bursey and Richard Johnson both advised me on finer points of grammar, and Linda Scott came to my rescue innumerable times with her technical expertise.

I am very grateful to everyone at Paulist Press, especially Lawrence Boadt, CSP, Paul McMahon, and most especially Michael Kerrigan, CSP.

Finally, I would like to thank all the students at Cuesta College who have taken my Philosophy 5 course, "Introduction to the Bible." Their thoughtful comments and challenging questions have had a tremendous effect on both the tone and the content of this book.

List of Abbreviations

BIBLICAL AND APOCRYPHAL BOOKS

1–2 Chr	1–2 Chronicles	Job	Job
1–2 Cor	1–2 Corinthians	Joel	Joel
1–2 Kgs	1–2 Kings	Jonah	Jonah
1–2 Pet	1–2 Peter	Josh	Joshua
1–2 Sam	1–2 Samuel	Jude	Jude
1–2 Thess	1–2 Thessalonians	Judg	Judges
1–2 Tim	1–2 Timothy	Lam	Lamentations
1–3 John	1–3 John	Lev	Leviticus
1–4 Macc	1–4 Maccabees	Luke	Luke
Acts	Acts of the Apostles	Mal	Malachi
Amos	Amos	Mic	Micah
Col	Colossians	Mark	Mark
Dan	Daniel	Matt	Matthew
Deut	Deuteronomy	Nah	Nahum
Eccl	Ecclesiastes	Neh	Nehemiah
Eph	Ephesians	Num	Numbers
Esth	Esther	Obad	Obadiah
Exod	Exodus	Phil	Philippians
Ezra	Ezra	Phlm	Philemon
Ezek	Ezekiel	Prov	Proverbs
Gal	Galatians	Ps	Psalms
Gen	Genesis	Rev	Revelation
Hab	Habakkuk	Rom	Romans
Hag	Haggai	Sir	Sirach
Heb	Hebrews	Song	Song of Songs
Hos	Hosea	Titus	Titus

Isa	Isaiah	Tob	Tobit
Jas	James	Zech	Zechariah
Jer	Jeremiah	Zeph	Zephaniah
John	John		

BIBLE TRANSLATIONS

NRSV New Revised Standard Version Bible (1989)
RSV Revised Standard Version Bible, Second Edition (1971)

Part I
INTRODUCTION

1

The Bible as Literature and as History

I. THREE WAYS OF APPROACHING THE BIBLE

Before we begin our discussion of the Bible, it is important that the reader have a clear idea of the nature and purpose of this book. In order to achieve this, it will be helpful to consider some of the various ways in which different people approach the Bible.

The Devotional Approach

Some people take what may be called a devotional approach to the Bible. This is the approach taken by those who look to the Bible as a source of inspiration and guidance. Those who take a devotional approach to the Bible typically practice either the Jewish or the Christian faith, and they regard the Bible as having a transcendent origin and value—that is, they believe that the biblical authors were divinely inspired to write the Bible as they did. Some who take a devotional approach to the Bible regard the Bible as historically accurate, and so read the Bible literally; those who believe that historical events occurred exactly as they are related in the Bible are thus called literalists. On the other hand, many people who take a devotional approach to the Bible do so without believing that the Bible must be regarded as true in the literal sense—that is, as historically accurate in all its claims. Such people believe that the Bible's truths lie more in its themes than in its account of historical events.

The Deflationary Approach

A very different way of approaching the Bible is what we might call the deflationary approach. One could be said to take a deflationary approach to the Bible if one's sole purpose in studying the Bible is to undermine or deflate the Bible's importance and value. For example, a student of the philosopher Karl Marx might argue that the Bible is merely a form of capitalist propaganda that encourages economically oppressed people to anticipate a pleasant existence in the afterlife—and thus to accept their lowly economic situation in this life. Similarly, a student of the psychoanalyst Sigmund Freud might argue that the Bible is nothing more than a complicated form of wish fulfillment; human beings invented religion as a way of making themselves feel more secure, and the Bible is simply one part of this elaborate self-deception. The goal in any deflationary approach to the Bible is to deny the possibility that the Bible might have a transcendent origin and value.

The Academic Approach

Distinct from both the devotional and the deflationary approaches is what we shall call the academic approach to the Bible. The academic approach is concerned with raising and answering questions about the Bible. Some of these questions are literary in nature, having to do with the Bible's contents, themes, and literary styles. Other questions are historical: Who wrote the Bible? When? Where? For whom? Under what circumstances? The academic approach thus regards the Bible as a work that was produced, preserved, and transmitted by human beings, and its goal is to understand as much as possible about the various stages of the Bible's development. Yet this interest in answering literary and historical questions about the Bible is not aimed at undermining the Bible's importance or its meaning. On the contrary, the academic approach to the Bible remains open to the possibility that the Bible has a transcendent origin and value. In other words, a person who approaches the Bible academically neither assumes that the Bible is divinely inspired nor assumes that the Bible is not divinely inspired, but instead remains neutral on this issue.

This book will take the academic approach to the Bible. Our goal will be to understand what biblical scholars have said about the Bible, and why. This will require us to be willing to think the way biblical scholars do when they are thinking about the Bible, which means trying to achieve and maintain a certain form of scientific objectivity. Scholars who are concerned with historical questions about the Bible must consider and weigh data provided by ancient texts (both biblical and nonbiblical), by historians, by archaeologists, by sociologists, and so on. Because they do not wish their evaluation of such data to be unduly tainted by their own personal beliefs and commitments, scholars attempt to distinguish what they may believe on faith from what they are able to assert based on objective, empirical evidence. Like such scholars, we must also be willing to "bracket" our own beliefs and consider the scholarly theories with scientific detachment.

At this point the reader might ask, what is the value of this academic approach to the Bible? After all, one need not approach the Bible academically in order to find it meaningful and valuable. Indeed, most Jews and Christians throughout history have derived inspiration from the Bible without subjecting it to literary or historical analysis. Does this not suggest that the academic approach to the Bible is, at best, an unnecessary exercise in scholarly eggheadedness or, at worst, a dangerous distraction from the response to the Bible that persons of faith regard as most appropriate—namely, devotion?

Three Reasons for Taking the Academic Approach

It is certainly true that one need not take the academic approach to the Bible in order to find the Bible meaningful and valuable. But this is not to say that the academic approach does not have its own meaning and value. On the contrary, there are at least three reasons why the academic approach to the Bible is important—even for persons of faith.[1] First, it is difficult to understand *any* ancient text without some sense of the historical context

5

in which that text was written, the meaning of the text's words in their original language, and so on. What is true of ancient texts in general is no less true of the Bible. Indeed, for persons of faith, understanding what a biblical author was trying to say to his or her contemporary (ancient) audience is crucial to a complete understanding and appreciation of the Bible, since that ancient author's intended message was surely part of what Jews and Christians believe is the Deity's inspired communication with human beings.

Second, both Judaism and Christianity—the religions that are based on the Bible—need some means of refuting misinterpretations of their scriptures. Literary and historical analysis of the Bible can shed light on what the biblical authors' words may have meant, what they most probably meant, and what they most certainly did not mean. Thus, the academic approach can provide good reasons for rejecting interpretations of the Bible that are clearly misguided.

Third, people who practice the Jewish faith or the Christian faith sometimes feel the desire or the need to justify the beliefs of their respective religious communities, both to themselves and to those outside their communities. In doing so, they often appeal to biblical evidence. But the Bible is not accepted as an authoritative source—indeed, it typically is not accepted as even a credible source—by those who are not members of the Jewish or Christian communities, that is, by those who do not share the faith experience of Jews or Christians. For this reason, it is beneficial to Jewish and Christian believers to develop methods of understanding and interpreting the Bible that satisfy the rational standards of the secular world. The academic approach to the Bible provides such methods.

The Goal

Our goal in this book will be to put aside temporarily whatever views we may have about the Bible and to see it as scholars try to see it, namely, as a work that was produced—at least in part—by human beings about whom we can raise historical questions, questions to which we may seek answers that can be supported by the available evidence. But it is important to bear in mind that the purpose of this book is not to undermine or even to challenge anyone's religious beliefs. The scholars whose theories we shall be studying certainly do not wish to challenge or undermine faith, since most of them are devoutly religious people—they are theologians, rabbis, priests, nuns, ministers, and so on. Rather, the aim of biblical scholarship, and thus of this book, is to make it possible for both religious and nonreligious persons to have *informed* views about the Bible and its history.

II. THE BIBLE AS A LITERARY WORK

While scholars have many different ways of studying the Bible, the methods that will be employed in this book can be divided into two categories: literary criticism and historical criticism. Literary criticism is the means by which scholars study the Bible as a piece of literature, a work of art. Historical criticism is the means by which scholars attempt to answer questions about the Bible's history. This section will introduce the basic questions and concepts of literary criticism; the next section will introduce historical criticism.

To think of the Bible as a literary work is to think of it as a work of art, an expression of meaning. When we study the Bible as a work of art, we are concerned with such things as its content, its themes, and the various literary styles found within it. Such literary questions are said to be synchronic—meaning "with time"—because we answer them by immersing ourselves in the text and reading it on its own terms; that is, we read it as if we were there when the words were written, reacting to the ideas those words express.[2] Our goal in this section is to gain a sense of just what we mean when we talk about the Bible as a work of art.

The word *Bible* literally means "books"; it is derived from the Greek word *biblia,* which referred to the scrolls on which ancient peoples did their writing. Today, we use the word *Bible* to refer to those writings that were collected and preserved as the scriptures (sacred writings) of the Jewish and Christian communities. Thus, the Bible is actually a number of distinct books that have been put together over a long period of time.

The Jewish Scriptures

The twenty-four books of the Bible that constitute the Jewish scriptures are collectively called the *Tanak*.* This name derives from the Hebrew names for the three main subdivisions of the Jewish scriptures: the *Torah* (Law); the *Neviim* (Prophets); and the *Kethuvim* (Writings). The word *Tanak* itself has no translation, because it is an acronym: *Torah* + *Neviim* + *Kethuvim* = T + N + K = TaNaK. The Torah (Law) is made up of the first five books of the Bible: Genesis, Exodus, Leviticus, Numbers, and Deuteronomy. Because it contains five books, the Torah is also called the Pentateuch, from the Greek expression meaning "five parts." The Torah tells the story of the prehistory of the nation of Israel, beginning with the creation of the world and ending with the arrival of the Israelites at the promised land of Canaan, later known as Palestine. The Neviim (Prophets) divide into the Former Prophets and the Latter Prophets. The Former Prophets (Joshua, Judges, 1&2 Samuel, 1&2 Kings) offer an interpretive history of the nation of Israel during a period when prophets were important advisors to the leaders of that nation. The Latter Prophets themselves divide into two categories: the Major Prophets (Isaiah, Jeremiah, Ezekiel) and the twelve Minor Prophets, which are also collectively referred to as the Scroll of the Twelve. The books of the Latter Prophets are those in which the actual teachings of prophets are said to have been recorded, either by the prophets themselves or, in some cases, by their followers. The Kethuvim (Writings) include a number of different types of literature, such as poetry, wisdom lore, and short stories.

The Christian Scriptures

The Christian scriptures divide into the Old Testament and the New Testament. The books that Christians call the Old Testament include the books of the Jewish scriptures, though they are arranged in a different order. In other words, all the books of the Tanak are

---

* The twenty-four books of the Hebrew Bible become thirty-nine books in the Christian Bible because the latter divides the books differently. For instance, the Hebrew book of Samuel is divided into two books—1 Samuel and 2 Samuel—in the Christian Bible.

regarded as sacred by both Jews and Christians. There are also a number of other books (or sections of books) that are not part of the Jewish scriptures, but which some Christians consider to be part of the Old Testament. Those Christians who consider these works to be part of the Old Testament—primarily Roman Catholic and Eastern Orthodox Christians—refer to them as the Deuterocanon (second canon); those who do not consider these works to be part of the Old Testament—mainly Protestant Christians—refer to them as the Apocrypha (hidden writings).

The other part of the Christian scriptures, the New Testament, consists of twenty-seven early Christian writings. These writings can be divided into four types. First, the New Testament contains four gospels (Matthew, Mark, Luke, and John), which are narrative accounts of the life and teachings of the founder of Christianity, Jesus of Nazareth. Second, the Acts of the Apostles is a narrative history of the early Christian church. Third, the New Testament contains twenty-one epistles (letters). Most of these letters are attributed to the apostle Paul, and are thus called the Pauline epistles. Finally, the New Testament contains one apocalyptic work, the Book of Revelation, which presents us with a vision of cataclysmic events preceding the end of time.

Development of the Canon

Many of the books contained in the Bible began as oral traditions; rather than being recorded on paper, the stories preserved in the Bible were first passed from person to person by word of mouth. Eventually, the stories were written down, copied, and translated into different languages. The Bible contains the books that it does because, at various points in its history, it has gone through a process called canonization. Canonization is the means by which a community adopts a text as authoritative or sacred; in other words, a canonical text is one that a community regards as having been divinely inspired. A collection of such works is called a canon.* The

---

* The English word *canon* derives from the Greek *kanon*, which itself derived from the Hebrew *qaneh*. The Hebrew term *qaneh*, which literally means "reed," was used to refer to a straight stick that could be used as a measuring device. Thus, generally speaking, a canon is a standard of excellence against which things may be measured.

process by which the books of the Bible achieved canonical status seems to have been very informal; in other words, it is *not* the case that the biblical texts became canonized because some sort of governing body within a religious community passed judgment on them and declared them to be authoritative. Rather, the biblical texts typically became canonized because so many people in a community regarded them as authoritative that their use became widespread; once most of the people in a community were using a text as part of their worship, and agreed that the text was important, then that text was considered part of the canon.

Because different parts of the Bible were written at different times, they also achieved canonical status at different times. The first part of the Hebrew scriptures to be canonized was the Torah (Law); the Jewish community had come to regard the Torah as authoritative by as early as 400 BCE.* The Neviim (Prophets) achieved canonical status sometime in the second century (200–100) BCE. Various parts of the Kethuvim (Writings) were canonized at different times, but the entire canon of Hebrew scriptures (Torah, Neviim, and Kethuvim) as we have it today seems to have been fixed by the end of the second century CE. Of the New Testament books, the first to achieve canonical status were the Pauline epistles, which Christians had come to regard as scripture between 150 and 200 CE. The four New Testament gospels were also regarded as canonical by the end of the second century CE, but the entire twenty-seven-book New Testament as we have it now did not achieve canonical status until late in the fourth century CE.[3]

Approaching the Bible as a literary work will require us to ask the same sort of questions about it that we might ask about any work of art, such as a novel. For instance, we shall want to discuss the themes, characters, setting, and plot of the various stories in the Bible. Analysis of these elements of stories is called narrative criticism.[4] We shall also want to understand the various types of literature by which the biblical authors convey their ideas. This

---

* As do many contemporary biblical scholars, we shall use the abbreviations BCE (Before the Common Era) and CE (Common Era) instead of the theologically loaded BC (Before Christ) and AD (*anno Domini*, "in the year of the Lord").

will involve identifying and analyzing a number of different literary forms, such as myths, legends, short stories, songs, and so on. The study of such literary forms is called rhetorical criticism. Narrative criticism and rhetorical criticism are both examples of literary criticism, for they are means by which scholars try to achieve a better understanding of the Bible as a work of art.

III. THE BIBLE AS A PART OF HISTORY

To regard the Bible as a part of history is to regard it as a product of historical events. It is to realize that the development of the Bible is a part of human history. At various points in the distant past, various human beings wrote, collected, edited, copied, and translated the many different books of the Bible. Thus, regarding the Bible as a part of human history means raising questions about who these people were, when and where they lived, and why they wrote what they wrote. Such questions are said to be diachronic—meaning "through time"—for they reflect an awareness that the Bible is something that has developed over the course of history. Answering such questions means placing both the production of the Bible and the events recounted in the Bible in their historical contexts.

Israel's History

The Bible tells the story of the nation of Israel. When we speak of the nation of Israel, we do not mean the modern political state of Israel or the land that that state occupies (which in ancient times was called Canaan and, later, Palestine). Rather, the nation of Israel is a group of people, namely, the twelve tribes that claimed to have descended from a single ancestor, Jacob (who was also known as Israel). Since our interest in the Bible as a part of history involves a desire to place the events recounted in the Bible in their historical context, we shall need to learn something about the historical periods in which the biblical stories are set. The events recounted in the Bible occurred over a very long stretch of time, so we shall be concerned with a number of distinct his-

11

torical periods. The table below gives a brief overview of these historical periods. Note that all dates are approximate!

1750–1300 BCE	Ancestral Period	Israel's ancestors migrate from Mesopotamia to Palestine.
1300–1250 BCE	Mosaic Period	Some of the people who would become the nation of Israel are enslaved in Egypt. They eventually escape and migrate back to Palestine.
1250–1020 BCE	Period of the Judges	The tribes of Israel struggle to gain control of Palestine.
1020–922 BCE	United Kingdom	Israel becomes a unified monarchy under the rule of kings Saul, David, and Solomon. Jerusalem becomes the kingdom's capital city, and a great Temple is constructed there.
922–722 BCE	Divided Kingdom	Israel splits into two rival kingdoms; ten tribes in the northern part of Palestine form a kingdom called Israel, and the remaining two tribes in the south form a kingdom called Judah.
722–586 BCE	Southern Kingdom	The northern kingdom of Israel is conquered by Assyria in 722 BCE; the southern kingdom of Judah (which includes Jerusalem) survives.
586–539 BCE	Babylonian Exile	In 586 BCE, the southern kingdom of Judah is conquered by the Babylonians, who destroy Jerusalem and its Temple and take many of the Jews into forced exile in Babylon.

539–333 BCE	Persian Period	In 539 BCE, Babylon is conquered by Cyrus the Great of Persia, who allows the Jews to return to Palestine and rebuild Jerusalem and the Temple.
333–166 BCE	Hellenistic Period	In 333 BCE, Alexander the Great and his Greek armies conquer Persia, Palestine, and Egypt.
166–63 BCE	Hasmonaean Dynasty	The Jewish Hasmonaean family leads a successful revolt against the Seleucid Empire (Alexander's successors in Syria, who were in control of Palestine at the time). Israel achieves autonomy, which lasts for a century.
63 BCE	Roman Period Begins	Troops of the Roman Empire, under the command of General Pompey, occupy Palestine and establish Roman control of the Near East.
6–4 BCE	Roman Period	Jesus of Nazareth is born.
29–33 CE	Roman Period	Jesus of Nazareth is executed.
66–73 CE	Roman Period	Jews revolt against Roman occupation forces; in 70 CE, the Romans level Jerusalem and destroy the second Jerusalem Temple.

Scholars' Methods

Scholars have a number of methods by which to answer historical questions about the Bible. First, scholars seeking to understand who wrote the Bible, and how and when that writing took place, can study the Bible itself for internal clues regarding the process by which the Bible developed. For example, traditions criticism seeks to reconstruct, as accurately as possible, the original oral versions of the stories that were later recorded in the Bible. Similarly, source criticism attempts to identify the written sources to which biblical authors might have appealed for information and/or as literary models. Finally, redaction criticism attempts to discern how various texts were redacted (edited) into their final form. We shall see examples of these types of criticism as we examine individual books of the Bible.

Second, scholars can seek to answer questions about the historical context in which the Bible was written, and about the events the Bible recounts, by appeal to the empirical historical method. This method provides a way of approaching the study of history scientifically. Like the empirical method used in the natural sciences, the empirical historical method involves both the formulation of hypotheses—theoretical explanations of how and why things happened—and the careful consideration of empirical evidence. For historians, empirical evidence takes the form of data provided by ancient documents, archaeological discoveries, and insights into human nature provided by such sciences as anthropology and sociology. Thus, the biblical scholar who approaches the Bible historically seeks to explain both the production of the Bible itself and the events described in the Bible by means of a theory that is supported by the best available evidence.

The various means of literary and historical analysis described above are favored by those scholars who take the academic approach to the Bible. Since our goal is to gain an understanding of and appreciation for the Bible from the academic perspective, most of the ideas we shall discuss will be conclusions drawn by scholars who have applied these methods in their studies of the Bible. In the next chapter, we shall briefly survey the history of biblical interpretation, charting the development of the methods of literary criticism and historical criticism that are used by many modern biblical scholars.

2

A Brief History of Biblical Interpretation

While historical criticism is a relatively recent development in biblical analysis, efforts to interpret the Bible date all the way back to biblical times. Indeed, some parts of the Jewish and Christian scriptures are themselves interpretations of scriptures. For instance, the two books of Chronicles in the Tanak are largely a reworking of material from the books of Samuel and Kings. Galatians 4:21–26 contains the apostle Paul's interpretation of the story of Hagar and Sarah (in Gen 16) as speaking of two covenants, one based on the Jewish law, the other based on Christian beliefs about Jesus. The seventh chapter of the Letter to the Hebrews interprets the significance for Christians of the mysterious character of Melchizedek, who is mentioned at Genesis 14:17–20.

This chapter will present a brief summary of how people in different historical periods have read and understood the Bible. Because the history of biblical interpretation spans a great length of time, and encompasses the work of many individual interpreters, our discussion can be no more than a survey that highlights some of the most significant contributions to biblical studies. In other words, the history of biblical interpretation presented here is by no means exhaustive!

I. EARLY JEWISH INTERPRETATION

Even before the canon of Hebrew scriptures was fully established, Jewish thinkers and writers began producing works that were not simply copies of the Hebrew scriptures, but rather interpretations of those scriptures.[1] The first effort at such interpretation was probably the production of the *targumim* (plural of *targum*, the Aramaic word for translation or interpretation). Written in the last few centuries BCE, the *targumim* were translations of the Hebrew scriptures into Aramaic, the language commonly spoken throughout the Near East at that time. But rather than being simply word-for-word translations, the *targumim* often paraphrase the original Hebrew, and they even add material that was not contained in the Hebrew versions of the scriptures.

Midrash

From about the first to the fifth centuries CE, Jewish rabbis also produced many interpretations of the Hebrew scriptures. The most common type of rabbinic interpretations were the *midrashim* (plural of *midrash*, the Hebrew word for inquiry or investigation). The *midrashim* were commentaries on the Hebrew scriptures, most of which were written between 70 and 500 CE, although later rabbis continued to add material to them. The goal of the *midrashim* was both to explain any unclear or obscure passages in the scriptures, and also to interpret the meaning of the scriptures in a way that made clear how their themes were relevant to a contemporary (first- to fifth-century CE) audience. The rabbis who produced the *midrashim* believed that any given passage of scripture could mean many different things at the same time, and their commentaries on biblical passages often explored multiple possible meanings—even, in some instances, contradictory meanings.

Mishnah

Another major rabbinic work was the *Mishnah*, a collection of sixty-three essays that interpret the Jewish religious laws. These essays are divided into six sections, each of which deals with a particular area of the Jewish law: agriculture, feast days, marriage and divorce, tort law (payment of damages), Temple sacrifice, and ritual purity. The essays that make up the *Mishnah* were compiled and edited by Rabbi Judah the Patriarch of Palestine around 200 CE, but most of the material contained in them was probably developed between 70 and 135 CE. Later rabbis produced a large commentary on the *Mishnah* known as the *Talmud*. In addition to analyzing and interpreting the *Mishnah*, the *Talmud* also offers interpretations of the Hebrew scriptures and edifying stories about particular rabbis. There are two versions of the *Talmud:* the Palestinian *Talmud*, which was completed in the fifth century CE, and the Babylonian *Talmud*, which was completed in the sixth century CE.

Philo

A discussion of early Jewish biblical interpretation would not be complete without mention of Philo, a Jewish theologian and philosopher who lived in Alexandria, Egypt, from roughly 15 BCE to 50 CE. In his commentaries on the Torah, Philo interprets the Jewish scriptures allegorically—that is, as having a deeper meaning than is evident in the words themselves. His reason for doing so lies in the fact that Philo was strongly influenced by ancient Greek philosophy, especially that of Plato (428–348 BCE). Thus, Philo's goal in interpreting the Torah allegorically was to show that the ideas contained in the Jewish holy books were compatible with the rationally derived conclusions of philosophy. For example, in his commentary on the creation of heaven and earth in the Book of Genesis, Philo takes heaven—which is not physical—to represent the human mind or power of reason, and earth—which is physical—to represent the human body (or, more specifically, the body's power of sensation). He thus interprets the biblical Creation story as meaning that the very two parts that Plato had said constitute a human being—namely, a reasoning mind and a sensing body—were created by God. This method of interpreting the Jewish scriptures allegorically, pioneered by Philo of Alexandria, would have a profound influence on the earliest Christian interpreters of the Bible.

II. EARLY CHRISTIAN INTERPRETATION

The early period of Christian biblical interpretation, from roughly the second through the fifth centuries CE, is often referred to as the patristic period (from the Latin word for father, *pater*). This is because the men who produced the most influential Christian interpretations of scripture during this period eventually came to be revered as fathers of the church.[2]

Efforts to Understand the Tanak

The earliest Christian interpreters of the Bible were guided by the practical needs of the early Christian church, which included preaching, instructing new converts, and defending the faith against both nonbelievers and heretics (holders of distorted Christian beliefs). For this reason, most of the earliest Christian efforts at biblical interpretation were directed toward the Hebrew scriptures; early Christian writers like Justin Martyr (100–165 CE) and Tertullian (160–225 CE) were primarily concerned to find passages in the Tanak that could be interpreted as referring to—and thus foretelling—the coming of Jesus of Nazareth. This effort required early Christian interpreters to read the Hebrew scriptures in a way that went far beyond the literal meaning of the words themselves. Indeed, much of the biblical interpretation carried out by the early fathers of the church was typological. A typological interpretation is one that takes the persons and events discussed in a text as types or symbols that represent later persons and events. Thus, early Christian interpreters read stories in the Tanak as symbolically foreshadowing events in the gospel accounts of the life of Jesus. An example of this interpretive method would be to regard Jonah's three days and nights in the belly of a fish (Jonah 1:17) as foreshadowing the three days and nights that passed, according to the gospels, between the death and resurrection of Jesus.

Origen

One of the most prolific writers of the early Christian church was Origen (185–254 CE), head of a Christian theological school in Alexandria. Origen believed that the Hebrew scriptures contained much more meaning for Christians than was evident in the words themselves, and thus offered an allegorical interpretation of those scriptures intended to make their underlying meaning clear and relevant to his Christian contemporaries. The third- and fourth-century theologians who succeeded Origen at Alexandria continued to follow his example of interpreting the Hebrew scriptures allegorically, but they also engaged in other forms of literary criticism, such as philology, which is the study of the meaning and grammar of the Hebrew scriptures in their original language.

The School at Antioch

In the third century CE, another Christian theological school was established in Antioch, Syria. To a certain extent, the school at Antioch emerged as a reaction against the school at Alexandria. For, while the theologians at Antioch agreed with those at Alexandria that the Hebrew scriptures had a deeper meaning for Christians than the literal meaning of the texts suggests, they generally believed that the Alexandrian theologians went a bit overboard in their allegorical interpretations of the Tanak. Thus, Antiochene theologians such as Lucian of Samosata (who died around 312 CE), Diodorus of Tarsus (who died around 392 CE), John Chrysostom (347–407 CE), and Theodore of Mopsuestia (350–428 CE) focused on the fact that human authors had written the Hebrew scriptures for particular audiences at particular times, and asked what meaning those authors had intended their words to have for their audiences. In other words, the theologians at Antioch were more concerned than those at Alexandria with trying to understand the Hebrew scriptures in their historical contexts.

Augustine

The last major figure of the patristic period, and the theologian who would have the most lasting influence of all the fathers of the church, was Augustine of Hippo (354–430 CE). Augustine believed that all the most important questions about human existence were answered, either literally or figuratively, in the Hebrew and Christian scriptures. But he also believed that the Bible could be very difficult to understand correctly. He thus argued that the scriptures needed to be interpreted by theologians who could read them in their original languages, and who had been trained in logic and rhetoric (the studies of argumentation and persuasive speech, respectively). Augustine also called attention to problems that arise in a strictly literal reading of the New Testament gospels. Since the gospels disagree with each other on points of chronology, Augustine argued that they should be understood as "recollections" of events, not as strictly chronological histories. Similarly, since the gospels do not always agree with each other in the words they attribute to Jesus, Augustine argued that the gospels should be regarded as recording, not verbatim accounts of Jesus' actual words, but merely the basic sense or meaning of things Jesus said.

III. MEDIEVAL AND REFORMATION INTERPRETATIONS

Throughout the medieval period—roughly the fifth through the fifteenth centuries CE—Jewish and Christian thinkers alike turned increasingly to philology and philosophy as means of interpreting and understanding the Bible.[3] In this period, biblical interpreters gained a clearer understanding of the vocabulary and grammar of biblical Hebrew and Greek, which helped them to appreciate more fully the meaning of the original biblical texts.

Medieval Jewish and Christian theologians also sought to reconcile the truths of their respective faiths with the conclusions of the ancient Greek philosophers. Their reason for doing so was based in the idea that there is only one truth; while revealed scriptures and rational arguments may pursue that truth by different means—and may even seem to contradict each other—the scriptures and human reason must ultimately arrive at the same conclusions. Demonstrating this compatibility between faith and reason often required medieval theologians to interpret the Bible in ways that went beyond the literal meaning of the texts. Thus, medieval Jewish and Christian thinkers generally agreed that scripture had multiple meanings and could be read in many different ways.

Maimonides

The most influential Jewish theologian of the medieval period was Rabbi Moses Maimonides (Moshe ben Maimon), who lived from 1135 to 1204. Maimonides was born in Spain but later settled in Fostat (Old Cairo) in Egypt. Having lived most of his life in countries ruled by Arabic Muslims, Maimonides was well versed in the works of such Arabic philosophers as Avicenna (980–1037) and Averroes (1126–98), who were themselves strongly influenced by the ancient Greek philosopher Aristotle (384–322 BCE). Thus, Maimonides offered interpretations of the Hebrew scriptures aimed at demonstrating that the biblically based beliefs of the Jewish faith are compatible with the doctrines of Aristotelian philosophy. For instance, Maimonides argued that the God whose existence is revealed in the Tanak could also be proved to exist by rational argument from Aristotelian principles.

The Christian Approach

Like their Jewish counterparts, medieval Christian theologians also sought to reconcile the beliefs of their faith with the rational conclusions of Platonic and/or Aristotelian philosophy, and thus interpreted the scriptures as containing multiple layers of meaning. Most medieval Christian interpreters regarded the Bible as having four distinct senses: (1) the literal or historical sense; (2) the allegorical sense; (3) the moral or anthropological sense; and (4) the eschatological sense, which has to do with God's ultimate plan for human beings at the end of time. This distinction had first been made by John Cassian (360–435), who explained that scriptural references to Jerusalem could be understood as (1) literal references to a city in Palestine; (2) allegorical references to the Christian church; (3) anthropological references to the human soul; and (4) eschatological references to heaven.

The Reformation

Whereas medieval Christian theologians often engaged in biblical interpretation for the express purpose of justifying the doctrines of the Catholic (Universal) Christian Church, the Reformation of the sixteenth century was largely a reaction against the centralized authority of that church. A key premise in the reformers' arguments was the principle of *sola scriptura* (scripture alone), the idea that Christian faith should rest not on the traditions or doctrines of the church, but on the Bible itself. For this reason, the reformers focused on the literal meaning of the biblical texts; they were skeptical of allegorical readings of scripture, and they denounced the medieval distinction between four different senses of scripture as misguided. Leaders of the reform movement such as Martin Luther (1483–1546), Ulrich Zwingli (1484–1531), and John Calvin (1509–64) studied the Bible in its original languages, paying careful attention to grammar, wording, and historical context. Because the different reformers all approached the Bible from their own theological perspectives, they ended up producing quite different—indeed, often conflicting—interpretations of the scriptures. Nonetheless, the reformers' attempts to understand the Bible in both literary and historical terms helped to pave the way for the still-more-critical biblical studies yet to come.

IV. MODERN BIBLICAL INTERPRETATION

The trends in biblical interpretation that would ultimately give rise to the emergence of historical criticism began in the seventeenth and eighteenth centuries.[4] At this time, a number of factors encouraged scholars to think about the Bible in new ways. One of these factors was philosophical; as seventeenth-century philosophical movements such as Rationalism and Empiricism focused more and more on theories of human knowledge (raising questions about what constitutes knowledge, how knowledge is attained, and so on), scholars began to think more critically about the status of the Bible as a source of historical information. Another factor was the scientific revolution that occurred during the seventeenth and eighteenth centuries; because empirical science was able to understand and explain the physical world so successfully, many people—scholars and nonscholars alike—came to regard the world as scientists understood it, namely, as a set of physical things and processes wholly governed by natural laws. On this understanding of the world, many people began to regard biblical stories about angels, miracles, and the like as difficult to believe.

Early Pioneers

Thus, in the seventeenth and eighteenth centuries, thinkers began studying the Bible in more critical ways than it had ever been studied before. One such thinker was Richard Simon (1638–1712), often regarded as the father of modern biblical criticism. Simon approached the Bible as one would any ancient literary work, and was thus the first person to produce a study of the Bible based solely on literary and historical analysis (as opposed to theological interpretation). Another early pioneer in modern biblical criticism was Johann Semler (1721–91). Semler distinguished the ideas or themes of the Bible, which he regarded as divinely revealed and thus infallible, from the *words* by which those ideas and themes had been expressed, which are the work of human authors and thus fallible. Such a distinction enabled Semler (and others) to study the biblical books as parts of human history, as things that emerged and changed over time, without thereby denying that those books were sacred. A third important figure in eighteenth-century biblical studies was Hermann Reimarus (1694–1768). Reimarus was a deist, meaning that he believed in the existence of a deity but not in divine revelation or miracles. Thus, in his studies of the Bible, Reimarus questioned any and all stories that seemed to conflict with a rational, scientific view of the world. For this reason, he distinguished between what he called the Jesus of history (a person who actually existed) and the Christ of faith (the main character of the gospels, to whom Christians attribute divine status).* Reimarus's study of the gospels led him to conclude that the Jesus of history was a Jewish revolutionary who had been crucified by the Roman authorities, while the Christ of faith was a deception invented by Jesus' followers after his death. Although all serious biblical scholars now reject Reimarus's conclusions, he is significant because of

---

* This distinction will be discussed at length in chapter 10.

the method he used: Reimarus distinguished the historical data contained in the Bible from the biblical authors' theological interpretation of that data. Even if Reimarus's theory on the origin of Christianity was incorrect, that theory "could be answered only by theologians allowing themselves to be drawn on to Reimarus's rational ground, and arguing *historically,* [that is,] non-supernaturally.... Once a devastating rational hypothesis had been presented it could only by countered by better historical hypotheses."[5]

The Nineteenth Century

The historical criticism in which many contemporary biblical scholars engage came into prominence in the nineteenth century. The classic formulation of its method and purpose was given in 1817 by Wilhelm de Wette (1780–1849). Because he regarded the events recounted in the Bible as historical phenomena, de Wette thought that they should be subject to the same types of study as any other historical events. He thus argued that biblical criticism should be both literary and historical. Literary criticism of the Bible should focus on the Bible's content (language, style, genre, and so on). Historical criticism, on the other hand, should focus on the Bible as a set of historical documents, and thus seek to answer questions regarding the context in which those documents were written: Who wrote them? When? Where? Under what circumstances? This latter effort, de Wette thought, could and should appeal to sources of information beyond the Bible, such as archaeology.

New Gospel Insights

Applications of this method of historical criticism led to a number of significant advances in biblical studies during the nineteenth century. One such advance had to do with the authorship of the New Testament gospels. In 1838, two scholars published works on the books of Matthew, Mark, and Luke. Christian Wilke (1786–1854) compared the Greek texts of the three gospels to each other in parallel columns. Noting that both Matthew and Luke contain virtually all the material found in Mark, but that Mark does not contain all the material found in Matthew and

Luke, Wilke argued that Mark was written first, and that Matthew and Luke both used Mark as a source for their own gospels. Christian Weisse (1801–66) agreed with Wilke that Mark was written before Matthew or Luke, but noted that Matthew and Luke also share material in common with each other that is missing in Mark. He thus argued that Matthew and Luke made use of two distinct sources in writing their gospels: one was the Gospel of Mark, the other was a (now lost) collection of sayings attributed to Jesus. Since its classic formulation in 1863 by H. J. Holtzmann, this theory has been known as the Two Source Hypothesis.*

The Documentary Hypothesis

Another major advance in nineteenth-century biblical criticism was the development of the Documentary Hypothesis, a theory about the authorship of the Hexateuch (the first six books of the Tanak—the Torah plus the Book of Joshua). The Documentary Hypothesis, to which many biblical scholars contributed, argues that the Hexateuch is a compilation of four distinct works, which are usually referred to by the single letters J, D, E, and P. The most complete version of the Documentary Hypothesis was developed by Julius Wellhausen (1844–1918). Wellhausen's significant contribution to this theory was the chronological order in which he arranged the writing of these four sources. The stories related in the Hexateuch all take place early in the history of Israel, long before the Babylonian Exile. For this reason, biblical scholars had generally assumed that these books were the earliest of the biblical books to have been written. In order to test this assumption, Wellhausen conducted a careful study of other biblical books, some of which are thought to have been written prior to the Exile, some of which are thought to have been written after it. He concluded that the P source—from which came many of the religious laws of Judaism, including virtually all of the Book of Leviticus—was not written until *after* the Babylonian Exile, on the grounds that there is evidence of these laws in the postexilic writings, but

---

* A later and more fully developed version of this theory, called the Four Source Hypothesis, will be discussed in chapter 11.

not in those biblical works written prior to the Exile. Wellhausen's version of the Documentary Hypothesis thus forced biblical scholars to rethink both the history of Israel's religious institutions and the chronology they assigned to the writing of the biblical books.*

Twentieth-century Advances

Thus, by the late nineteenth century, historical criticism had become a widely accepted method of biblical analysis among scholars. In the twentieth century, the application of that method would become increasingly effective, largely as the result of significant advances in other fields. The sciences of archaeology, ethnology, sociology, and anthropology provided biblical scholars with a clearer understanding of biblical peoples, lands, languages, and events. By the late twentieth century, historical criticism had joined literary criticism as one of the interpretive tools of choice for many biblical scholars, both Jewish and Christian. Because historical criticism was developed primarily by Christian scholars, contemporary Jewish biblical scholars sometimes challenge Christian biblical interpretations as being too strongly guided by the principles of Christian theology, but many Jewish biblical scholars use the same methods of literary and historical interpretation as do their Christian counterparts. The twentieth century would also see the emergence of new methods of interpreting the Bible, such as feminist criticism. Feminist biblical critics have called attention to the significance of female biblical characters, a significance that nonfeminist critics often overlook. They have argued that many of the negative views of women that interpreters have attributed to the Bible are in fact imposed upon the Bible by those interpreters themselves, and they have offered readings of the Bible on which the Deity can be understood as being neither male nor female, but beyond gender altogether.

We must now bring our brief history of biblical interpretation to a close. As we have seen, the story of how people in dif-

---

* We shall discuss the Documentary Hypothesis at greater length in the next chapter.

ferent historical periods have tried to understand and interpret the Bible is long and varied. In the next chapter, as we begin our examination of the Bible itself, we should bear in mind that the literary and historical ideas we encounter are the cumulative result of centuries of scholarship.

Part II
THE JEWISH SCRIPTURES

3

Prehistory: Creation and Ancestral Legends

I. THE DOCUMENTARY HYPOTHESIS

We shall begin our discussion of the Torah, the first part of the Tanak, with a brief description of the Documentary Hypothesis. The Documentary Hypothesis is a theory about the authorship of the Torah. According to this theory, the Torah is a compilation of distinct texts that were written by at least four different authors. Scholars have come to think that at least four authors contributed to the Torah as the result of both source criticism and redaction criticism; by comparing various sections of the Torah to each other, scholars have discovered that some passages strongly resemble each other in terms of vocabulary, literary style, and theme, while others do not. All of these similarities and differences taken together suggest that those sections that resemble each other were written by the same person or group of people. Because they have been able to distinguish four such resemblance-bearing sets of passages, scholars believe that the Torah incorporates material drawn from four distinct sources. The material from these sources was eventually woven together into the continuous narrative that we now find in the Torah.

The J Source

Each of the four sources posited by the Documentary Hypothesis has a name, and each of those names is usually abbreviated by a single letter. The first is called the Yahwist source, and is abbreviated by the letter J. The Yahwist source gets its name from the fact that the passages attributed to it usually use the divine name YHWH (Yahweh) when they refer to the Deity.* The J source tends to present the Deity in a very anthropomorphic (humanlike) way; YHWH walks and talks on the earth just like human beings do. The J source also stresses the importance of Israel's ancestral leaders, and seems to be very nationalistic. Scholars believe that the J source was written in Jerusalem during the tenth or ninth century BCE—that is, during the reign of King Solomon (962–922 BCE) or shortly thereafter. This was a time when things were going very well for Israel, and the author seems to be writing a story about Israel's past that reflects its (then) current success. Thus, in the passages written by the J source, YHWH is always there to take care of the beloved nation Israel. Some of the passages attributed to the J source are the second Creation story (Gen 2:4b–25), the story of the first sin and the expulsion from the garden (Gen 3), the covenant between God and Abraham (Gen 12:1–3), and the story of Joseph (Gen 37—50).

The E Source

The second source is called the Elohist source, and is abbreviated by the letter E. The Elohist source gets its name from the fact that the passages attributed to it tend to use the word *Elohim* to refer to the Deity. *Elohim* is actually the plural form of the Canaanite/Hebrew word for god, *el*. The fact that the E source refers to the Deity by means of a plural word is peculiar, as that word is clearly meant to denote a single divine being. Several explanations may be offered as to why the E source uses a plural term to denote the Deity. It may be that the term is a remnant of earlier times when the ancestors of the nation of Israel, like their Canaanite neighbors, worshiped multiple deities; in this case, the plural word *Elohim* simply came to take on the characteristics of a singular, proper name. Or, the E source's use of the plural could reflect the belief that the Deity was not alone in heaven, but was

---

* The Yahwist source is abbreviated as J rather than as Y because the Documentary Hypothesis was first developed in Germany in the nineteenth century. The German word for Yahweh is *Jahve*.

attended by a heavenly court of semidivine beings. This would explain why the Deity says such things as "Let us make humankind in our image" (Gen 1:26). Finally, the term *Elohim* may have been intended to stress the power and importance of the Deity in a way akin to the royal *we*, by which Queen Victoria famously referred to herself in the assertion, "We are not amused."

Whereas the Yahwist's Deity is anthropomorphic, the Elohist presents a more abstract, spiritual Deity. For example, in the Elohist's passages, the Deity rarely appears in visible form; instead, the Deity communicates with human beings in their dreams or by means of messengers. Scholars believe that the E source was written in the northern kingdom of Israel during the period of the Divided Kingdom (922–722 BCE), in part because this would explain many of the stylistic and thematic differences between E and J. For instance, scholars believe that certain peculiarities in the vocabulary and grammar of the E source reflect the fact that its author spoke a dialect of Hebrew that developed in the northern kingdom after its split from the southern kingdom, and which was slightly different from the form of Hebrew spoken in Jerusalem.[1] Passages attributed to the E source include the story of Abraham and Sarah at Gerar (Gen 20), the promise of a nation to Abraham's son Ishmael (Gen 21:8–21), and the near sacrifice of Isaac (Gen 22:1–13).

The D Source

The third source, which is called the Deuteronomic source and is abbreviated D, has a bit of a story behind it. Chapters 22—23 of 2 Kings tell us that, during the reign of King Josiah of Judah (roughly 640–609 BCE), a book was found in the Jerusalem Temple that purported to contain the Law of Moses. The king read the book to the people and inaugurated a period of religious reformation. Scholars refer to this book as the Deuteronomic Code. They believe that the Deuteronomic Code, much of which is thought to be preserved in our Bible as the book of Deuteronomy, was written by priests serving at the Jerusalem Temple in roughly 650 BCE. Like the J source, the D source refers to the Deity as YHWH. Unlike the J source, the D source presents the Deity as a stern lawgiver. Again, whereas the material from the J and E sources is mostly narrative in style—meaning that J and E like to tell stories—the material in the D source typically takes the form of long sermons, most of which are attributed to Moses. Finally, the D source tends to emphasize things that would have been of concern to priests serving in the Jerusalem Temple during the mid-seventh century BCE, such as the importance of having a centralized place of worship, and the dire consequences of failing to worship properly—that is, of failing to listen to the priests!

The P Source

The fourth source is called the Priestly source and is abbreviated P. The Priestly source refers to the Deity as both YHWH and *Elohim*, but always presents that deity as powerful, majestic, and transcendent. The P source emphasizes the idea that all things happen according to God's will and through God's power. The P source sometimes uses stories, but also summarizes events by means of genealogies and lists (Gen 5:1–32; 11:10–30). The P source is very much concerned with the cultic aspects of the Jewish faith, that is, the rules and rituals of worship. It takes pains to stress the importance of proper cultic procedures and the crucial role of the priests therein (Exod 25—31). The P source also seems concerned that Israel should work to preserve its identity as a people; for example, it discourages the intermarriage of Israelites with non-Israelites (Gen 27:46—28:9). Given these themes, most scholars believe that the P source was compiled and edited by priests during or shortly after the Babylonian Exile (586–539 BCE), although much of the material within it may have existed earlier in oral and/or written versions. Because the Jews who were exiled to Babylonia found themselves both without a political state (Judah having been conquered) and without a place of centralized worship (the Jerusalem Temple having been destroyed), the careful practice of the cultic aspects of their religion was one of the few means by which they could preserve their unique identity. The P source thus emphasizes such cultic practices. Passages attributed to the P source include the first Creation story (Gen 1:1—2:4a), the revelation of the divine name YHWH to Moses (Exod 6:2–12), and most of the Book of Leviticus.

Redaction

These four sources, which first existed as distinct works, were ultimately woven together to produce the Torah as we have it today. This process involved a good deal of cutting and pasting; passages from each of the four sources have been blended together to form a continuous narrative. Because some person or group of people must have compiled these works into their current form, some scholars think we should specify a fifth source for the Torah, namely, the editor who wove the four written sources together. This hypothetical fifth source is called the Redactor (a scholarly word for editor), and that name is abbreviated by the letter R. However, many scholars believe that the person or persons who edited the Torah were actually the same priest or priests who produced the Priestly source. Thus, many scholars do not think we need to posit a distinct R source, since they believe that R is actually the same as P.

II. THE CREATION AND PREHISTORY

The Book of Genesis begins with the creation of the world by God. But instead of just one Creation story, Genesis presents us with two Creation stories, each of which could stand alone as an account of how the Creation took place.

Creation: Part One

The first Creation story occurs at Genesis 1:1—2:4a. In this story, God creates the world in stages that are very orderly and balanced. On the first three days, God creates light, then the sky and the sea, and then the land and vegetation. Over the next three days, God populates the areas created on the first three days: God first makes bodies of light (sun, moon, and stars), then birds and sea creatures, and finally land animals (including human beings). The literary style of this account of Creation is very formulaic, in that the author regularly repeats particular phrases as if filling in the blanks of a formula: "And God said.... And God saw that it was good.... And there was evening and there was morning, the [*n*]th day". The first Creation story refers to the Deity as *Elohim* (God), and presents that Deity as a powerful creator who rules over a perfectly ordered world. Because of these stylistic and thematic elements, this first Creation story is attributed to the Priestly source.

Creation: Part Two

The second Creation story (Genesis 2:4b–25) differs from the first in some interesting ways. Whereas the first Creation story refers to the Deity as God *(Elohim)*, the second Creation story refers to the Deity as LORD God *(YHWH Elohim).** According to the first story, human beings were created after all the other living things had been created, and male and female human beings were created at the same time. According to the second story, however, God creates a male human being first, then other animals, and then a female human being. In the first story, Creation unfolds according to an orderly plan; in the second story, Creation is more of a piecemeal, trial-and-error process. For example, in the second Creation story, God creates a man, decides he should not be alone, and then creates animals; but God then decides that the animals are not suitable companions for the man, and so creates a woman to be his partner. Because the Deity in this second story is much more humanlike than the majestic creator presented in the first story, and because this second story uses the divine name YHWH, it is thought that this second account of Creation comes from the J source.

The question arises, Why did the person or persons who edited the four sources of the Torah into one book choose to keep

---

* When the word LORD appears in an English Bible with all its letters capitalized, it marks a place where, in the original Hebrew text, the divine name YHWH had been used. Sometime after the Babylonian Exile, probably around the third century BCE, Jews stopped pronouncing the divine name, regarding it as too holy to be uttered aloud by human beings. In place of YHWH, Jews reading the scriptures aloud would substitute the Hebrew word *adonai* (My Lord). Eventually, the vowels of *adonai* were added to the consonants of YHWH in Hebrew Bibles as a reminder to readers that they should make this substitution. The artificial word that resulted (often mistranslated in the past as "Jehovah") is now translated in most English Bibles as LORD (or, in some English Bibles, as GOD).

two distinct accounts of the Creation, especially when those two accounts seem to have quite different takes on the same subject matter? The editors probably thought that each of the stories conveyed something true, and that either story by itself would be missing something important. The first of the two stories presents God as powerful, transcendent, and somehow distant. The second story presents God as a person who is deeply concerned about human beings and who is intimately involved in the events of the world. Since the Israelites believed that both sets of qualities pertained to the Deity, the editors of the Torah probably thought that the message of each story was important enough to warrant putting both stories into the text.

Prehistory Stories

Chapters 3 through 11 of Genesis continue the prehistory of Israel by recounting events that are presented as having transpired between the Creation of the world and the time when God begins to establish a relationship with Abraham. These stories include the first sin and the expulsion from the garden (Gen 2—3), Cain's murder of his brother Abel (Gen 4:1–16), Noah and the great flood (Gen 6—9), and the Tower of Babel (Gen 11:1–9). It is interesting to observe that these stories seem to follow a pattern. First, human beings rebel against God: Adam and Eve eat the fruit that God has forbidden them to eat; Cain murders his brother Abel, and so on. God then confronts the human beings, who make excuses for their behavior: Adam blames Eve; Eve blames the serpent; Cain pretends not to know what has become of his brother. Finally, God punishes his rebellious creatures by imposing some form of alienation on them: Adam and Eve are cast out of the garden; Cain is condemned to wander the earth. It is also worth noting that, in all but the last of these stories, God mitigates the human beings' punishment somehow: God clothes Adam and Eve so that they will not be ashamed of their nakedness; God puts a mark of protection on Cain so that no one he encounters on his wanderings will kill him. Clearly the authors of these stories want us to remember that, even when God is punishing human beings, God loves and cares about them, too.[2]

III. THE ANCESTRAL LEGENDS

The stories contained in Genesis 12—50 are collectively referred to as the ancestral legends, because they tell tales of particular individuals from whom the ancient Israelites believed themselves to have descended. In these stories, God establishes a relationship with a specific group of people and begins to guide the course of events for those people. In order to understand the ancestral legends, we must first understand the nature of the relationship that God establishes with Israel's ancestors. We shall then briefly consider the roles played by some of those ancestors.

A. The Covenant

A covenant is an agreement or contract made between two or more parties, each of which agrees to do something for the others. For example, your relationship with a dry-cleaning store is a type of covenant relationship; the store agrees to clean your clothes for you, and you agree to pay for this service. The relationship that God establishes with Israel's ancestors in the ancestral legends is just such a covenant relationship. It is an agreement between two parties, each of which makes certain pledges to the other.

Covenant: Version One

The ancestral legends contain two distinct versions of the initial covenant between God and the ancestors of Israel. Each version is established by means of a theophany. A theophany is a manifestation of the Deity—it is a powerful experience of the presence of God, whether that experience is visual, auditory, or tactile. In both versions of the establishment of the covenant, God speaks to an ancestor and makes that ancestor some sort of offer or promise. In the first version of the covenant, at Genesis 12:1–3, God makes three promises to the ancestor Abraham. First, God promises to provide Abraham with a land that he can call his own. Second, God promises to "make of [Abraham] a great nation," that is, to give Abraham many descendents. Third, God promises to make Abraham and his people a blessing to all nations.

38

In other words, God not only promises to take good care of Abraham and his descendents; God also promises that this people of Abraham will somehow make the world a better place for everyone in it. Note that, in this first version of the covenant, God does not seem to be asking much in return for the things God is promising. Presumably, Abraham's people will keep up their end of the covenant by worshiping God, but just how they are to worship is not specified. This first version of the covenant is thought to come from the Yahwist source.

Covenant: Version Two

A second account of the covenant is recorded at Genesis 17:1–14. God again promises Abraham both a land and a people; the third promise of a blessing, though not explicitly stated, could be said to be implied. Here, however, emphasis is placed on the idea that this is an *everlasting* covenant, one that is to hold not only between God and Abraham, but between God and all the successive generations of Abraham's descendents (17:7, 13). This second version of the covenant also makes specific what God expects the people of Abraham to do as their part of the agreement: All the males among them, whether freeborn or slave, must be circumcised (17:10–14). Any male among them who is not circumcised must be cast out, for God will regard that male as being in violation of the covenant.

Why are there two accounts of the covenant, only the latter of which stresses its permanence and specifies an obligation on the part of Abraham's people? Scholars believe that the second covenant account comes from the Priestly source. Recall that the Priestly source was produced during or shortly after the Babylonian Exile. This was a time when the Jews, having lost both their political autonomy and their Temple, were struggling to maintain their identity as a people. Thus, it is thought that the authors of the P source crafted a new version of the older Yahwist covenant story, modifying it in ways that were relevant and important at the time. By stressing the idea that the covenant between God and Abraham is everlasting, the Priestly source assured the exiled Jews that they were still the chosen people of

God, even if things had not been going well for them lately. By specifying circumcision as a covenant obligation of the people of Abraham, the Priestly source offered the exiled Jews—who had been practicing circumcision for a long time—a powerful boost to their sense of identity. The fact that the exiled Jews practiced circumcision set them apart from non-Jews, but it also provided them with a means of fulfilling their covenant obligations to God even though they lacked a temple in which to offer sacrifices.

The most important theme in the ancestral narratives, which we see in both accounts of the covenant, is that God has chosen a specific group of people—namely, Abraham and his descendents—with whom to establish a special relationship. Whereas the first eleven chapters of Genesis dealt with the general prehistory of the world, the focus of the story has now shifted to the ancestors of the nation of Israel; God has singled them out and taken control of their destiny. How God effects such control, and how the ancestors themselves respond to it, is explored in the stories of the individual ancestors.

B. The Ancestors

Abraham and Isaac

Each of the ancestors of Israel responds to the relationship offered by God in his own way. God first approaches Abram, whose name God later changes to Abraham, with the offer of the covenant relationship. Abraham consistently responds to God with tremendous faith. Abraham is already seventy-five years old when God tells him to leave his homeland of northern Mesopotamia and head to Canaan, but Abraham obeys without a moment's hesitation. When God tells Abraham that he and his elderly wife Sarah will have a son, Abraham is shocked and somewhat incredulous, but he nonetheless does as God asks, circumcising his entire household. Later, when God demands that Abraham kill that very son (Isaac) as a sacrifice, Abraham is heartbroken. Not only does Abraham not wish for his son to die, but Isaac's death would presumably mean that God's promise to make a great nation of Abraham will never be fulfilled. Still,

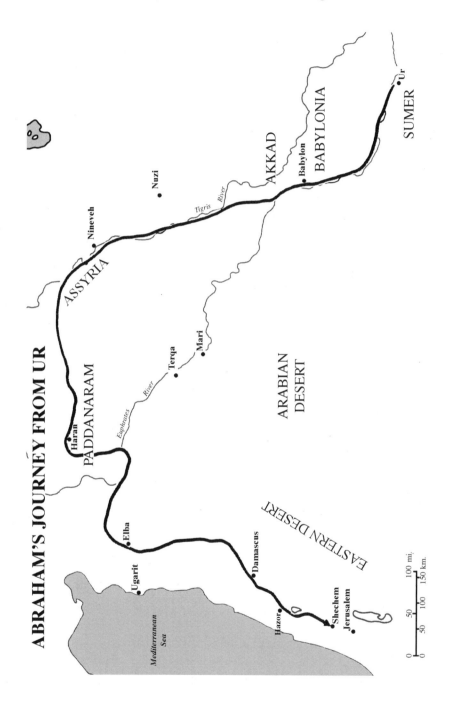

ABRAHAM'S JOURNEY FROM UR

Abraham resolves to carry out God's will, and Isaac is spared the sacrificial knife only by the last-minute intervention of a messenger sent from God.

Jacob

When Isaac is an adult, he and his wife Rebekah have twin sons, Jacob and Esau. The biblical authors make fairly clear to us that Esau, Isaac's firstborn and favored son, is a bit dim-witted. They also make clear that Jacob is a bit conniving. Jacob talks Esau into trading his birthright—his right as firstborn to inherit a double share of their father's wealth—for a bowl of stew. Later, Jacob and Rebekah trick Isaac into giving Jacob a blessing that he had meant to give to Esau. (A blessing, like a curse, invokes the power of the Deity, and thus cannot be taken back or changed once it has been uttered.) Fearing retribution from his brother, Jacob goes to live with his uncle Laban. He stays with Laban fourteen years, marries Laban's two daughters, Leah and Rachel, and—with his wives and their slaves—produces twelve sons.

Most interesting about Jacob are his interactions with God. When he is on his way to his uncle's house, Jacob has a dream in which the Lord speaks to him, renewing the threefold promise of land, descendents, and a blessing that had been made to Abraham. The next morning, Jacob responds to this dream, but his response is not the unconditional faith of his grandfather Abraham. Rather, Jacob makes his response to God conditional upon getting what he wants: "*If* God will be with me, and will keep me in this way that I go, and will give me bread to eat and clothing to wear, so that I come again to my father's house in peace, *then* the LORD shall be my God" (Gen 28:20–21; emphasis added). This is a rather self-serving response to God's offer, but one that should not surprise us, given Jacob's past behavior; Jacob is a manipulator, so why should he not try to manipulate God?

Jacob's "Conversion"

While he is away from home, however, the conniving Jacob gets a taste of his own medicine at the hands of his uncle Laban (Gen 29:15–30). The resulting change in Jacob's personality is significant. On his way back to the land of his father, Jacob humbles himself before his brother (Gen 32:3–5) and before God (Gen 32:9–10). Jacob also has a profound experience in which a mysterious man appears and wrestles with him all night, but is unable to subdue him. In the morning, Jacob refuses to let the man leave until he has obtained a blessing from him; obviously, Jacob has figured out that this is no ordinary man with whom he has been struggling. The man asks Jacob his name; when Jacob tells him, the man responds, "You shall no longer be called Jacob, but Israel, for you have striven with God and with humans, and have prevailed" (Gen 32:28). (The name that the mysterious wrestler gives to Jacob, *Israel*, means something like "God strives.") Thus, the story of Jacob relates how a rather deceptive and arrogant young man ultimately comes to have a profoundly personal relationship with God.

The story of Jacob's son Joseph (Gen 37—50) is significant for two reasons. First, it explains how the people of Abraham come to be in Egypt, which is where we shall find them when the Book of Exodus begins. Second, the story of Joseph is considered to be the first short story in the Bible; it has a sustained story line in which a complex plot develops over time. Unlike the many shorter episodes in Genesis, it would be very difficult to follow the story of Joseph if any part of that story were omitted.

IV. HISTORY AND PURPOSE

From the academic perspective, neither the biblical accounts of prehistory nor the stories about the ancestors can be regarded as historical in the strict, modern sense of that term. That is, most biblical scholars do not regard the stories contained in the Book of Genesis as presenting an objective, fact-based description of historical events. Rather, they regard the stories about the Creation and other prehistoric events (Gen 1—11) as myths, and they regard the stories about the ancestors (Gen 12—50) as legends. Let us consider what each of these terms means, and why scholars apply them to the Book of Genesis.

Myths

To assert that the stories in Genesis 1—11 are myths is not to assert that those stories are false or incorrect. Rather, it is to assert that those stories fall into a literary genre to which such adjectives as "true" and "false" do not really apply. Myths are stories about gods and human beings that are set in the distant past. Such stories describe *transhistorical* events, that is, events that occur outside the spatiotemporal world of our experience. Because transhistorical events—such as the actions of a deity in creating a universe—occur outside space and time, they also occur outside history as a subject of scientific inquiry. Thus, transhistorical events are events for which there is not, and could not possibly be, the sort of empirical evidence to which modern historians must appeal. It is because the stories in Genesis 1—11 describe such events that scholars regard them as myths.

Myths were not unique to the ancient Israelites. Indeed, many of the motifs used in the biblical myths can also be found in the myths of other ancient Near Eastern cultures. For instance, like Genesis, ancient Babylonian writings such as the *Enuma Elish* and *Gilgamesh* epics also make reference to creation out of chaos, a tree of life, deceptive serpents, food of the gods bringing wisdom if eaten, and a great flood survived by only one family (which was chosen by the Deity to gather animals together on a boat).[3] This is not to say that the authors of the Book of Genesis plagiarized the works of their neighbors, but simply that these sorts of mythical ideas were in wide circulation among the various cultures of the ancient Near East. Nor is this surprising, when we consider that myths serve an important etiological function. Etiology is the explanation of causes or origins; an etiology attempts to explain how something came to be. Myths serve an etiological function because they explain things in the world of our experience by linking that world to prehistoric, transhistorical events. We can see this etiological function in the prehistory myths of Genesis. For example, the first and second Creation stories explain the institutions of the Sabbath and marriage, respectively (2:1–3, 24); the story of the first sin explains why human

44

beings are mortal (3:19); the story of the Tower of Babel explains the existence of different languages (11:9).

Legends

Whereas myths focus on transhistorical characters and events, legends are stories that focus on the lives of human beings who lived in the distant past, and that are presented in the form of an historical narrative. Again, to assert that a biblical story is a legend is not to say that it is false; rather, it is to admit that there is no extrabiblical evidence that the story is historical in our modern sense of that term. None of the characters of the ancestral legends (Gen 12—50) appear in any other ancient Near Eastern documents. This means that scholars lack the sort of objective confirmation they would need in order to assert that people like Abraham, Isaac, and Jacob were historical figures. Of course, scholars have no confirmation that these characters were *not* historical figures, either. The general consensus of scholarly opinion, however, is that the ancestral legends should not be regarded as objective accounts of historical events.

Oral Traditions and Their Purpose

One reason why scholars do not regard the ancestral legends as historical is the fact that those legends are not confirmed by any extrabiblical sources. Another important reason has to do with the fact that, before they were written down, the ancestral legends seem to have existed for a long time as an oral tradition.[4] It is a common feature of oral traditions that multiple versions of a single story or idea will develop simultaneously, since each family or tribe that participates in the oral tradition gives its own twist to parts of the story. Scholars find evidence of such variant development in the ancestral legends. There are, for instance, two accounts of Jacob's name changing (Gen 32:28; 35:10), two accounts of the naming of Beer-sheba (Gen 21:31; 26:33), two accounts of the naming of Bethel (Gen 28:19; 35:15), and three stories in which one of Israel's male ancestors tries to pass his wife off as his sister (Gen 12:10–20; 20:1–18; 26:6–11). Another common feature of oral traditions is anachronism, that is, errors in chronology.

Anachronism occurs in oral traditions because the practitioners of an oral tradition often insert elements of the world as they experience it into stories about the distant past, where those elements do not belong. Evidence of such anachronism can be found in the ancestral legends. For example, Genesis 26:1 identifies Abimelech as king of the Philistines, but the Philistines did not arrive in Canaan until the twelfth century BCE, centuries later than the time when the events in the ancestral legends are supposed to have transpired (namely, the eighteenth to the fourteenth centuries BCE).

Thus, evidence internal to the ancestral narratives themselves suggests that those narratives were passed on orally before they were recorded in written form. This is significant because of what modern social science has come to think about oral traditions in general. Anthropologists and sociologists who have studied cultures with oral traditions find that the main purpose of those traditions is not the preservation of historical facts. Rather, the purpose of an oral tradition is to preserve a culture's values, to pass those values on to successive generations. For this reason, events and characters may be invented or modified for narrative purposes. Because it is the moral behind the story that really matters, practitioners of an oral tradition feel free to modify a story when doing so helps to get its point across more clearly or powerfully. Since research suggests that this is true of oral traditions in general, biblical scholars conclude that it is likely true of the oral tradition that produced the ancestral legends as well.

Historical Foundations

The foregoing paragraphs give us some idea why scholars are not inclined to regard the ancestral legends as accurate accounts of historical events. Still, while they do not regard the ancestral narratives as historically accurate, scholars do believe that the ancestral legends are connected to the distant past in important ways. Whether the specific people mentioned in the ancestral narratives existed or not, those narratives seem to have been influenced by—and to reflect—empirically verifiable historical facts. For instance, archaeology tells us that a large group of Semitic

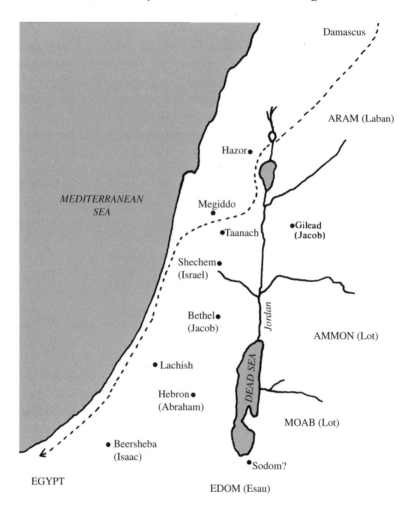

Damascus

ARAM (Laban)

Hazor

MEDITERRANEAN
SEA

Megiddo

Gilead
(Jacob)

Taanach

Shechem
(Israel)

Jordan

Bethel
(Jacob)

AMMON (Lot)

Lachish

DEAD SEA

Hebron
(Abraham)

MOAB (Lot)

Beersheba
(Isaac)

Sodom?

EGYPT

EDOM (Esau)

ROUTES, SANCTUARIES, AND TERRITORIES CONNECTED WITH THE PATRIARCHS AND THEIR FAMILY

(Jacob) = patriarch

MOAB = territory

people* migrated from Mesopotamia to Canaan in roughly 2100 BCE. This is significant because, in Genesis, Abraham and his family were living in northern Mesopotamia when God told them to go to the promised land of Canaan.[5]

It is also worth noting that the names given to the ancestors in the ancestral narratives seem to be genuinely ancient names, since none of them were in common use among Israelites during the Iron Age (1200–586 BCE), which is when scholars believe the ancestral legends were first written down. Had the biblical authors simply invented the stories they recorded, they probably would have given the characters in those stories names that were in common use at the time the authors were writing. The fact that they did not do so suggests that these stories date back to a more ancient time, when such names were actually in use.[6]

Even more significant are the clues that the ancestral legends give us about the religious and social customs of the ancestors of Israel. The stories refer to several practices that Jewish law would later reject. For example, the ancestral narratives suggest that Israel's ancestors used to erect sacred trees (Gen 21:33) and sacred stones (Gen 28:18–22), both of which practices would later be associated with idolatry (Exod 34:13; Deut 7:5; 12:2–4). The story of Jacob tells us that he married two sisters, Leah and Rachel, although the practice of marrying two sisters would later be forbidden (Lev 18:18). Since it is unlikely that the Israelites would have invented stories in which they attributed to their ancestors practices that the Israelites themselves regarded as improper, such stories suggest at least a distant memory of historical realities.[7]

Perhaps most important are the various names used for God in the ancestral narratives. According to the Book of Exodus, the divine name YHWH was first revealed to Moses (6:2–3), and was thus unknown to Israel's ancestors. This latter assertion seems to be confirmed by the Book of Genesis, in which Israel's ancestors typically refer to the Deity as *El*—which was both a title (the God) and a proper name. To this name they often attached a descriptive

* The term *Semitic people* (or *Semites*) refers to various groups in the ancient Near East who spoke very closely related languages. The ancient Semitic languages included—but were not limited to—Arabic, Aramaic, Assyrian, Babylonian, and Hebrew.

epithet. For instance, God is referred to as *El Elyon* (God the Most High) at 14:18–20, as *El Shaddai* (God the Almighty) at 17:1, and as *El Olam* (God the Everlasting) at 21:33. When Jacob builds an altar upon his return to Canaan (33:20), he names it *El-Elohe-Israel* (El is the God of Israel). The fact that the ancestral legends use all these different names for God suggests that at least some of the stories contained in them date back to pre-Israelite times, that is, to a period in time before the people who would come to be known as Israel united in the worship of a deity they called YHWH. Thus, although they do not regard the details of the ancestor stories as accurate accounts of historical events, many scholars nonetheless believe that those stories may have originated in the very period they are said to describe.[8]

Let us conclude our discussion of Genesis with a review of its major themes. The Creation myths not only establish the authority of God as creator of the world, but also stress the importance of human beings in God's creation. The prehistory myths make clear that, although God loves and cares for human beings, there is tension in that relationship; human beings have a tendency to rebel against God rather than to obey God. Finally, the ancestral legends link the general prehistory of Genesis 1—11 to the more specific story of a people with whom God chooses to have a special relationship. The stories about the ancestors offer studies in the sort of faithfulness that this relationship demands of the chosen people, and they bring the saga of that people to its next stage: the sojourn in Egypt.

4

The Exodus Tradition

Exodus, Leviticus, Numbers, and Deuteronomy (books two through five of the Torah) collectively preserve what is known as the Exodus tradition. The importance of this tradition, both for the nation of Israel and for the Jewish faith, cannot be overstated. It is in this part of the biblical narrative that Israel emerges as a nation of people unified by their shared faith in YHWH, and it is in these books that the religious laws of Judaism are made explicit. The Exodus tradition tells of YHWH's deliverance of the chosen people from their slavery in Egypt, the establishment of a covenant between YHWH and the people of Israel, and the journey of those people to the land YHWH promised to them. (This third part of the story, the conquest and occupation of the promised land, is completed in the books of Joshua and Judges.) We shall focus first on the story of the deliverance of the chosen people from Egypt, and then on the covenant relationship.

I. DELIVERANCE: EXODUS 1—18

Exodus begins with the Hebrews, the descendents of Jacob, working as forced laborers in Egypt. The first eighteen chapters of Exodus tell of how YHWH planned and executed their escape from this bondage. Let us review the elements of the biblical narrative first, and then consider some of the available historical evidence.

A. The Narrative Account

By the time the story of Joseph is finished, Jacob and all his descendents have relocated to Egypt. Exodus begins by reminding us of this, and asserts that Jacob brought a total of seventy people to Egypt with him. Some time has passed since Jacob's death; Joseph and his whole generation—all of Jacob's other sons—have died, though their descendents have multiplied greatly. So great have their numbers become, in fact, that the Egyptians begin to fear them. Eventually, a pharaoh rises to power "who did not know Joseph" (Exod 1:8), and things quickly turn ugly for Jacob's people. The pharaoh presses the Hebrews into forced physical labor, and ultimately orders the Egyptians to kill all newborn Hebrew boys.

Moses

In the midst of this unhappy situation, the main character of the Exodus tradition enters the story. Moses is the child of a Levite couple, that is, descendents of Jacob's son Levi. His mother hides him from the Egyptians after his birth, and then sets him adrift in a basket on the river. Ironically, he is found by the pharaoh's daughter, who adopts him and rears him in the pharaoh's house. The story then skips ahead to Moses as an adult. Moses kills an Egyptian who was beating a Hebrew, and is forced to flee the pharaoh's wrath. He goes to Midian (in the Arabian Desert, opposite the Sinai Peninsula), where he enters into the service of a Midianite priest named Jethro, marries Jethro's daughter, has a son, and settles into the life of a desert nomad.

The Divine Name

While tending Jethro's flock in Midian, Moses has a powerful theophany experience; he sees a bush that is on fire but that is not burning up, and from this bush the voice of the Lord speaks to him. The Deity identifies itself to Moses in a familiar way, namely, as the God of Moses' ancestors: "I am the God of your father, the God of Abraham, the God of Isaac, and the God of Jacob" (Exod 3:6). The Lord commissions Moses to go to Egypt and lead the Hebrews out of their bondage. The Lord promises to

51

facilitate the Hebrews' escape by striking Egypt with wonders, and gives Moses several powerful signs that Moses can use as proof that the Lord has indeed appeared to him.

What is perhaps most significant about this theophany experience, however, is that the Lord reveals the divine name to Moses. When Moses asks the Lord what he should say if people ask him the name of the one who sent him, the Lord answers, "I AM WHO I AM" (Exod 3:14). This is a rendering of the Hebrew word *YHWH*, for which there is no clear translation, in part because there is no clear interpretation even in Hebrew. The word derives from the Hebrew verb *hawah* (to be), so can be thought to mean something like "I am" or "The one who is" or "The one who causes to be."* However it is interpreted, the divine name is quite unlike the familiar description by which the Deity first identifies itself to Moses. Indeed, the divine name seems designed to convey the sense that its bearer is not familiar at all, but is instead mysterious, powerful, and transcendent. Moses is supremely privileged in having the divine name revealed to him; at Exodus 6:2–3, the Lord tells Moses that he is the first person to hear the divine name, because the Lord had not revealed it to Abraham, Isaac, or Jacob.

Plagues

Moses does as YHWH has commanded him. He returns to Egypt and—with the help of his brother Aaron—calls forth wonders in an effort to persuade the pharaoh to set the Hebrews free. Thus begin the ten plagues of Egypt. The first nine of these plagues fail to impress the pharaoh, in part because his own magicians are able to duplicate some of them. But the tenth plague has the desired effect; the Lord strikes dead all the firstborn human beings and animals in Egypt, except those of the Hebrews. (The Hebrews are spared by marking their doorposts with the blood of a lamb, a sign that the Lord should pass over that house; thus the Jewish holiday of Passover is instituted.) The pharaoh relents, telling Moses to

---

* The divine name YHWH is sometimes referred to as the Tetragrammaton (Greek for "having four letters") because it is composed of four Hebrew consonants: *yod* (y), *he* (h), *vav* (v), and *he* (h). In ancient Hebrew, *vav* was pronounced like the letter W.

take his people and be gone. The Lord then leads the Hebrews—according to Exodus 12:37–38, some 600,000 men, plus women and children—into the desert, so as to avoid the warlike Philistines along the Mediterranean coast. The Lord orders the Hebrews to camp near the Red Sea so that the Egyptians will think that they are lost. Then, just as the pursuing Egyptian army is closing in, the Lord divides the waters of the Red Sea so that the Hebrews may pass through. The Egyptians give chase, but the Lord closes the waters upon them, and they drown.

Note that, while Moses is a towering figure in the Exodus tradition, the Lord is the real hero of the story. Bearing in mind that Egyptian pharaohs claimed to be divine, we can see that what looks like a conflict between Moses and the pharaoh is really one between the Lord and a false god, a pretender to divinity. Again, though Moses performs many wonders both prior to and during the Hebrews' flight from Egypt, it is the power of the Lord that effects those miracles; Moses is simply an instrument through which the Lord operates. That the authors of the Exodus tradition regard the Lord in such heroic terms can be seen in the victory song of Exodus 15, where the Lord is praised as a mighty warrior.

B. Historical Evidence

Two Difficulties

Linking the elements of the Exodus story to empirically verifiable historical events is extremely difficult, for two reasons in particular. First, the biblical narrative is lacking in the sort of details that would enable scholars to pinpoint the times, persons, and places it describes. For example, none of the Egyptian pharaohs mentioned in the Exodus narrative is identified by name. The Book of Numbers does give names to three Transjordanian rulers (King Sihon at 21:21; King Og at 21:33; King Balak at 22:4), but these rulers are unknown outside the Bible.* Similarly, while the Exodus narrative makes reference to places in Egypt, it tends to

---

* The term *Transjordan* refers to the lands opposite Canaan on the eastern side of the Jordan River and the Dead Sea, including Edom, Moab, and Ammon.

use generic rather than specific place names. Consider Pithom and Rameses, the supply cities that Exodus 1:11 tells us the Hebrews were forced to build. Pithom's name derives from the Egyptian *Pr-'Itm* (Per Atum), which means the "Temple [or Estate] of [the god] Atum." In Egyptian usage, this term would not have been used in isolation to refer to a place, but would instead have been used in conjunction with a place name—for example, the "Temple of Atum at Karnak." Again, the Rameses referred to in Exodus could be Per Rameses, the Nile Delta capital of Pharaoh Rameses II (1279–1213). But because many cities used Rameses' name even after his death, that name alone is not enough to identify the city.[1]

A second reason why the Exodus tradition is difficult to place in historical context is that there are no other ancient Near Eastern texts that provide independent witness to the events recounted in the biblical narrative. Since the biblical narrative does not easily lend itself to historical analysis, and because no extrabiblical accounts exist that could corroborate the biblical narrative, scholars must simply look for parallels between the events described in the Exodus tradition and the generally accepted history of the ancient Near East. In the following paragraphs, we shall survey some of the parallels that pertain to the historicity of the Israelite sojourn in Egypt, the existence of Moses, the date of the Exodus, and the wonders of the Exodus tradition.

Israel in Egypt

There is good reason to think that the Hebrews could indeed have been in Egypt. Strong historical evidence shows that Asiatic settlers began entering northern Egypt by force in roughly 1700 BCE. (*Asiatic* was the Egyptians' term for people from Syria and Canaan.) These settlers were Semitic and originated in Canaan. By the mid-seventeenth century BCE (around 1650), the Asiatic settlers had political control over most of northern Egypt, and their control continued to spread into middle Egypt as the century wore on. The Egyptians called these people *heqaw khasut* (rulers from foreign lands), which later Greek authors rendered as *Hyksos*. These Hyksos ruled over northern Egypt until around 1550 BCE, when

Khamose and Ahmose—Egyptian rulers from Thebes—led a successful revolt against them and reestablished native control over the north. Whether or not the Hebrews of the biblical narrative are the Hyksos of Egyptian history is a matter of debate among biblical scholars. However, if the Hebrews and the Hyksos are the same people, then the mid-sixteenth century revolt led by Khamose and Ahmose could mark the point at which the Hebrews' fortunes in Egypt began to take a sharp turn for the worse.[2]

The Hyksos were not the only non-Egyptians in Egypt; there is also evidence that large numbers of Asiatics entered Egypt during the second half of the second millennium (1500–1000) BCE. During part of this period, Egypt ruled an empire that included Canaan. This meant that many Asiatics and others came to Egypt as slaves, the spoils of Egyptian military conquests, or tribute payments made by vanquished states. But many came freely as well, for instance, as traders by land or by sea.

Another piece of indirect evidence for the historicity of Israel's sojourn in Egypt is worth noting. As B. S. J. Isserlin has observed, the fact that the people who would become the nation of Israel claimed to be descendents of liberated Egyptian slaves is "most unusual." Since the majority of ancient peoples claimed to have descended either from gods or from semidivine heroes, the fact that the Israelites claimed descent from lowly slaves at least suggests that this claim has an historical basis.[3]

Although there may have been Hebrews in Egypt, the numbers cited in the biblical narrative are surely exaggerated. According to Exodus 12:37–38, some 600,000 men made the journey out of Egypt, plus women, children, and animals. That many men plus women and children would be roughly 1.5 million people, at the least. The Sinai Desert could never have supported such a large number of people; its scarce water supply suggests that this number is logistically impossible. More importantly, such a large group of people could have easily conquered Egypt itself or any other ancient Near Eastern state; Rameses II's largest army was only about twenty thousand soldiers. A more reasonable number for the group of Hebrews that escaped from Egypt is suggested by Exodus 1:15; if only two midwives were sufficient to meet the needs of the whole Hebrew population of

Egypt, then the Hebrews who made the Exodus probably numbered around one thousand or so.[4]

The Existence of Moses

Outside the Bible, there is no direct evidence to support the existence of an individual named Moses; no archaeological finds or extrabiblical texts offer any trace of him. Indeed, some elements of his life story seem to have been adapted from other ancient Near Eastern legends. For example, the story of the pharaoh's daughter rescuing the infant Moses from the river very closely parallels an earlier Mesopotamian legend about the infancy of Sargon the Elder, whom the Akkadians of Mesopotamia believed had founded their empire.[5]

Still, there is some compelling indirect evidence that the character of Moses is historically grounded. Moses, his brother Aaron, and Aaron's grandson Phinehas all have names of Egyptian origin. Moses' name (*Moshe* in Hebrew) comes from the Egyptian root *mys* (born). For instance, the name Ramose (*Ra-mys*) means "the god Ra is born" or "born of Ra," and the name Ptahmose *(Ptah-mys)* means "the god Ptah is born" or "born of Ptah." Egyptian usage typically attached *mys* to the name of a god; Egyptians almost never used the shortened form as a name by itself. Thus, although the name *Moses* lacks a divine element, it most likely would have had one originally. That divine element may have been dropped later, either by Moses himself or by those who preserved his story.[6]

It is also conceivable that a non-Egyptian like Moses could attain a life of wealth and privilege in Egypt. Egyptian documents attest to the fact that Asiatics often rose to relatively powerful and prestigious positions. This was due, at least in part, to the fact that Egyptian kings often took the children of conquered rulers as hostages. This was a common practice among ancient empires; after conquering a foreign kingdom, the empire would leave the ruler of that kingdom on the throne as a client king, but would also take the king's children back to the empire's homeland as hostages to ensure that the client king behaved as the empire demanded. Such children were not treated as prisoners; rather, the children that Egypt took as hostages were reared in Egyptian homes as Egyptian children, and they often rose to positions of power when they grew up. Thus, the idea that a Hebrew like Moses might have grown up in the household of an Egyptian pharaoh is not implausible.

Another piece of historical evidence lends support to the Exodus tradition's assertion that Moses experienced his first theophany in Midian. According to Exodus 6:2–3, Moses is the first person to whom the Lord reveals the divine name YHWH. As we have seen, the ancestors of Israel had worshiped the Lord under a variety of titles (God the Most High, God the Almighty, God the Everlasting), probably because they lacked a proper name for the Lord. Historical evidence suggests that there may have been worship of a deity named YHWH very early among the people of Midian. An inscription of Pharaoh Amenophis III (1408–1372 BCE) describes the area east of the Sinai Peninsula as the "land of the Shosu [Bedouin], the tribes of Yhw." While this is not evidence that the Midianites were monotheists, it does at least give us reason to believe that Moses may have first heard the divine name during his time in Midian.[7]

Dating the Exodus

The Exodus tradition is so difficult to align with historical data that scholars have proposed a number of hypotheses regarding when the Israelites' Exodus from Egypt might have taken place, each of which has certain strengths and weaknesses. The date for the Exodus that is most widely accepted among scholars, however, is the mid-thirteenth century BCE, during the reign of Pharaoh Rameses II. One reason this date meets with wide acceptance has to do with what archaeology has determined about Canaanite settlements. Israelites are known to have occupied villages in the hill country of southern Canaan by around 1025 BCE. Most of those villages in the hill country had been founded around 1200, and had a material culture simpler than that of the large cities already existing on the Canaanite plains. It is thus reasonable to think that the Israelites themselves probably founded those villages, which would mean that the Exodus from Egypt must have occurred slightly earlier, around 1250 or so.[8]

A mid-thirteenth century date for the Exodus also accords well with several other relevant pieces of information. First, historians know that the Egyptian Empire was beginning to unravel by the mid-thirteenth century, which means that Egypt's control over Canaan was considerably less than it had been in preceding centuries. If the Exodus is dated earlier than the mid-thirteenth century, then both the Israelites' escape from Egypt and their settlement in Canaan occurred at a time when all of Canaan was firmly under the military and political control of Egypt. Such an upset is highly unlikely, and is not reflected in the biblical narrative itself.[9]

Second, a mid-thirteenth century date for the Exodus fits well with the biblical claim that, by the time the Exodus occurred, the Israelites had been in Egypt 430 years (Exod 12:40). If the Exodus occurred around 1250, then 430 years earlier would have been very close to 1700, the generally agreed upon date for the entry of the Hyksos into Egypt.[10] Thus, if the Hebrews of the biblical narrative are the Hyksos of Egyptian history, a mid-thirteenth century date for the Exodus would mean that the Hebrews' original arrival in Egypt is dated to the same point in time by both the Bible and Egyptian history.

Third, a mid-thirteenth century date for the Exodus accords well with an important piece of historical data: the Merneptah Stele. The Merneptah Stele is a carved stone in the funerary temple of Pharaoh Merneptah (who ruled 1213–1203 BCE) in Thebes, and it is significant because it contains the only extrabiblical reference to Israel by name prior to the ninth century BCE. The stone mentions Merneptah's military victories over four Canaanite enemies: Ashkelon, Gezer, Yanoam, and Israel. The hieroglyphics used in this reference identify the first three of these enemies as foreign countries (that is, city-states), while those used for Israel identify it as a foreign *people* (meaning a rural or nomadic tribe). Thus, the Merneptah Stele gives us reason to believe that, by the late thirteenth century, Israel was clearly in Canaan, was strong enough militarily to be worthy of mention alongside three city-states, but did not yet have the status of a

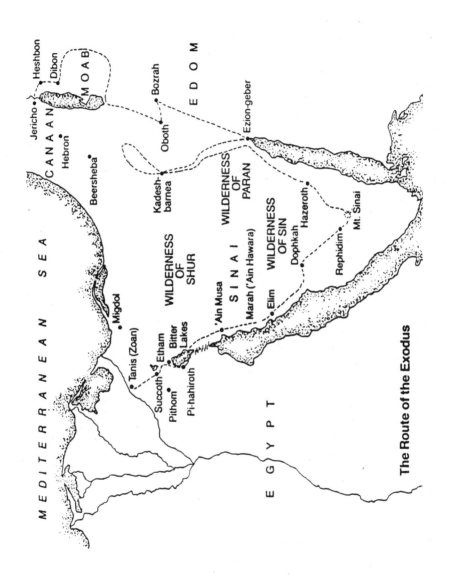

The Route of the Exodus

political state. This is most likely what Israel's situation would have been in the *late* thirteenth century if the Exodus had occurred in the *mid*-thirteenth century.[11]

Attempts to Explain the Exodus Miracles

A great deal of effort has been made to understand and explain the many wonders or miracles recounted in the Exodus tradition. Some of this effort has been directed to showing that natural, rational explanations can be given for the sorts of events that the Exodus tradition attributes to the divine power of the Lord. For example, it has been noted that, in recounting the plagues brought upon the Egyptians by the Lord, biblical authors might have been giving theological interpretations of naturally occurring events in Egypt. Thus, the turning of the Nile to blood is explained as an effect of microorganisms in the water—that is, a red tide; the plague of darkness is explained as a sandstorm; the death of the firstborns is explained as some sort of child epidemic; and so on.

Similar efforts have been made to understand and explain the parting of the Red Sea. Here it is pointed out that the Hebrew term *yam suf*, which is translated as Red Sea, literally means "Sea of Reeds." It is thus thought that the body of water referred to here was actually one of many marshy areas in Egypt where strong winds and tides could dramatically change the water levels. Possible locations include the marshes between the Gulf of Suez and the Great Bitter Lake, the reed beds of the northeast Nile Delta, and Lake Sirbonis on the Mediterranean Sea, which has an historical precedent of trapping and destroying troops.[12]

Here it is important to remember that biblical authors thought differently about history than we do today. Their concern was not history in our modern sense, that is, an objective record of empirically verifiable facts. The biblical authors' goal was not simply to record events, but also to interpret them. Such interpretations were theological, for the biblical authors wished to show that God acts in history. This being the case, it is not unreasonable to think that biblical authors might have regarded the shifting of historical particulars as permissible when doing so served their theological ends.[13] Thus, even if the wonders of the Exodus tradition can all be explained as naturally occurring events, this need not undermine the biblical authors' point. *That* such events took place may not have been, in itself, miraculous. What the biblical authors regarded as miraculous was *when* they took place, namely, just when they were needed in order to facilitate Israel's escape from Egypt. It is this miraculous timing that the biblical authors could be said to attribute to the divine power of YHWH.

II. THE SINAI COVENANT: EXODUS 19—DEUTERONOMY

After their escape from Egypt, the Israelites camp at Mount Sinai, where they enter into an explicit covenant agreement with the Lord. The establishment of this Sinai Covenant—also known as the Mosaic Covenant or the Mosaic Law—is recounted in Exodus 19 through Deuteronomy. The Sinai Covenant is crucial to the self-identity of the Israelites, for it defines Israel as a nation in which membership is based, not on blood relations or place of birth, but on obedience to the divine will. We shall consider both the covenant itself and some of the narrative elements of this part of the Exodus tradition. But first, a note on the books of Leviticus, Numbers, and Deuteronomy is in order.

Leviticus, Numbers, and Deuteronomy

The Book of Leviticus is so called because it is primarily concerned with the Hebrew priesthood, which was Levitical in that it was traditionally restricted to descendents of Moses' brother Aaron, a member of the tribe of Levi. Leviticus explains how the priesthood was inaugurated, how sacrifices should be performed, what sort of ritual-purity standards priests should maintain, and so on. Because of its emphasis on the priesthood, Leviticus is thought to be the work of the Priestly source, which was written by priests during or shortly after the Babylonian Exile. Though the P source recorded religious legislation from its own period, it also incorporated much older doctrines as well, such as the Holiness Code (Lev 11:43–45; 17–26) and the Azazel (scapegoat) rite (Lev 16:8–10, 26).

The Book of Numbers takes its name from the fact that it begins with the Lord commanding Moses to take a census of the Israelites. Numbers contains narrative elements about the Israelites' camp at Sinai and wanderings in the wilderness, but it also contains laws. The book as a whole is thought to have been compiled by an editor who drew stories from the E and J sources and laws from the P source.

The Book of Deuteronomy gets its name from the Greek word *deuteronomos*, which means "second law." This is because chapters 12 through 26 of the Book of Deuteronomy contain a restatement and expansion of the Covenant Code recorded at Exodus 20:22—23:19. Deuteronomy is composed mostly of laws that are presented in the form of long sermons attributed to Moses. Scholars believe the author, known as the Deuteronomist, was a priest (or priests) serving at the Jerusalem Temple in the mid-seventh century BCE. They think that the Deuteronomist, who had been influenced by the work of some of the prophets, issued Deuteronomy as a call for errant Israelites to return to their covenant obligations.

A. History and Purpose

Recall that the covenant that the Lord had made with Abraham was rather one-sided. The Lord promised Abraham land, descendents, and a blessing, but did not ask for anything in return—except, in the later Priestly version, the sign of circumcision. The Sinai Covenant is different in that (1) it is a covenant between the Lord and the whole nation of Israel, and (2) it is *conditional*; the Lord promises to make Israel a "priestly kingdom and a holy nation" (Exod 19:6), *provided that* Israel keeps up its end of the agreement. The many laws laid down in the latter part of the Exodus tradition specify just what Israel must do if it is to remain in good standing with the Lord.

Ancient Near Eastern Vassal Treaties

It is interesting to note that the Sinai Covenant is very much like a treaty.[14] The treaties that existed between ancient Near

Eastern nations fall into two categories: Parity treaties established and defined relations between equally powerful states; vassal treaties established and defined relations between a lord state and a vassal (subject) state—for example, between a military conqueror and the conquered state. Ancient Near Eastern vassal treaties almost always contained the same basic elements:

1. A preamble in which the lord state is identified
2. An historical prologue, usually stressing the lord's past goodness to the vassal
3. Stipulations and demands—what the vassal must do to keep the lord happy
4. Provisions for the storing and reading of the treaty
5. Appeals to the gods of both the lord and vassal states to witness to the treaty
6. Blessings and curses, that is, an appeal to the gods to enforce the terms of the treaty by rewarding obedience and punishing transgression
7. A ritual sealing of the treaty

The Sinai Covenant may be seen to contain almost all the elements of a vassal treaty. Let us examine each in turn.

1. Preamble

The Exodus tradition contains a passage that may be regarded as a preamble to the Sinai Covenant, for it is a passage in which the lord of the treaty is identified. This is the theophany experience of Moses in Midian, where the Deity identifies itself to Moses both by familiar description as the God of Abraham, Isaac, and Jacob (Exod 3:6) and by the proper name YHWH (Exod 3:14). It is with this lord that the Israelites, through their representative Moses, will establish their covenant.

2. Prologue

In a sense, Genesis 12 through Exodus 18 could be regarded as one long historical prologue to the Sinai Covenant, since all the good things the Lord has done for Abraham and his descendents are recounted therein. But the Lord's goodness to the Israelites camped at Mount Sinai is summed up succinctly at Exodus 19:4 and 20:2, where the Israelites are reminded that it was the Lord who brought them out of their slavery in Egypt.

3. Stipulations

The short version of the Lord's demands on Israel can be found at Exodus 19:5–6, where the Lord tells the Israelites that they will be a priestly kingdom and a holy nation if they obey the Lord and keep the covenant. The long version, which spells out in detail what Israel must do in order to keep the covenant, takes the form of distinct (though related) collections of laws. Let us briefly survey some of these law codes.

A. THE TEN COMMANDMENTS

The Ten Commandments (Exod 20:1–17) are apodictic laws regarding ethics. They are apodictic (unconditional) laws because they make commands without qualification; they are ethical laws because they have to do with moral behavior.[15] The first few commandments have to do with divine/human relations, while the rest have to do with human/human relations. The Ten Commandments are also referred to as the Decalogue, from a Greek expression meaning "ten words." The Decalogue is central to the Jewish faith; obeying these ten laws is essential to keeping the covenant.

B. THE COVENANT CODE

The Covenant Code (Exod 20:23—23:33) contains casuistic laws, that is, laws that apply to specific cases. Thus, unlike the Ten Commandments, the laws of the Covenant Code are conditional, for they state what must be done when certain situations arise. In this sense, they may be seen as specific applications of the laws laid down in the Decalogue. For instance, whereas the Decalogue states that one should honor one's parents (Exod 20:12), the Covenant Code specifies that anyone who strikes or curses a parent should be put to death (Exod 21:15, 17). While the Decalogue states that one should not commit murder (Exod 20:13), the

Covenant Code specifies that, when a person is killed by a dangerous ox whose owner failed to restrain it, both the ox and its owner shall be put to death (Exod 21:28–29). Whereas the Decalogue states that one should not steal (Exod 20:15), the Covenant Code specifies the forms of punishment to be meted out for animal theft under various circumstances (Exod 22:1–5).

C. THE PRIESTLY CODE

The Priestly Code constitutes most of the material from Exodus 25 through Numbers 10. It is attributed to the P source because it is primarily concerned with cult practices and ritual purity. For example, the first three chapters of Leviticus explain how sacrifices should be performed. Leviticus 11 lays down a number of dietary laws; certain animals are pronounced unclean, and so must not be eaten or even touched by the Israelites. Leviticus 17:10–13 forbids the Israelites to ingest blood, indicating that blood is to be used only in making sacrifices to the Lord. The Israelites must observe these regulations regarding ritual purity so that the Lord may dwell among them in their desert camp (Lev 15:31) and, later, in the Jerusalem Temple.

It is important to note that ritual-purity laws are distinct from ethical laws. To the ancient Israelites, one's being ritually impure did not necessarily mean that one was sinful. Instead, being impure meant that one was not in the proper condition for approaching the Deity. Israelites regularly came into contact with things that would render them impure, such as childbirth (Lev 12:2–5), menstrual blood (Lev 15:19), semen (Lev 15:2), and corpses (Num 19:11). The means to rectifying one's ritual impurity was not repentance, but ritual cleansing, such as the immersion of one's body in water. As one biblical scholar has noted, the main purpose of these purity laws was to keep those processes most intimately connected to the life and death of mortal creatures away from that which was holy, unchanging, and eternal—namely, the presence of God.[16]

The Priestly Code also contains laws regarding moral conduct. It commands the Israelites to love their neighbors as they love themselves (Lev 19:18). It forbids the Israelites to oppress any aliens living among them, since the Israelites themselves were once aliens living under oppression in Egypt (Exod 22:21; 23:9; Lev 19:33–34). The Priestly Code also contains a clear example of *lex talionis*, which is Latin for "law of retaliation." Leviticus 24:17–21 states that those who do harm should be made to suffer the same harm—and no more—in turn, "life for life…eye for eye, tooth for tooth." The purpose of such laws of retaliation may have been deterrence; one should not do to another what one is not prepared to suffer in return. However, it is also possible that the purpose of these laws was to *limit* retaliation by the injured or their families, since such retaliation—if left unchecked—could easily spiral into a full-blown blood feud.

D. THE DEUTERONOMIC CODE

Finally, the stipulations of the Sinai Covenant include the Deuteronomic Code (Deut 12—26), which is attributed to the D source of the mid-seventh century BCE. The Deuteronomic (second law) Code is so called because it is largely a rewriting and expanding of the earlier Covenant Code. The laws of the Covenant Code are given longer and more detailed treatment in the Deuteronomic Code. Compare, for example, the law regarding the release of slaves at Exodus 21:2 to the more elaborate version at Deuteronomy 15:12–15, or the law regarding homicide at Exodus 21:12–14 to the more fully developed version at Deuteronomy 19:1–13.

As we can see, the Sinai Covenant is not only conditional, it is also thorough and complex. Indeed, during the Second Temple period (515 BCE–70 CE), members of a Jewish sect known as the Pharisees would conduct a count of the laws contained in the Torah. By their reckoning, the Torah specifies 613 distinct laws that the Jews had to obey in order to keep their covenant with the Lord![17]

4. Provisions for Storing the Treaty

The Sinai Covenant contains specific provisions for how the documents that preserve it are to be stored. In Exodus 25—31 and again in 35—40, detailed instructions are given for the construction of an ark (a box or chest) in which the treaty between the Lord and Israel was to be kept. This ark itself was to reside in a tabernacle, a tent or hut that served as a portable sanctuary and place of worship for the wandering Israelites. The repetition of this material—the first time as a set of commands (Exod 25—31), the second time as the execution of those commands (Exod 35—40)—stresses its importance. Construction of the ark and the tabernacle had to be correct, for it was on the "mercy seat"—the top of the ark of the covenant—that the presence of the Lord was thought to dwell when the Lord was among the chosen people (Exod 25:22).

5. Witnesses

This part of a standard ancient Near Eastern vassal treaty is not to be found in the Sinai Covenant, for obvious reasons. Since the Israelites are bound by their contract with YHWH to acknowledge no other gods, there are no neutral deities—gods who are not party to the agreement—who can be appealed to as impartial witnesses.

6. Blessings and Curses

At Deuteronomy 11:26-28, the Lord explicitly states that Israel will be blessed if it obeys the commandments the Lord has given, and cursed if it fails to do so. Deuteronomy 28 makes explicit what the Israelites can expect to befall them for obeying and for disobeying the Lord's commandments. This treaty will be divinely enforced!

7. Sealing Ritual

Most ancient Near Eastern treaties were made official by some sort of ceremony marking the institution of the agreement. A ceremony marking the institution of the covenant between YHWH and Israel can be found at Exodus 24:3-8, where Moses seals Israel's agreement to obey the Lord's commands by splashing the people of Israel, and their altar to YHWH, with the blood of sacrificial oxen.

Thus, the religious laws of Judaism are spelled out in a covenant agreement that seems to have been modeled on the vassal treaties of the ancient Near East. Note, again, that this Sinai Covenant is conditional, for God's continued benevolence toward Israel depends upon Israel's obedience to the divine will. Note also that the Sinai Covenant is an agreement between God and the whole nation of Israel. This means that one is an Israelite if and only if one enters into the agreement established at Sinai. It also means that disobedience by any individual Israelite can place the entire nation of Israel in violation of the covenant.

B. Narrative Elements

We should close our discussion of the Exodus tradition by highlighting an important element in the narrative accounts of the Israelites' stay at Sinai and their wanderings in the wilderness. The dominant theme of the narrative passages in Exodus 19 through Deuteronomy is that of rebellion and punishment.[18] In Exodus 32, Moses catches the Israelites worshiping an idol, and orders the sons of Levi to go on a bloody rampage; at his command, the Levites kill three thousand of their fellow Israelites. (Many scholars suspect that this story was a later invention, intended to explain and to justify the restriction of priestly duties to Levites. See Exod 32:29.) In Numbers 11, the Israelites clamor for meat, and complain that they were better off in Egypt. So the Lord sends them quails to eat, but also a plague that strikes many of them down. In Numbers 12, Moses' brother Aaron and his sister Miriam complain about Moses having married a non-Israelite woman, and about the Lord's favoring Moses over either of them. The Lord responds to their impudence by striking Miriam with leprosy; she recovers only after Moses has appealed to the Lord on her behalf. Thus, even as YHWH and Israel are forging the covenant that defines their relationship, Israel is already showing the ease with which it can fall into violation of that covenant, while YHWH emerges as a personal and jealous god who demands the loyalty of every Israelite.

Indeed, the Lord becomes quite frustrated with the Israelites' rebellions. As a result, the Lord decides to withhold the promised

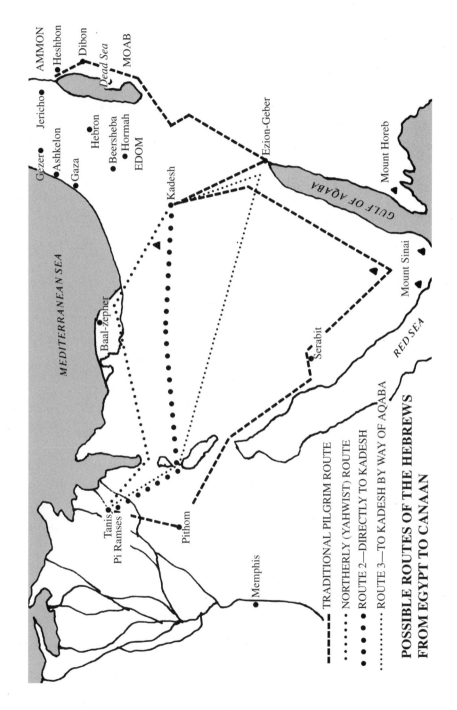

POSSIBLE ROUTES OF THE HEBREWS
FROM EGYPT TO CANAAN

TRADITIONAL PILGRIM ROUTE

NORTHERLY (YAHWIST) ROUTE

ROUTE 2—DIRECTLY TO KADESH

ROUTE 3—TO KADESH BY WAY OF AQABA

land from those who had been in Egypt. The Israelites will wander the desert for forty years—the standard Hebrew measure of a generation—so that the descendents of those Israelites who had been delivered from Egypt will inherit the promised land in their place (Num 14). Even YHWH's servant Moses is not to enter the promised land, as punishment for a seemingly brief lack of faith (see Num 20:1–13; 27:12–14). At Moses' request, the Lord appoints a successor to Moses in the person of Joshua, who will lead the Israelites into Canaan (Num 27:15–23). As the Book of Numbers draws to a close, Israel arrives at the plains of Moab, just east of the Jordan River, and is ready to cross into the promised land.

5

Conquest and Monarchy

In the Hebrew canon of scriptures, the books of Joshua, Judges, 1 and 2 Samuel, and 1 and 2 Kings are known collectively as the Former Prophets, because it is here that the official prophets first make their appearance. These books offer a continuous history of Israel from the death of Moses to the Babylonian Exile, a period of history that includes the Israelites' occupation of Canaan, the emergence of an Israelite monarchy, the division of that monarchy into two kingdoms, and the ultimate fall of both those kingdoms. Like the Deuteronomic Code (Deut 12—26), the books that constitute the Former Prophets emphasize the idea that the Lord is a lawgiver who rewards the Israelites for their obedience and punishes them for their transgressions. For this reason, biblical scholars refer to the Former Prophets as the Deuteronomic History, and they refer to the author/editor of these works as the Deuteronomic Historian—not to be confused with the Deuteronomist who authored the D source in the mid-seventh century BCE.[1] The Deuteronomic Historian is thought to have compiled his history of Israel from a number of different sources in the mid-sixth century BCE. As we shall see, the Deuteronomic Historian was concerned not simply to preserve the history of Israel, but also to interpret that history theologically.

I. CONQUEST AND EARLY MONARCHY: JOSHUA, JUDGES, 1 SAMUEL

The books of Joshua, Judges, and 1 Samuel recount Israel's conquest of the promised land and its transition from a loose affiliation of tribes into a unified monarchy. We shall review some of the narrative elements of these books, and then the historical elements. First, however, we should make clear what we mean when we refer to the *tribes* of Israel.

The Twelve Tribes

According to the biblical narrative, the nation of Israel was composed of twelve distinct tribes. Each of the tribes took its name from one of the twelve sons of Jacob, and the members of a tribe were thought to be the descendents of the son after whom their tribe was named. Actual listings of the tribes, however, are not always consistent with each other. Consider the following three lists:

Genesis 49:1–27	Numbers 1:5–15	Deuteronomy 33:1–29
Reuben	Reuben	Reuben
Simeon	Simeon	
Judah	Judah	Judah
Levi		Levi
Benjamin	Benjamin	Benjamin
Zebulun	Zebulun	Zebulun
Issachar	Issachar	Issachar
Dan	Dan	Dan
Gad	Gad	Gad
Asher	Asher	Asher
Naphtali	Naphtali	Naphtali
Joseph	Ephraim	Ephraim
	Manasseh	Manasseh

It is unclear what happened to Simeon. It may have been wiped out in the conquest of the promised land, or perhaps it was absorbed into the tribe of Judah (see Judges 1:3). After Exodus, the tribe of Joseph is usually replaced—as in the above lists from Numbers and Deuteronomy—by tribes named for Joseph's sons Ephraim and Manasseh, suggesting that one tribe may have split into two. Because the Levites had the privilege of performing religious duties on behalf of the entire nation of Israel (Num 3:5–9), they were not allotted a section of the promised land once it was under Israel's control (Num 18:21–24). Thus, although Levi ultimately lost its status as a tribe, it continued to exist in Israel as a class of religious servants.[2] As we shall see, the differences between Israel's tribes play an important role in the Deuteronomic History.

A. Narrative Elements

Joshua

The books of Joshua and Judges both recount Israel's occupation of Canaan, the fulfillment of YHWH's promise of a land to the descendents of Abraham. Yet the two books seem to preserve very different accounts of how the occupation occurred. The Book of Joshua gives us the impression that Israel conquered Canaan in a unified, lightning-fast military campaign. The Lord commands Moses' successor, Joshua, to cross the Jordan and take the promised land (1:2–6). The Lord then facilitates Israel's crossing of the Jordan by stopping the flow of its waters, so that "all Israel" crosses into Canaan on dry ground (3:14–17). The Lord delivers the city of Jericho into the hands of the Israelites (6), and then the city of Ai (8); in both cities, the Israelites slaughter virtually all the inhabitants. Next the Israelites defeat a combined force of five Amorite kings and their hosts, again with the Lord's help (10). Joshua 12:7–24 lists thirty-one Canaanite cities defeated by Joshua and the Israelites. Much of the remainder of the book deals with how all these captured lands were divided up among the Israelite tribes.

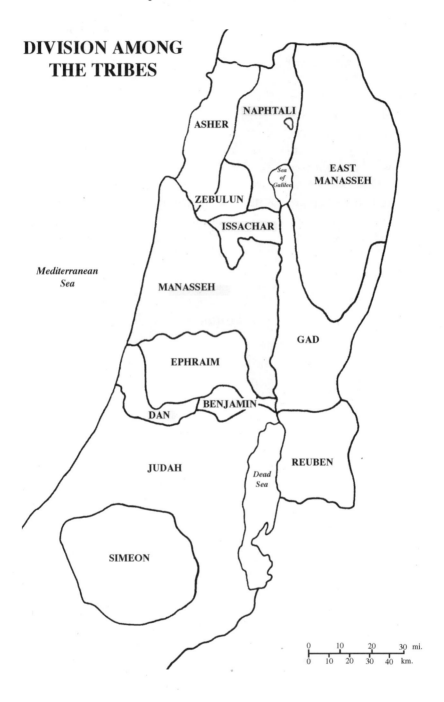

DIVISION AMONG THE TRIBES

ASHER

NAPHTALI

Sea of Galilee

EAST MANASSEH

ZEBULUN

ISSACHAR

Mediterranean Sea

MANASSEH

GAD

EPHRAIM

BENJAMIN

DAN

JUDAH

Dead Sea

REUBEN

SIMEON

0   10   20   30 mi.

0   10   20   30   40 km.

Judges

Whereas the Book of Joshua portrays the entire nation of Israel as sweeping through Canaan in an unstoppable blitzkrieg, the Book of Judges paints a different picture of Israel's occupation of the promised land. The narrative account in Judges begins after the death of Joshua, and recounts a conquest that is much slower and more piecemeal. Judges 1:1—2:5 gives us the strong impression that the various tribes' military campaigns were distinct— that is, different groups of Israelites were waging war independently of each other, rather than all of them fighting together in a unified group. Consider also the Song of Deborah recorded in Judges 5, which is thought to be one of the oldest passages in the Bible (dating to roughly 1125 BCE). In this poem, some of the tribes of Israel (Ephraim, Benjamin, Machir [Manasseh], Zebulun, Issachar, and Naphtali) are lauded for their participation in a battle against the Canaanites, while others (Reuben, Gilead [Gad], Dan, and Asher) are chastised for having failed to lend their assistance. It thus seems that the tribes were acting more or less autonomously during this period. The passage at Judges 1:1—2:5 also emphasizes—in a way that Joshua does not—the incompleteness of Israel's conquest. It points out precisely all of the places that the various Israelite tribes were *not* able to capture and all the indigenous peoples that the Israelite tribes were *not* able to defeat. The Book of Judges offers a theological reason as to why Israel met with such limited success: YHWH was punishing the Israelites for their violations of the Sinai Covenant (2:2–3).

Why Keep Both Accounts?

Why would the Deuteronomic History paint two such different pictures of Israel's occupation of the promised land? Could such a unified and successful military force become divided and ineffective so quickly after Joshua's death? Scholars have two answers to these questions. One is that, in compiling and editing this history of Israel, the Deuteronomic Historian appealed to a number of different oral and written sources, and sometimes preserved variants of the same story. For example, the Book of Joshua asserts that the Israelites conquered the Negev Desert, the hill country and lowlands of Israel, and the cities of Jerusalem, Hebron, Taanach, and Megiddo (11:16–19; 12:7–24). In the Book of Judges, however, these same places are listed among those over which the Israelites could not gain control (1:8–10, 20–27). Similarly, Judges 4 tells us that two or perhaps three tribes fought against the Canaanites at Kishon, whereas Judges 5 tells us that six tribes did so. Thus, it seems that the Deuteronomic Historian had access to more than one account of how Israel came to occupy Canaan. In one of those accounts, the power of the Lord made it a quick and easy affair for Israel. In the other, the tribes fended for themselves with limited success.[3]

A second reason why the Deuteronomic History might preserve two different views on Israel's occupation of Canaan is that the Deuteronomic Historian deliberately wished to stress two different ideas. On the one hand, he wanted his readers to know that the Israelites' ultimate success in Canaan was the result of the Lord's acting on their behalf; YHWH delivered the promised land to Israel in fulfillment of the covenant. This is the idea stressed in Joshua. On the other hand, he also wanted his readers to know that Israel's conquest of the promised land was a long and difficult process, primarily because Israel continually violated its covenant agreement with the Lord. This is the idea stressed in Judges, where the Deuteronomic Historian's theological interpretation of events follows a discernible pattern: Israel sins; YHWH delivers Israel into the hands of a Canaanite oppressor; the people cry out to the Lord for help; YHWH sends a deliverer (judge)* to rescue them; there is peace while the judge lives, but then the judge dies, and the people sin again. For an example of this pattern, see Judges 3:7–11; the whole process begins anew at 3:12. Thus, while affirming the miraculous aspect of Israel's conquest—and thereby the fidelity of the Lord—the Deuteronomic Historian also interprets Israel's difficulties as divine punishment for the nation's failures to obey the divine will.[4]

---

* The English word *judge*, from which the Book of Judges gets its name, is a translation of the Hebrew word *shophet*, which means something like "ruler." Thus, Israel's judges are best thought of as military leaders, heads of clans, or tribal chieftains.

Emergence of the Israelite Monarchy

The Deuteronomic History contains a similar blending of divergent views with regard to the establishment of the monarchy in Israel. The Book of 1 Samuel seems to alternate between two portraits of Israel's first king, one very flattering and the other very unflattering. In chapter 8, the people of Israel come to the prophet Samuel and ask him to appoint them a king. The Lord clearly seems to think that this is a bad idea, and instructs Samuel to warn the people that having a king would make them slaves. In chapter 9, the Lord guides Saul to Samuel, instructs Samuel to appoint Saul king, and says that Saul will save the Israelites from the Philistines. Chapter 10 begins with Samuel anointing Saul king over Israel, but then tells us that Saul is selected to be king by a drawing of lots. In chapter 11 Saul is portrayed as a successful military leader, saving the town of Jabesh-gilead from the Ammonites. But in chapter 13, Saul performs a sacrifice, which was the duty of priests, not kings. Saul is then told by Samuel that his reign is over, and that the Lord has picked someone else to rule. Again, in chapter 15, when Saul fails to kill every living thing in one of the cities he attacks—as the Lord had commanded him to do—the Lord expresses regret at having made him king, and rejects him. But despite having been twice rejected by the Lord, Saul continues to rule until his death.[5]

The Deuteronomic History seems to have preserved two different views of the Israelite monarchy. On the one hand, the flattering elements of Saul's story suggest that the monarchy was a gift from the Lord, part of the divine plan for Israel. On the other hand, the unflattering elements of Saul's story suggest that the monarchy was a mistake, something God never intended for the chosen people and even regretted having allowed. Again, scholars believe that the Deuteronomic Historian may have intertwined two distinct accounts of the establishment of the monarchy, each with its own interpretation of events. These two accounts are referred to as the early source and the late source. The early source is thought to have been written sometime during the reign of King Solomon (962–922 BCE). This was a time when Israel was thriving under its king. Thus, the early source is promonarchy; it characterizes the kingship as a blessing and salvation, portrays Saul as a hero, and downplays the role of Samuel. The late source is thought to have originated late in the period of the Divided Kingdom or early in the period of the Judean Kingdom (roughly 750–650 BCE). It regards the monarchy as a mistake; the centralization of power in the person of a king has divided Israel politically and degraded it religiously. This later source seems to think that power should rest with Israel's religious authorities. Thus, it presents Saul in unflattering terms, while celebrating Samuel as the true judge and religious leader of Israel.

B. Historical Elements

There is no doubt that, between 1250 and 1000 BCE, the Israelites came to dominate Canaan. Archaeology confirms that there was an extraordinary increase in settlements and population in Canaan during the twelfth and eleventh centuries. Exactly how this occupation occurred, however, is still a matter of debate. The available evidence allows for the formulation of hypotheses, but it neither completely confirms nor completely refutes the biblical accounts of the occupation. Although scholars have offered many different theories regarding how Israel came to occupy the promised land, all those theories are variations on one of three basic models: the Conquest Hypothesis, the Peaceful Infiltration Hypothesis, and the Social Revolution Hypothesis. Let us consider each of these theories in turn.[6]

The Conquest Hypothesis

First is the Conquest Hypothesis. On this theory, the Israelites—who were ethnically and religiously distinct from the Canaanites—invaded and took control of Canaan by means of military force. Obviously, this theory fits well with the account found in Joshua. Archaeological evidence suggests that both widespread destruction and subsequent cultural changes occurred in Canaan around 1200 BCE. Unfortunately, that evidence does not reveal whether or not it was Israel who wrought the devastation; the ruins could have been the result of Egyptian attacks, inter-Canaanite conflicts, or even earthquakes. Moreover, most of the towns destroyed during this period were also burned, but Joshua 11:13 suggests that the burning of towns was not a common practice of the Israelites. Archaeology has also shown that the walled city of Jericho had been destroyed in roughly 1550 BCE; by the early thirteenth century, it was an unwalled and impoverished settlement, and by the early twelfth century it had been abandoned altogether.[7] Again, archaeological finds strongly suggest that a number of the cities that the Deuteronomic History claims to have been conquered by the Israelites (such as Heshbon, Dibon, Ai, and Arad) were not even occupied in the late thirteenth and early twelfth centuries. If the Israelites took these cities, it was not by force, for there was no one there to resist them!

The Peaceful Infiltration Hypothesis

Second is the Peaceful Infiltration Hypothesis, also known as the Pastoral Nomad Hypothesis. On this theory, the nation that would come to be known as Israel was made up of various nomadic peoples who practiced sheep and goat husbandry; these peoples migrated into Canaan in small groups and settled there. Such nomads could have established relatively peaceful relations with the indigenous Canaanites, since they would have led their flocks into sparsely populated regions where they would neither pose a threat to—nor be under the control of—the Canaanite city-states. Still, while these nomads did not invade Canaan by force, they may have come into armed conflict with the indigenous Canaanites from time to time. One problem with this theory is that it is difficult to imagine large numbers of nomadic peoples suddenly deciding to settle down, which must have happened if this theory is to account for the increase in settlements. Another problem, both for this theory and for the Conquest Hypothesis, is the abundance of archaeological evidence indicating that the early Israelites were very similar to the indigenous Canaanites in terms of their religious beliefs, poetry, pottery styles, and house design. If the Israelites were both religiously and ethnically distinct from the Canaanites, as both the Conquest and Peaceful

79

Infiltration models contend, then the cultural similarities between Israelites and Canaanites are difficult to explain.

The Social Revolution Hypothesis

Third is the Social Revolution Hypothesis, formerly known as the Peasant Revolt Hypothesis. On this theory, the people who ultimately came to be known as Israel included not only a small group of former slaves from Egypt, but also people already living in Canaan. Some of these might have been Hebrews who had remained in Canaan when Jacob's people relocated to Egypt, but the majority were probably indigenous Canaanites. This theory holds that the "conquest" of Canaan was actually a revolt by oppressed Canaanite peasants against their feudal lords—that is, against the kings of the Canaanite city-states. It is reasonable to believe that the arrival of the Yahwist faith in Canaan could have served as a catalyst for the socially, economically, and politically oppressed to withdraw to as-yet unoccupied areas and take up arms in defense of those areas. This would mean that Israel's ranks swelled by the admission of Canaanite converts to the Sinai Covenant. While many scholars consider this theory to be highly plausible, there is no historical evidence that supports it directly.

A Little of Each

It is important to note that very few scholars favor one of these hypotheses to the point of rejecting the other two. Instead, most scholars think that a reasonably historical explanation of the Israelites' occupation of Canaan probably involves elements of all three theories. The early Israelites probably had some military victories, but Israel's rise to dominance in Canaan was probably a gradual, peaceful process overall. Some Israelites arriving from the Exodus through the wilderness may very well have reunited with other Hebrews in Canaan who had never relocated to Egypt. Once in Canaan, Israel probably absorbed other Canaanite groups, such as oppressed peasants, into the covenant with YHWH. Finally, it is not unthinkable that the Israelites could have integrated and peacefully coexisted with at least some of the indigenous Canaanite peoples.

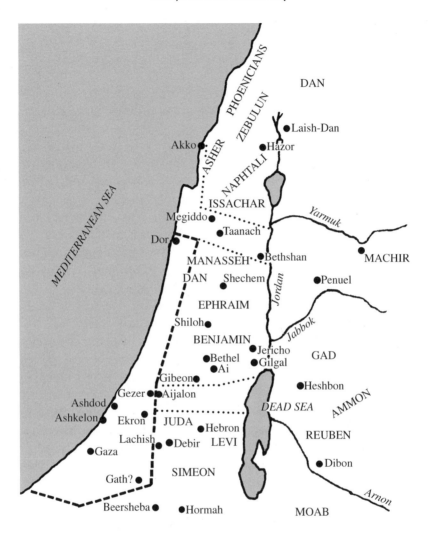

THE TRIBES AT THE TIME OF THE CONQUEST

Canaanite Population Barriers ··············

Possession of the Peoples of the Sea ━ ━ ━ ━ ━

The Philistines

However Israel's occupation of the promised land is to be understood, the biblical narrative suggests that true control of Canaan did not belong to the Israelites until, sometime in the late eleventh century BCE, they proved to be a military match for the Philistines. The Philistines were part of a fierce group of seafaring peoples whom the Egyptians referred to collectively as the Sea Peoples. The Philistines originated in the area of the Aegean Sea, but abandoned their original home when the Mycenaean Civilization collapsed in the late Bronze Age (1550–1220 BCE). They moved southward along the eastern end of the Mediterranean Sea, destroying a number of cities along the coast as they went. By 1190 or so, they had occupied the southern coast of Canaan. They tried to take Egypt in 1175 BCE, but the forces of Pharaoh Rameses III repelled them. The Philistines' territory was organized into a pentapolis, meaning that it was governed by five well-fortified cities: Ashdod, Ashkelon, Ekron, Gaza, and Gath.[8]

By the second half of the eleventh century BCE, the Philistines posed a considerable threat to the fledgling state of Israel. Evidence of this is reflected in the biblical narrative. Judges 18 tells us of the migration of the tribe of Dan to the area previously known as Laish, northeast of the Sea of Galilee. According to Judges 18:1, the Danites were looking for a place to settle because "until then no territory among the tribes of Israel had been allotted to them." But Joshua 19 tells us that the tribe of Dan *had* been allotted a section of the promised land to the west of Jerusalem, on the edges of the Philistine pentapolis. Dan's relocation to the extreme northeast of Canaan was probably motivated by the forceful encroachment of the Philistines on the Danites' territory.

Thus, although there is no extrabiblical data about King Saul, scholars have some reason to believe that Israel may have united under its first monarch in the latter half of the eleventh century. The loosely affiliated tribes of Israel probably found it very difficult to repel such a well-trained and well-equipped military as that of the Philistines. Israel's centralization of power in the person of a king would have made possible, perhaps for the first time, a coordinated response to enemy attacks.[9]

II. THE UNITED KINGDOM: 2 SAMUEL, 1 KINGS 1—11

Did Saul, David, and Solomon Really Exist?

There is very little extrabiblical evidence to confirm the existence of kings Saul, David, and Solomon, and that which does exist is inconclusive. For example, two inscriptions from the period of the Divided Kingdom—the Tel Dan inscription (made by one of the kings of ancient Syria, around 800 BCE) and the Mesha Stele (erected by King Mesha of Moab, 850–800 BCE)—seem to refer to the southern kingdom of Judah as the "House of David." While these inscriptions were written roughly 150 years after David's lifetime, they seem to offer indirect historical evidence that David was the founder of a dynasty in Israel. Some scholars, however, are skeptical of such indirect evidence. They also note that, because the relevant passage of the Mesha Stele is damaged and difficult to read, its interpretation is debatable.[10]

It is possible to argue that Saul, David, and Solomon were historical figures on the basis of indirect evidence in the Deuteronomic History itself. For instance, Stephen McKenzie has noted that many of the stories about David and Solomon in the Deuteronomic History have the strongly apologetic tone of royally commissioned propaganda; they seem intended to defend David and Solomon against charges of unworthiness and to justify those monarchs' reigns. Such propaganda was often commissioned by ancient Near Eastern monarchs—especially by those who had usurped the throne. McKenzie observes that, throughout David's rise to power and his reign, people who stand in David's way (such as Saul, Nabal, Abner, Ishbaal, and Absalom) tend to die at times that are very convenient to David, yet the Deuteronomic History takes pains to stress that David was not responsible for any of their deaths. Similarly, the account of Solomon's succession to the throne (instead of his older brother Adonijah) records the executions of two persons who probably opposed that succession (Joab and Shimei), but it attributes the order for their execution to David—thereby exonerating Solomon. These stories suggest that David and Solomon were regarded by some as being ruthlessly murderous, and that the authors of the stories were trying to paint both kings in a more favorable light. As McKenzie observes, it is unlikely that an author would invent such charges about fictional characters only to explain those charges away. Rather, the apologetic tone of these stories suggests that they were intended to clear the names of real historical figures about whom such charges had rightly or wrongly been made. Still, while this reading of the Deuteronomic History gives us some reason to believe that Saul, David, and Solomon really existed, it does not prove that they existed.[11]

Because the biblical and the extrabiblical evidence for Israel's first kings is inconclusive, biblical scholars are divided on whether or not the biblical stories about them contain historically reliable information. Some scholars, called maximalists, would argue that the Deuteronomic History preserves a great deal of historically accurate data about Saul, David, and Solomon. Other scholars, known as minimalists, would argue that the Deuteronomic History's stories about Saul, David, and Solomon are mostly—if not completely—theologically motivated legends. Since the biblical narrative offered in the books of Samuel and Kings is the only source we have to work with, we shall take a middle-of-the-road approach. We shall survey the data provided by these books on the assumption that they preserve at least a basic core of historical data, while bearing in mind that the Deuteronomic Historian probably interpreted and embellished that data for theological reasons.

King David

The biblical narrative makes clear that, while Saul may have been the Israelites' first king, it was during the reigns of his successors David (1000–962 BCE) and Solomon (962–922 BCE) that Israel emerged as a geopolitical power in the ancient Near East. According to the Deuteronomic History, David came from Bethlehem in Judah. He proved himself an able warrior against the Philistines, and was put in charge of Saul's armies. Eventually, he became a member of the royal court through marriage to Saul's daughter Michal. But Saul grew jealous of David's success, and of the people's love for him. After Saul made several attempts on his life, David fled Saul's capital at Gibeah (in the territory of Benjamin) and took to the hills, where he raised a heavy infantry force and continued to harass the Philistines. When Saul died, David marched his forces to Hebron (the principal city in the territory of Judah), where the Judeans anointed him as their king. He ruled over the tribe of Judah for seven years, and then the rest of the tribes anointed him as king of all Israel.

Many accomplishments are attributed to King David. One of his first moves was to attack and seize Jerusalem, the last city in Canaan still under Canaanite control. Having taken the city, David made it his political capital. This was a very strategic maneuver for a new king ruling over a confederation of twelve distinct tribes. Rather than governing from his homeland of Judah, David chose as his capital a city lying *between* Judah and the northern tribes. Because Jerusalem was not under the control of any of the tribes prior to its capture, it was neutral territory from which David could assert his authority over all the tribes equally (see 2 Sam 8:15).[12] David then brought the ark of the covenant to Jerusalem, making the "City of David" both the political center and the religious center of Israel. David is also thought to have expanded the borders of Israel through military conquest. He pushed the Philistines back to Philistia once and for all, and he conquered the Transjordanian lands of Edom, Moab, Ammon, and Aramea (Syria).

The Davidic Covenant

Theologically speaking, nothing in the Deuteronomic History's account of David is more important than the covenant that the Lord establishes with him. When David expresses his desire to build a Temple to house the ark of the covenant, the Lord responds through the prophet Nathan that David should not build a Temple, but leave it for his successor to do. The Lord then says that he will not withdraw his love from David's successor, and that David's house and kingdom "shall be made sure forever" (2 Sam 7:14–16). This is a profound covenant, not just for David, but for all of Israel. The Lord has promised the Israelites an everlasting kingdom to be ruled forever by the family of King David.

As beloved and successful as David was, he also had his flaws. The Deuteronomic History records the sordid tale of David's affair with Bathsheba, and his complicity in the death of Bathsheba's husband, Uriah. But, in typical Deuteronomic fashion, the Lord makes David pay dearly for his sin (see 2 Sam 12:7–14): His first child with Bathsheba dies; Amnon (David's son) rapes his own half sister Tamar (David's daughter by a different wife); Tamar's brother Absalom kills Amnon; Absalom then plots to usurp the throne from David, forces David temporarily into exile, and is finally killed by David's general Joab.

King Solomon

When David died around 962 BCE, he was succeeded by his son Solomon. Like his father, Solomon did a great deal to solidify the military and political status of Israel. He strengthened Israel's army by establishing standing chariot and cavalry forces, he constructed a defensive wall and an armory for Jerusalem, and he fortified the cities of Megiddo, Gezer, and Hazor. Solomon also secured Israel against its neighbors through shrewd diplomacy. For example, he allied Israel to Egypt by marrying the pharaoh's daughter, and he negotiated trade treaties with King Hiram of the Phoenician seaport of Tyre. He reorganized the kingdom by dividing it into Egyptian-style tax districts, and he established a bureaucracy to help him collect taxes and administer the affairs of state. He also constructed the first Temple of Jerusalem, a permanent dwelling place for the presence of the Lord. The Temple and adjoining royal palace were so elaborate that their construction took twenty years (1 Kgs 9:10).[13]

Although Solomon ruled over an enormously wealthy and powerful Israel, he too had his dark side. The massive building projects undertaken during his reign required tremendous labor, which Solomon extracted from forced-labor gangs. While Solomon certainly had plenty of foreign subject peoples from among whom to conscript laborers, 1 Kings is unclear on whether or not he also conscripted Israelites; 1 Kings 9:22 says he did not, but 5:13, 11:28, and 12:10–11 imply that he did.[14] Solomon's public works projects, military buildup, and government bureaucracy

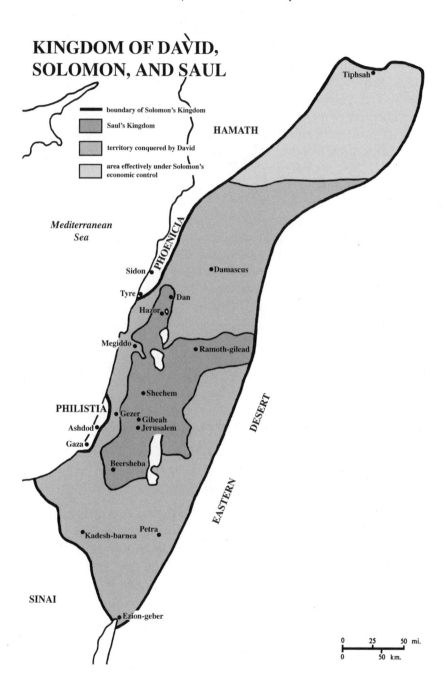

KINGDOM OF DAVID, SOLOMON, AND SAUL

— boundary of Solomon's Kingdom

Saul's Kingdom

territory conquered by David

area effectively under Solomon's economic control

HAMATH

Mediterranean Sea

PHOENICIA

Tiphsah

Sidon

•Damascus

Tyre

Dan

Hazor

Megiddo

•Ramoth-gilead

•Shechem

DESERT

PHILISTIA

Gezer
•Gibeah
•Jerusalem

Ashdod

Gaza

Beersheba

EASTERN

Kadesh-barnea

Petra

SINAI

•Ezion-geber

0   25   50 mi.

0   50 km.

were all expensive, and thus resulted in heavy taxation. And his reorganization of the kingdom into tax districts, each of which was under the control of a royal governor, undermined the relative autonomy previously enjoyed by the tribes of Israel.[15] The effect of all this was a growing disenchantment with Solomon's rule among the northern tribes. Theologically speaking, Solomon's greatest failing resulted from his polygamy. Solomon is said to have had one thousand wives, but this was not yet regarded as improper in itself.* Solomon's polygamy was sinful because most of his wives were non-Israelites of various faiths, and Solomon built altars and temples to their various gods (1 Kgs 11:1–8).

Like David, Solomon is punished by the Lord for his transgressions. First the subject peoples in Edom and Aramea rebel against Israelite control and win their freedom. Then Jeroboam, the former taskmaster of Solomon's labor gangs, leads a rebellion against Solomon—which fails—and flees to Egypt. (We shall hear more about Jeroboam below.) The most severe punishment, however, is to come after Solomon is dead, for the Lord promises to tear the kingdom out of the hand of Solomon's son (1 Kgs 11:11–13). How this rending of the unified kingdom occurred is the topic of the next section.

III. THE DIVIDED KINGDOM: 1 KINGS 12—22, 2 KINGS

The Meeting at Shechem

After Solomon's death in 922 BCE, his son Rehoboam ascended the throne. Rehoboam probably doubted whether the northern tribes, who had been disenchanted with his father's rule, would now be willing to accept his authority. The Deuteronomic History tells us that Rehoboam called for a meeting of the leaders of the twelve tribes at Shechem in Ephraim, near the southern bor-

---

* Polygamy was permitted by the Torah (see Deut 21:15–17), though it is unclear whether it was ever a common practice among the ancient Israelites. By the time of the Babylonian Exile, monogamy seems to have been regarded as the moral ideal (see Mal 2:14–16).

der of Manasseh. The purpose of this meeting was for "all Israel" to anoint Rehoboam as king. Among those in attendance was Jeroboam, freshly returned from his exile in Egypt. When Rehoboam arrived at Shechem, the representatives of the northern tribes—including Jeroboam, an Ephraimite—expressed their dissatisfaction with Solomon's policies and demanded to know whether Rehoboam would make things better for them. Acting on the bad advice of his young friends, Rehoboam gave the answer the northern tribes least wanted to hear: "My father made your yoke heavy, but I will add to your yoke; my father disciplined you with whips, but I will discipline you with scorpions" (1 Kgs 12:14). On hearing this, the northern tribes seceded from the unified monarchy, and Rehoboam was forced to flee back to Jerusalem. The northern tribes then anointed Jeroboam as their king. From this point forward, the Israelites would be divided into two kingdoms: the ten tribes in the northern part of Palestine formed a kingdom called Israel, while the remaining two tribes in the south (Judah and all or most of Benjamin) merged to form a kingdom called Judah.

Accounts of the Northern and Southern Kings

Most of what we know about the Divided Kingdom comes from the books of 1 and 2 Kings. These books seem to contain a great wealth of historical information, in part because the Deuteronomic Historian appealed to a number of official records that have since been lost, including the *Book of the Acts of Solomon* (1 Kgs 11: 41), the *Annals of the Kings of Israel* (1 Kgs 14:19), and the *Annals of the Kings of Judah* (1 Kgs 14:29). Still, it is important to remember that the Deuteronomic History is not just a record of events, but also a theological interpretation of those events. That the Deuteronomic Historian is concerned to evaluate the events he describes is evident in the formulaic way in which 1 and 2 Kings are structured. Virtually every account of an individual king's reign follows the same formula. First, a reference is made to the king who was reigning in the other kingdom when the king under discussion ascended the throne; this was a means of dating the beginning of the king's reign. Second, the length of the king's reign is given. Third, we are told what the king did that was evil in the eyes of the

Lord. The northern kings are typically condemned for having failed to depart from "the sins of Jeroboam," that is, idolatry. This is because, after the split of the united monarchy into two kingdoms, the people in the northern kingdom of Israel no longer had access to the Temple in Jerusalem. Thus, at the southern city of Bethel and at the northern city of Dan, King Jeroboam had established new centers of worship where, according to the Deuteronomic Historian, he proceeded to erect idols (1 Kgs 12:28). Fourth, a reference is sometimes made to one of the above-mentioned annals, directing the reader to a source of further information. Finally, the king's death and succession are reported. For an example of this formula, see 2 Kings 15:1–7.

This same formula is applied to both northern and southern kings, with two exceptions. First, the accounts of the southern kings usually mention the name of the king's mother. This is probably because the *Annals of the Kings of Judah* contained this information, whereas the *Annals of the Kings of Israel* did not. Thus, the Deuteronomic Historian only had access to the names of the southern kings' mothers. Second, *all* the northern kings are condemned for having done evil in the sight of the Lord, whereas not all the southern kings are so condemned. While most of the southern kings are said to have done evil, important exceptions are made for those southern kings who were religious reformers, such as Asa (1 Kgs 15:9–24), Hezekiah (2 Kgs 18:1—20:21), and Josiah (2 Kgs 22:1—23:30).

When Were They Written?

Scholars suspect that the Deuteronomic History's account of the kings of Israel and of Judah is drawn from two distinct sources. One was a history of the northern kings that was probably written in the southern kingdom after the fall of the northern kingdom to Assyria. That this history of the northern kingdom of Israel was written in Judah after Israel had already fallen is suggested by the fact that its author condemns all of Israel's kings; the author *blames* Israel's fall on its kings by suggesting that their sinfulness caused the Lord to abandon the northern kingdom to destruction. The Deuteronomic Historian also made use of a history of the southern kingdom of Judah. This history was written during or after the Babylonian Exile. In this source, the author attributes blame for the Babylonian Exile to those southern kings who did evil in the eyes of the Lord, but not to those who tried to reestablish good relations with the Lord through religious reforms.[16]

We shall have an opportunity to look into some of the historical details of the northern and southern kingdoms in the next chapter, when we discuss the prophets. We will close this chapter with a brief sketch of Israel and Judah.

Profile: The Northern Kingdom

The northern kingdom of Israel had twice the population and three times the area of Judah. Its capital was first at Shechem, but was moved north to Tirzah by King Jeroboam, and was later moved to Samaria by King Omri. It had two main centers of worship, one at Dan in the northern part of the kingdom and one at Bethel in the southern part. Both were meant to replace Jerusalem as the center of worship for citizens of the northern kingdom.[17] Because of its size and location, Israel was almost always at war—with Judah, with rebellious subject peoples, with the Philistines, or with the Assyrian Empire. Israel was also plagued by internal violence and dynastic instability; many of Israel's kings were usurpers rather than heirs. Consider the example of Zimri, recounted in 1 Kings 16. In roughly 882 BCE, Zimri was the commander of half of King Elah's charioteers. He killed King Elah at Tirzah, wiped out all of Elah's relatives who could claim to be a rightful heir to Elah, and seized the throne. Now most of Israel's army was off fighting the Philistines when this occurred. When news of Zimri's usurpation reached the troops, they proclaimed their commander Omri to be king, marched on Tirzah, and laid siege to it. Zimri barricaded himself in the palace and then—according to the Deuteronomic History—burned it to the ground. (It is more likely that Omri's troops torched the palace with Zimri trapped inside.) The reign of King Zimri of Israel lasted seven days.[18]

The dynastic instability of Israel is evident even in its number of kings. Israel went through nineteen kings in 201 years. Compare this to the twenty kings that ruled Judah for 335 years.[19]

DIVIDED KINGDOM

PHOENICIA

ARAM

Dan●

Mediterranean
Sea

Sea
of
Galilee

ISRAEL

●Samaria

● Shechem

AMMON

● Bethel

Jerusalem●

JUDAH

Dead
Sea

● Beersheba

MOAB

PHILISTIA

EASTERN

DESERT

● Kadesh-barnea

EDOM

WILDERNESS

0   15   30 mi.
0   20   40 km.

Israel's end came in 722–720 BCE. Israel had already been ravaged by the Assyrian king Tiglath-pileser III (745–727 BCE), who had forced many of the Israelites in the territories he conquered to relocate to other parts of the Assyrian Empire. In 722 BCE, the Assyrian king Shalmaneser V (727–722 BCE) captured the Israelite capital of Samaria. In 720 BCE, after a brief revolt against Assyria by Israel and Syria, Samaria was besieged and recaptured by the Assyrian king Sargon II (722–705 BCE). With the conquest of Israel complete, Sargon II deported most of the remaining Israelites to other parts of the Assyrian Empire, and repopulated northern Palestine with foreigners. Those Israelites whom the Assyrians deported were never heard from again, presumably because they were eventually assimilated into Assyrian culture. They are often referred to as the ten "lost tribes" of Israel.[20]

Profile: The Southern Kingdom

The southern kingdom of Judah was smaller, less populous, and thus weaker than Israel, but it enjoyed more peace than did its northern neighbor. This was due in part to dynastic stability. With only a few exceptions, the house of King David continued to rule Judah from the capital at Jerusalem until the kingdom fell. Judah also enjoyed peace because it capitulated to the more powerful states of the ancient Near East, making vassal treaties with the Assyrian Empire, and later with Egypt, and finally with Babylon. The end came for the southern kingdom in 586 BCE, after a failed revolt against Babylonian rule. On orders from King Nebuchadnezzar, the Babylonians besieged Jerusalem, destroyed the Temple, executed the leaders of the revolt, and deported most of the prominent Judeans to Babylonia. Thus began the Babylonian Exile.

6

The Prophets

I. INTRODUCTION

When people in our contemporary world hear the word *prophet*, they often envision some sort of fortune-teller who uses supernatural power to predict future events. This is not really what the word means in its biblical usage. The English word *prophet* comes from the Greek word *prophetes*, which means "one who speaks on behalf of another." The word that the Hebrew scriptures use for the prophets is *navi*, which means "one who is called" or "one who announces." Both of these definitions capture part of the biblical idea of a prophet. Israel's prophets were people who were called by the Lord to speak on the Lord's behalf. As we shall see, the prophets were important figures in the history of Israel, and the Israelites regarded them as both very holy and very powerful. Before we examine some of the individual prophets, a few introductory remarks are in order.

Former Prophets and Latter Prophets

The books of the Tanak that deal with the prophets divide into two groups: the Former Prophets and the Latter Prophets. The Former Prophets (Joshua, Judges, 1 and 2 Samuel, 1 and 2 Kings) are so called because it is in these books that prophets begin to play an important role in shaping the destiny of Israel. Thus, the Former Prophets contain stories about Samuel, who anointed Saul king; Nathan, who served David and Solomon; Elijah, who served King Ahab of Israel; and Elisha, who served the Israelite kings Jehoram, Jehu, Jehoahaz, and Jehoash. The Latter

Prophets differ from the Former Prophets in an important way: Whereas the books of the Former Prophets contain stories *about* prophets, the books of the Latter Prophets were written *by* prophets (or their followers). For this reason, the Latter Prophets are sometimes referred to as the Literary Prophets or the Writing Prophets. The Latter Prophets themselves divide into two categories: the Major Prophets (Isaiah, Jeremiah, Ezekiel) and the twelve Minor Prophets, which are also collectively referred to as the Scroll of the Twelve.

Basic Themes

While different prophets had different concerns and emphases that varied according to the circumstances in which each individual prophet was working, there are a few basic themes shared by virtually all the books of the Latter Prophets. The primary goal of most of the writing prophets was to call erring Israelites back to their covenant obligations. This involved (1) reminding the Israelites what those obligations were, and (2) warning the Israelites what the consequences would be if they continued to be derelict in their duties to the Lord. It is this latter aspect of biblical prophecy that is often mistaken for fortune-telling. Unlike a fortune-teller, however, the biblical prophet's messages about the future are conditional; he tells the Israelites what sort of punishment they can expect *if* they do not change their ways. The fact that this prediction is conditional, and is offered as a warning, means that the prophet hopes the people will change their ways and thereby avoid the punishment he has foreseen for them. The prophets as a whole also stress the ethical dimension of the Yahwist faith. By emphasizing issues of social justice and care for the oppressed, the prophets tried to convince their audience that personal morality is just as important to the Lord as proper maintenance of the cultic aspects of worship.

Let us now examine the roles played by prophets working in the periods of the Divided Kingdom, the Babylonian Exile, and the Restoration. In each of the sections that follow, we shall consider some of the literary elements of the prophetic books and also the historical elements of the periods in which the prophets lived.

II. PROPHECY IN ISRAEL

During the period of the Divided Kingdom, a number of prophets served as advisors to the kings of the northern kingdom of Israel. The first two major prophets of this period were Elijah and Elisha, who worked in the mid-to-late ninth century BCE. Before we discuss the prophets themselves, it will help to have a sense of the historical context in which they prophesied.

Elijah

King Omri of Israel (876–869 BCE) had sought to strengthen Israel's ties with the Phoenicians by marrying his son and successor Ahab (869–850 BCE) to Jezebel, the daughter of Ethbaal, king of the chief Phoenician cities of Sidon and Tyre. Jezebel was a worshiper of Baal, the Canaanite god of fertility. When Ahab became king, he not only allowed Jezebel to continue worshiping Baal, but also institutionalized the worship of Baal in Israel—by building temples and altars to Baal, and by maintaining a large body of Baalist prophet-priests. According to 1 Kings 18, Jezebel brought hundreds of prophets of Baal into the royal court (v. 19), while Israel's Yahwist prophets were being executed at Jezebel's command (v. 4). The strength and success of Baalism in Ahab's Israel implies that many Israelites must have been worshiping Baal either instead of—or in addition to—worshiping YHWH (see, for example, 1 Kgs 18:21).

Elijah (873–843 BCE) confronted the Israelites and their king over the issue of Baalism, reminding them that tolerance of the Baal cult—not to mention participation in it—was a violation of their covenant with the Lord. Elijah warns Ahab that a drought is coming, YHWH's punishment for the Israelites' idolatry (1 Kgs 17:1). A drought was a particularly effective show of force against Baalism, since Baalists held that their god controlled the rain. After the drought has gone on for three years, during which time Elijah was in hiding, Elijah goes to Ahab and proposes a challenge: He alone will confront the 450 prophets of Baal at Mount Carmel, to see whether Baal or YHWH will answer the prophets' calls for fire to light a sacrifice. The prophets of Baal dance and sing themselves to exhaustion, but their efforts are in vain; no fire comes down from the skies to light their sacrifice. Elijah taunts the Baalists, suggesting that perhaps their god is asleep, or has "wandered away"—a euphemism for ducking into the brush to relieve oneself. When Elijah's turn comes, he shows off a bit by having his sacrificial offering doused three times with water before he calls upon YHWH, who immediately sends down a consuming fire. Having proven to those present that YHWH is their true lord, Elijah leads the people in the slaughter of the prophets of Baal (1 Kgs 18:1–40).

Elisha

After Elijah ascended into heaven (2 Kgs 2:1–11), his prophetic work was continued by Elisha (849–785 BCE), his chosen successor (1 Kgs 19:19–21). Elisha seems to have been what biblical scholars call a teaching prophet, that is, the head of a school of prophets who are the students and disciples of the leader (see references to the "company of prophets" at 2 Kgs 2:3, 15; 9:1). The biblical accounts of Elisha's ministry tend to focus on his actions rather than his teachings, especially his working of wonders. Consider, for example, 2 Kings 2, in which Elisha parts the Jordan River (vv. 13–14), purifies a well (vv. 19–22), and invokes a violent punishment of some ill-behaved boys (vv. 23–25).

One important aspect of Elisha's ministry is his involvement with the usurper Jehu.[1] Jehu was a military commander in the army of King Jehoram of Israel. In roughly 842 BCE, Jehu was pronounced king by the army at the military outpost in Ramoth-gilead, an advanced position in Israel's conflict with Syria. Jehu and his troops then set out for Jezreel, where King Jehoram was recovering from wounds he had received in fighting against the Syrians. When Jehu arrived at Jezreel, he went on a killing rampage: He killed King Jehoram; Jehoram's nephew, King Ahaziah of Judah—who happened to be in Jezreel to visit his wounded uncle; the queen mother Jezebel, Ahab's widow; seventy sons of Ahab; forty-two relatives of Ahaziah; and assorted officers, friends, and priests of the Ahab dynasty (2 Kgs 9–10).

The effects of this usurpation were damaging to both kingdoms. The death of King Ahaziah of Judah opened a path to the

Judean throne for Athaliah, who was a daughter of Ahab and Jezebel and the mother of Ahaziah. Athaliah secured the throne by ordering the execution of Ahaziah's children. Joash, the only prince to escape this slaughter, would gain the Judean throne seven years later by means of a coup (2 Kgs 11:1–16). The gruesome death of Jezebel (2 Kgs 9:30–37) meant the end of friendly relations between Israel and Phoenicia. The internal chaos in Israel also weakened it externally; Israel soon lost its Transjordanian territories of Gilead, Ammon, and Moab to Syria (2 Kgs 10:32–33). And, according to an Assyrian obelisk, the Assyrian King Shalmaneser III attacked and subdued Israel in 841 BCE, forcing it into a tribute-paying vassal state.

According to 2 Kings 9:1–6, Jehu was anointed king of Israel on orders from Elisha, and was commissioned by Elisha to overthrow the dynasty of King Ahab. The Deuteronomic History characterizes Jehu's rampage as punishment, willed upon Israel by the Lord, for the transgressions of Jezebel and the other Baalists (2 Kgs 9:7). It is interesting to note, however, that this is the last time a prophet is so politically active as to be a kingmaker; from this point forward, those prophets who participate in political decision making will limit themselves to the role of advisors.

Amos

The next great prophet of the northern kingdom was Amos, who worked in the mid-eighth century BCE, during the reign of King Jeroboam II (786–746 BCE). The reign of Jeroboam II was a time of relative peace and prosperity for Israel, partly because Jeroboam had defeated Israel's enemies in Syria, and partly because the Assyrian Empire was weak at this time. Amos himself was not a northerner, but a Judean shepherd called by the Lord to go to the northern kingdom and denounce the idolatry that still thrived there—despite the efforts of Elijah, Elisha, and Jehu to eradicate it.

The prophecy in the Book of Amos attacks the Israelites for their idolatry, their extravagant ways of living, and their neglect of the poor and the afflicted (2:6–8; 6:4–6). It points out the hypocrisy of those who engage in the cultic rituals of worship but do not practice personal morality (5:21–24). It asserts the authority of the Lord over all nations, not just Israel (1:3, 6, 9, 11, 13). The Book of Amos is also the first to put in writing a concept that is thought to have been long in use among the Israelites: the day of the Lord. This is what theologians call an eschatological term (from the Greek *eskhatos,* "last things"), because it expresses beliefs about the ultimate destiny of humankind. It seems that some Israelites envisioned the day of the Lord to be a time in the future when God would finally crush Israel's enemies and begin a golden age during which Israel would be exalted. The Book of Amos corrects this view, warning that the day of the Lord is not something to be desired, but something to be feared; it will not be a day of exaltation for Israel, but a day when the Lord will judge and punish Israel for its sins (5:18–20).

Hosea

The last of the prophets of the northern kingdom was Hosea, who worked around 740–730 BCE. By this time, Assyrian power was surging, and the end of Israel was within sight. One of the interesting things about Hosea is that he does not simply preach his prophetic message, but also lives that message by means of symbolic actions. At the Lord's command, Hosea marries an adulterous woman named Gomer. His marriage to a presumably unfaithful wife is meant to symbolize the Lord's continued fidelity to an unfaithful Israel. Hosea and Gomer have three children, to whom Hosea—again at the Lord's command—gives symbolic names. The first is named *Jezreel,* the site of Jehu's massacre, for which the Lord will make Israel suffer. The second is named *Lo-ruhamah* (Not pitied), signifying that the Lord no longer forgives Israel. The third is named *Lo-ammi* (Not my people), suggesting that the Lord's covenant with Israel is dissolved. Still, there is hope even in these actions, for the Lord looks forward to a time when the proper relationship between Israel and the Lord will be restored (Hosea 1—3).

An interesting stylistic device can be found in Hosea 4, where the prophecy takes the form of a covenant lawsuit. Here the prophet acts as the Lord's prosecuting attorney, trying the Israelites for their failure to abide by their agreement with the Lord. Thus, chapter 4 begins with a summons in which the people of Israel are called to hear the charges against them (v. 1a). Those charges are then listed: lack of faith, lack of loyalty, ignorance of God, and so on (vv. 1b–2). Next, circumstantial evidence is offered in the form of the visible effects of Israel's guilt: "…the land mourns, and all who live in it languish…. My people are destroyed" (vv. 3–6a). Finally, a verdict is handed down: The Lord rejects the priests of Israel and vows to punish the people for their ways (vv. 6b–11a). For other examples of covenant lawsuits, see Jeremiah 2:4–13, Micah 6:1–8, and Psalm 50.

III. PROPHECY IN JUDAH

Three Isaiahs

The first of the major prophets to work in the southern kingdom of Judah was Isaiah of Jerusalem. Here we must note that, because of internal variations in style and context, scholars believe that the biblical book of Isaiah is a compilation of works by three different people or groups of people writing in three different periods. These different people or groups are referred to as First Isaiah, Second Isaiah, and Third Isaiah. Chapters 1—39 of the Book of Isaiah are attributed to First Isaiah, a prophet living in Jerusalem in the latter part of the eighth century BCE. Chapters 40—55 are attributed to Second Isaiah, a disciple (or disciples) of Isaiah of Jerusalem who lived and wrote after 586 BCE, during the Babylonian Exile. Chapters 56—66 are attributed to Third Isaiah, another prophet (or group of prophets) who lived in Jerusalem after the exile, during the Restoration (late sixth/early fifth centuries BCE).

First Isaiah

Isaiah of Jerusalem (First Isaiah) was born around 770–760 BCE. His commission as a prophet is vividly recorded in the call narrative of Isaiah 6. (A call narrative is a story recounting God's calling of an individual to serve as a prophet; see also Jeremiah

1:4–10.) The call begins with a theophany experience, in which the Deity reveals itself to Isaiah (vv. 1–4). Isaiah responds by lamenting his own unworthiness (v. 5). The Lord then reassures Isaiah that he is worthy by purifying him with glowing charcoal (vv. 6–7), and enjoins him to speak to the people on the Lord's behalf (vv. 8–13).

Isaiah was a counselor to the kings of Judah during some very turbulent times. During the reign of King Ahaz (735–715 BCE), King Pekah of Israel and King Rezin of Damascus formed a coalition to rebel against the Assyrian Empire, of which both Israel and Syria were vassal states. Failing to persuade Ahaz to join in their cause, Pekah and Rezin attempted to force Judah into their coalition by attacking Jerusalem in 734. Ahaz responded to this pressure by sending tribute to King Tiglath-pileser III of Assyria—making Judah a voluntary vassal of Assyria—and asking for Assyria's help. Assyrian troops then swept through Syria, Phoenicia, and down the coast to Gaza; when they turned eastward toward Jerusalem, the forces of the Israel-Damascus coalition withdrew (see 2 Kgs 16:1–9). According to Isaiah 7:1–9, Isaiah counseled Ahaz against appealing to Assyria, probably because he foresaw the religious corruption that such vassalage might bring—such as Ahaz's erection of Assyrian idols in the Jerusalem Temple (2 Kgs 16:10–18).[2]

King Ahaz was succeeded by his son Hezekiah (715–687 BCE). Around 705 BCE, Assyria's King Sargon II died on the battlefield in Anatolia (Asia Minor). Seizing on the momentary weakness of Assyria, Hezekiah organized a rebellious coalition of Judah, Syria, Phoenicia, and Philistia—all of which were vassals of the Assyrian Empire—with the promise of Egyptian military support. Isaiah warned Hezekiah, through both words and actions, not to rely on Egypt for help (Isa 20; 30:1–5; 31). Hezekiah readied Jerusalem for the inevitable onslaught by building a new defensive wall and by digging a tunnel that linked the city to an external water source. It was not until 701 that the new Assyrian king, Sennacherib, made his move. The Assyrian forces marched through Syria toward the coast, then down through Philistia to the border of Egypt, where they pushed back the Egyptian troops who tried to come to the coalition's aid. Turning inland, the Assyrians made for Jerusalem, taking and destroying a number of fortified cities along the way (see Isa 1:7). As Sennacherib's forces were closing on Jerusalem, Isaiah counseled King Hezekiah to be strong, prophesizing that the City of David would not fall (Isa 37:5-7, 21-35). When the Assyrians reached Jerusalem, they laid siege to the city, but did not take it. Instead, Hezekiah seems to have negotiated a surrender to Sennacherib, under the terms of which Judah returned to Assyrian vassalage and lost control of much of its territory to Assyrian vassal kings in Philistia, but Jerusalem was spared.[3]

Like Amos and Hosea before him, Isaiah of Jerusalem criticized his contemporaries for their luxurious lifestyles (3:16-17; 32:9-14), their idolatry (2:6-9; 31:6-7), and the hypocrisy of their superficial faith (1:10-17; 10:1-4). He, too, warns of the devastating punishment that is sure to come if the Judeans do not change their ways (5:26-30). But Isaiah also went beyond his predecessors. Perhaps the most interesting part of the message of First Isaiah is his idea that historic events, both those within and those outside Judah, are part of the Lord's plan. He sees the Assyrian Empire as a tool in the hands of the Lord, a weapon that the Lord wields against the unfaithful people of Judah (10:5-11). In a reference to this divine weapon, Isaiah names his second son *Maher-shalal-hash-baz*, which means something like "hasten the plundering" (8:1-4). He seems to regard Hezekiah's trust in Egyptian aid as a lack of faith in God's control over world events (30:1-5). He even suggests that Jerusalem's material defenses—such as Hezekiah's wall and water tunnel—are worthless without the Lord's will to protect Jerusalem (22:8b-11).

Isaiah of Jerusalem also emphasized the Lord's concern to fulfill the promises of the Davidic Covenant (9:6-7). Isaiah named his first son *Shear-jashub*, which means "a remnant shall return" (7:3). He held out hope that, despite the suffering that the Lord was soon to inflict upon the erring Judeans, a remnant of righteous people would be preserved and protected by the Lord (10:20-23). To these people the Lord would send a leader from the Davidic line—a "shoot...from the stump of [David's father] Jesse"—who would rule them with wisdom and justice (11:1-5). This leader, blessed by the Lord, would usher in an age of unprecedented peace (11:6–9) in which the northern and southern kingdoms would be reunified (11:13) and would quell their enemies permanently (11:14–16).

Micah

Another prophet of the southern kingdom was Micah (730–701 BCE). Unlike his older contemporary Isaiah, who was both a counselor to kings and the head of a prophetic school, Micah was a poor commoner living in Moresheth, the foothills south of Jerusalem. Micah was critical of what he regarded as the pretentious and morally corrupt life of Jerusalemites, who took advantage of the poor (2:1–3) and had no concern for justice (3:9–11). Micah went beyond Isaiah in that he prophesied the fall of Jerusalem itself (3:12). Still, like Isaiah, Micah also looked forward to a period in which Israel would be restored (4:1–3), a Davidic monarch returned to the throne (5:2), and an era of peace initiated (5:4b–5).

Zephaniah and Nahum

The next two prophets to serve in the southern kingdom of Judah both did so in the time of King Josiah, the great religious reformer who reigned from roughly 640 to 610 BCE (2 Kgs 22—23). The prophet Zephaniah, who claims to have been a descendent of King Hezekiah, tells his audience explicitly that the word of the Lord came to him during Josiah's reign (Zeph 1:1). The book of Zephaniah is highly eschatological; the prophet describes the coming day of the Lord—a time of judgment for Israel and for other nations—as "a day of wrath...of distress and anguish...of ruin and devastation" (1:15). Still, Zephaniah's message is also one of hope; after the day of judgment, the Lord will see to it that the "remnant of Israel...shall do no wrong and utter no lies,...and no one shall make them afraid" (3:11–13).

The prophet Nahum most likely lived and worked toward the end of King Josiah's reign. The Book of Nahum is a prophetic description of the fall of Nineveh, the largest and most important city in Assyria. According to Nahum, Nineveh's destruction will be the work of the Lord, an act of divine justice and vengeance

(1:2–3) that the Lord will undertake for the sake of the chosen people (1:15; 2:2). Since the city of Nineveh was indeed destroyed by the Babylonians in 612 BCE, the prophet Nahum most likely wrote his book around that time.

Jeremiah

The last major prophet of the southern kingdom was Jeremiah (627–580 BCE), who was a witness both to the religious reforms under King Josiah and to the tumultuous events culminating in the fall of Jerusalem. By Jeremiah's time, the Assyrian Empire was crumbling, succumbing to attacks from the emerging Neo-Babylonian Empire to its south. King Josiah met his end in 610 BCE, when Assyria was in its death throes. Apparently thinking that Assyria's weakness meant a chance to push for Judean independence, Josiah marched his army out to intercept the Egyptian forces who were on their way to lend assistance to Assyria; by this time, Egypt had allied with Assyria against the growing Babylonian threat. Meeting the Egyptians at Megiddo, the Judeans were routed, and Josiah was killed by Pharaoh Neco II. Judah thus became an Egyptian vassal state.[4]

Josiah was succeeded by his son Jehoiakim (608–598 BCE), who was installed as a vassal king by Neco II. In 605 BCE, Prince (soon to be King) Nebuchadnezzar of Babylonia won a decisive victory against the combined forces of Assyria and Egypt at Carchemish, which lies on the Euphrates River in Syria. After this triumph of Babylonia over the Egyptian military, Jehoiakim voluntarily submitted Judah to Babylonian vassalage. Four years later, Nebuchadnezzar tried to invade Egypt itself, but was repelled. Jehoiakim saw this as an opportunity to escape Babylonian domination; he ceased sending tribute to Babylon, and allied Judah to Egypt once again. King Nebuchadnezzar responded by sending an army to lay siege to Jerusalem in 597 BCE. During this siege, King Jehoiakim died and was succeeded by his son Jehoiachin. With no help coming from Egypt, Jerusalem was forced to resubmit to Babylonian vassalage. The Babylonians then deported ten thousand Judeans to Babylonia, including Jehoiachin and his court, the military elite, and many skilled tradesmen (2 Kgs 24:11–16). Later, the

Babylonians installed Zedekiah—another of Josiah's sons—as their vassal king in Jerusalem. Against the advice of Jeremiah (Jer 27—28), Zedekiah plotted a rebellion against Babylon with the promise of Egyptian support. In 586 BCE, the Babylonians again laid siege to Jerusalem, this time much more thoroughly; the city and its Temple were destroyed, Judah's military commanders were executed, and tens of thousands of Judeans—including Zedekiah—were exiled to Babylonia (2 Kgs 24:17—25:30). Jeremiah was permitted to stay in Jerusalem and seems to have been treated well, on orders from Nebuchadnezzar himself (see Jer 39:11–14). He became a counselor to Gedaliah, the Jewish governor appointed by the Babylonians after the fall of Jerusalem. Within a few months, however, Gedaliah was assassinated, presumably for collaborating with Babylon. Jeremiah and others who had been close to Gedaliah fled to Egypt, where Jeremiah probably remained until his death (Jer 40:7—43:7).[5]

Jeremiah's prophecies include warnings of the doom that is coming for Judah because of her idolatry (11:9–13) but also hope for a future restoration of Israel (31:3b–17, 27–28). What is perhaps most significant about the work of Jeremiah is his shifting of religious emphasis from the nation to the individual. Although the Jews had always understood themselves as having a relationship with the Lord, that was a relationship in which they stood together as a group. The Sinai Covenant had been an agreement between the Lord and the whole nation of Israel, and the Israelites' worship had largely been carried out by priests who offered prayers and sacrifices on behalf of the entire nation. In his introspective confessions (12:1–3; 15:10; 17:14–18) and his vision of a new covenant that the Lord will write on the people's hearts (31:31–34), Jeremiah suggests that being one of the chosen people means more than being part of a nation; it means having an intimate personal relationship with the Lord.

Habakkuk

A contemporary of Jeremiah was Habakkuk, who prophesied in roughly 600 BCE. This was a time when the Babylonians were wreaking havoc throughout the ancient Near East. Habakkuk was a philosophical prophet whose work is an exercise in theodicy, the attempt to justify God's ways to human beings. Habakkuk's theodicy unfolds in the form of a dialogue between the prophet and the Lord. When Habakkuk protests against Judah's suffering at the hands of the barbaric Babylonians ("Chaldeans"), the Lord replies that the success of the Babylonians is the Lord's own doing (1:2–6). Habakkuk objects that such suffering is not something that a righteous and loving God would allow (1:12–17). The Lord then assures Habakkuk that, though justice may seem far away, he must simply "wait for it; it will surely come." Meanwhile, the righteous should "live by their faith," trusting that the Lord will not abandon them (2:2–4).

IV. PROPHETS IN EXILE

Although most of the poorer Judeans were left in Judah to eke out an existence from the land as best they could, the Babylonians deported tens of thousands of Judeans to Babylonia after Jerusalem fell. Some were taken to the city of Babylon; many others were settled in the war-torn borderlands between Babylonia and Assyria where, along with other peoples conquered and deported by the Babylonians, they set about redeveloping heavily damaged areas in more or less self-governing units. Lacking a temple in which to make sacrifices, the Jews of the exile sought to preserve their unique identity by carefully observing their other covenant obligations, such as circumcision and the Sabbath rest.[6]

Ezekiel

Two important prophets served the Jews during the Babylonian Exile. The first of these was Ezekiel (593–570 BCE). Ezekiel lived in Jerusalem before it fell, but is thought to have been among those deported to Babylonia with Jehoiachin in 597 BCE. In his ministry to the exiles, Ezekiel further developed Jeremiah's focus on the individual by stressing the importance of personal responsibility. He rejects the idea that guilt and punishment can be passed on from parents to children, asserting instead that the Lord judges each individual person according to his or her own merits (18:1–4, 14–20). This is a clear departure from the view of reward and punishment taken in the Torah and the Deuteronomic History, both of which assert that the Lord does indeed punish children for their parents' sins (Exod 20:5; 34:6–7; 2 Sam 12:14; 1 Kgs 11:11–12). Ezekiel stresses that, though the Lord will surely punish those who are wicked, the Lord would much prefer to see wicked people change their ways and be rewarded for their righteousness (18:21–23, 30–32). Ezekiel also offered his fellow exiles hope by describing the future restoration of Israel in vivid metaphors, such as the valley of the bones in chapter 37.

Second Isaiah

The second major prophet of the Babylonian Exile was Second Isaiah. Whether Second Isaiah was an individual prophet or a small group of prophets is unknown. It is also unclear exactly when Second Isaiah prophesied, although his references to Cyrus of Persia suggest a date around 540 BCE. What is clear is that Second Isaiah was a member of the school of prophecy established by Isaiah of Jerusalem, and that he carried on the spirit of First Isaiah's work among the exiles.

Like First Isaiah, Second Isaiah stresses the idea that the Lord is at work in the events of world history. This idea takes dramatic form in Isaiah 45, where the Lord's words are addressed to Cyrus the Great of Persia (559–530 BCE), who would capture Babylon and release the Jews from their forced exile. Cyrus is here described as the instrument by means of which the Lord will free the chosen people; though Cyrus does not know the Lord, he will be an unwitting player in events directed by the Lord for the sake of Israel. Cyrus is even referred to as the Lord's "anointed" (Hebrew *mashiah*, Greek *christos*), a word usually reserved for kings of Israel.* Indeed, this is the only place in the Bible where the term is applied to someone who is not Jewish.[7]

Another important aspect of Second Isaiah's work is what scholars call his theoretical monotheism. Monotheism is the belief

---

* For a discussion of the Hebrew term *mashiah*, see chapter 10, section IV.

that there is one, and *only* one, deity. From its very beginnings, Yahwism was—or, at least, was meant to be—practically monotheistic; the people of the covenant were to worship no god but YHWH (Exod 20:1-3). But the fact that the prophets were continually combating idolatry means that many if not most of the Israelites were theoretical polytheists; whether they actually worshiped other gods or not, many Israelites believed that other gods existed who could be worshiped in addition to, or instead of, YHWH.* Indeed, the persistence of Baalism in both Israel and Judah suggests that many Yahwists were hedging their bets for a successful life in Canaan by worshiping both YHWH and Baal, the local god of agriculture and fertility. Thus, Second Isaiah makes a concerted effort to eradicate theoretical polytheism by making explicit assertions of theoretical monotheism—that is, explicit assertions that no gods but YHWH exist (Isa 43:10; 44:6; 45:5-6, 20b-21).

Finally, Second Isaiah developed the idea of the suffering servant, an important message of hope for the exiled Jews. The prophet describes a servant whom the Lord will send to bring justice to the world (42:1-4). This servant is Israel itself (41:8; 44:1, 21; 48:20; 49:3), which shall be "a light to the nations" and a "salvation" for the whole earth (49:1-6). Rather than being exalted, this servant will suffer; it will be "despised and rejected," wounded and afflicted "like a lamb led to the slaughter." Yet it is the will of the Lord that the servant should suffer, for it is through this suffering that the world is saved. In suffering and dying, the servant shall "make many righteous" by bearing their sins for them (53:1-12). To the Jews of the exile, this prophecy of Second Isaiah sent the powerful message that the pain, death, and humiliation they had experienced in the fall of their kingdom and the loss of their homeland were part of the Lord's plan. Their suffering would have a vicarious effect on the sins of others, in fulfillment of the Lord's promise to Abraham that Israel would be a blessing to all nations.

---

* As evidence of this, consider the Song of Moses, which asserts that YHWH divided human beings into distinct nations by fixing their boundaries "according to the number of the gods" (Deut 32:8-9). See also Exod 15:11; Deut 32:43; 1 Sam 26:19; Mic 4:5; Ps 82:1, 6.

V. RESTORATION PROPHETS

In roughly 550 BCE, King Cyrus II of Persia rebelled against and conquered Media, to which Persia had been a vassal state. By 546 he had swept through Armenia, Cappadocia, and into Lydia (an ally of Babylonia) and the Ionian coast of Asia Minor. In 539, he marched virtually unopposed into Babylon. With the fall of the Babylonian Empire, Persia acquired all of Babylon's imperial holdings, including Syria-Palestine. Unlike the Babylonians, the Persians did not have a policy of forcibly deporting conquered peoples. After he had conquered Babylon, Cyrus issued a decree allowing all peoples deported by the Babylonians to return to their lands of origin. Thus, in 538 BCE, the first of the exiled Jews began making their way back to Judea.[8]

Haggai and Zechariah

Prophets continued to minister to the Jews during this period, which is known as the Restoration. Haggai and his younger contemporary, Zechariah, prophesied in the late sixth century BCE (520–515). Both prophets commented on the conditions of Jerusalem some fifteen years or so after the exiles had begun to return. Elaborate private homes had been constructed (Hag 1:4), but the Temple remained in ruins (Hag 1:2; 2:3; Zech 4:9). Haggai urged the people of Jerusalem to rebuild the Lord's house, and expressed the Lord's will that they should do so (Hag 1:8; 2:4–9). Zechariah assured them that the Lord would deal with them differently than in the past; there would be "a sowing of peace," and the Lord would make Judah a blessing among the nations (Zech 8:11–13). Finally, both Haggai and Zechariah preserve the idea that a descendent of David would arise to take the throne in Jerusalem and serve as God's regent on earth (Hag 2:20–23; Zech 3:8). It seems that Haggai, and probably Zechariah also, thought that this Davidic monarch would be Zerubbabel, the grandson of Jehoiachin whom the Persians had appointed as governor of Judea (Hag 2:23). This, however, was not to be; Zerubbabel disappears from the biblical record before the Temple is even completed.[9]

Malachi

Another prophetic work that dates to the Restoration is the Book of Malachi. Because the Hebrew word *malachi* literally means "my messenger," it is unclear whether it is used (at Mal 1:1) as a name or a description. The book is dated to the first half of the fifth century BCE (around 460), based on its assertions that Judah is under the control of a governor (1:8) and that the Temple has been rebuilt and sacrifices resumed (1:10; 3:1, 10).[10] Despite having returned to their homeland, the Jews seem to have become lax in their faith. Thus, Malachi denounces the men of Judah for divorcing their Jewish wives to marry Gentiles (2:10–16) and for failing to pay their Temple tithes in full (3:8–12). He also rebukes the priests for growing weary with their duties and for making sacrifices of poor quality (1:6—2:9).

Joel

Like Malachi, the prophet Joel was also concerned with the proper maintenance of the Temple cult (Joel 1:9, 13–14; 2:14). We know virtually nothing about this prophet, so dating his work is difficult. Since the prophet makes no references to a king or royal court in Jerusalem, nor to the Babylonians, the work seems to date to the postexilic period. If this is the case, its references to Temple worship mean that the Book of Joel must have been written no earlier than 515 BCE, the year the Second Temple was completed. Since the work was written at a time when the Phoenician city of Sidon still existed (Joel 3:4), it must have been written no later than 343 BCE, the year that Sidon was destroyed by the Persians. Joel's prophecy divides into two parts. In the first part (1:1—2:27), the prophet describes a plague of locusts and a drought that have befallen Judah, signaling the need for repentance (1:8, 14; 2:17). The second part (2:28—3:21) is eschatological; here the prophet describes the coming day of the Lord, on which day the righteous will be saved (2:32), Judah restored (3:1-2), and Judah's enemies vanquished (3:4-8).

Obadiah

The last two books of the Minor Prophets are difficult to date with any certainty, though many scholars believe that they were probably written in the postexilic period. The Book of Obadiah is an example of an oracle against a foreign nation, in this case Judah's southern neighbor, Edom. Judah and Edom had long been at odds, vying for control of the Negev Desert and, thereby, control of Red Sea trade routes. Still, the Judeans considered the Edomites to be distant kin; as the nation of Israel was traditionally thought to have descended from Jacob, so the nation of Edom was thought to have descended from Jacob's brother Esau. It was perhaps because of this belief in shared lineage that the Judeans were so outraged by Edom's actions when the Babylonians were besieging Jerusalem.[11] Rather than coming to Jerusalem's aid, the Edomites "stood aside" (Obad v. 11), and may have even lent assistance to the Babylonians (Obad v. 14). Once the siege had ended, the Edomites took advantage of Jerusalem's downfall, rushing in to seize areas of Judah left undefended because of the Babylonian Exile. Thus, the Book of Obadiah denounces Edom for her sins against Judah (vv. 10–14) and predicts that Edom itself will fall in an act of divine retribution (vv. 1–9). The Edomites were in fact conquered by the Nabataeans (Arabs) between the sixth and fourth centuries BCE. The imminent fall of Edom to the Nabataeans during the Restoration suggests that the Book of Obadiah may date to this period.[12]

Jonah

Finally, the Book of Jonah is different from the other books of the Latter Prophets in that, rather than preserving a prophet's oracles, it tells the story of his experiences. Jonah was commissioned by the Lord to go to Nineveh (in Assyria) and "cry out against it" (1:2). Rather than obeying, Jonah tries to escape his burden by boarding a ship for Tarshish. (The location of Tarshish is unknown, but its name may be a corrupted version of Tartessus, which was a town near Gibraltar in Spain.) This attempt fails, as a number of miraculous events bring Jonah back to land (1:3—2:10). The Lord commissions him again, and this time Jonah complies. He goes to

Nineveh and warns its citizens that their end is coming. The Ninevites take Jonah seriously; they begin fasting and lamenting their wicked ways. The Lord is impressed by this change of heart and, much to Jonah's annoyance, decides to spare Nineveh the destruction that Jonah had been sent there to foretell (3:1—4:5).

The authorship and date of the Book of Jonah are virtually impossible to determine. While there was a prophet by the name of Jonah in Israel in the mid-eighth century BCE (2 Kgs 14:23–25), few scholars would attribute the Book of Jonah to that prophet. Indeed, most scholars doubt that the story is based on historical events, not only because some parts of the story strain credulity, but also because no other sources attest to any mass conversion of Nineveh to Yahwism. The only internal evidence that might help to date the work is the sympathetic stance it takes toward Assyria. Prior to the rise of the Babylonians, the Assyrian Empire had been an aggressive superpower in the ancient Near East, toward which neither Israel nor Judah would have had any sympathetic tendencies. After the fall of Jerusalem and the Babylonian Exile, however, Jews came to regard Babylonia as the enemy of enemies. This meant that, in retrospect, Assyria no longer appeared quite so evil. Thus, the fact that the author of the Book of Jonah makes an Assyrian city the subject of God's mercy suggests that that book may date to the postexilic period of the Restoration.

7

Songs and Wisdom Literature

The Kethuvim (Writings) constitute the third and final section of the Tanak to be incorporated into the canon of Hebrew scriptures (130 BCE–100 CE). The Writings comprise a number of different literary genres, including songs, wisdom literature, short stories, historical narrative, and apocalypse. Our topic in this chapter will be the songs and wisdom literature of the Hebrew Bible.

I. ISRAEL'S SONGS

Music and songs were part of the Yahwist faith from the very beginning. Indeed, scholars believe that a number of the Hebrew songs recorded in the Tanak are among the most ancient parts of the Hebrew scriptures. For instance, the Song of the Sea (Exod 15:1–21), the Song of Deborah (Judg 5), and the Song of Moses (Deut 32) are thought to have been written between the twelfth and tenth centuries BCE; they all use archaic grammar, and they make only limited use of words and grammatical forms that, though absent in Canaanite speech, were common in later (biblical) Hebrew. In other words, these songs seem to date to a transitional period during which the Hebrew language as we know it in the Bible was still emerging from the language of the indigenous Canaanites.[1] In the Writings we find three books that are actually collections or anthologies of songs: the Psalms, the Song of Songs, and the Lamentations. We shall examine each of these books individually.

A. Psalms

Origin and Purpose

The Book of Psalms (also known as the Psalter) gets its English name from the Greek word *psalmos,* which referred to a poem sung to the accompaniment of musical instruments. The book's title in Hebrew is *Tehillim,* which means "songs of praise." Although there are many different types of songs in the Psalms, they are unified by the underlying theme of praise for the Lord that runs through virtually all of them. Tradition has attributed authorship of the Book of Psalms to King David, based on (1) the ascription "of David," which is attached to 73 of the 150 songs in the book, and (2) the attribution to David of an interest in religious music at 1 Chronicles 16. While some of the psalms may have been written by David, the ascription "of David" is somewhat ambiguous; the Hebrew could be translated to mean "for David," "pertaining to David," or "belonging to David."[2] At least a few of the psalms (such as Psalms 18 and 113) contain the sort of archaic elements mentioned above, which suggests that those psalms predate even the United Kingdom. However, linguistic and theological analysis suggests that most of the psalms originated later, and that they did not achieve their final form until the period between 400 BCE and 100 CE.[3] Most scholars think that the Book of Psalms is an anthology of smaller collections that already existed, in which case the ascription "of David" to a psalm might mean that the psalm came from a royal collection; "of Asaph" might mean that the psalm came from a collection attributed to a particular musician, and so on.

Whatever their origins, it seems clear that many of the songs in the Book of Psalms had a liturgical use—that is, they were set to music and incorporated into public worship at the Temple or local shrines. Many of the psalms begin with instructions to the musical director on how the songs should be performed. The mysterious word *Selah,* which occurs seventy-one times in the Psalms, also seems to have been part of these instructions. Although this word's meaning is no longer known, its placement suggests that it might have indicated natural breaks in the songs where musical interludes should be inserted.

Because there are a number of different types of psalms, each with its own specific purpose and way of approaching the Lord, it will be helpful to discuss some of these types individually. For each type of psalm that we discuss, we shall consider a specific example of that type in detail.[4]

Laments

One of the most common types of psalm is the lament, in which the singers describe a situation of distress and appeal to the Deity for assistance. Such laments might be sung by an individual or by a group of people. In an individual lament, the singer typically stresses the breakdown of her personal relationship with the Lord, and seeks to reestablish that relationship. Consider Psalm 22, which begins with the singer's distress at having been abandoned by the Lord (vv. 1–2). The singer then recalls help that the Lord has given in the past (vv. 3–5) and, despite the fact that she is being mocked by those around her (vv. 6–8), affirms her trust in the Lord (vv. 9–11). Verses 12 through 18 describe the singer's lamentable condition, which seems to include fever (vv. 14–15) and weakness (vv. 16b–18), suggesting that this was a psalm sung by a person suffering a physical illness. Verses 22 through 31 then offer a promise of future thanksgiving; the singer vows to praise and glorify the name of the Lord whose aid is sought.

Like individual laments, communal laments also manifest the idea that well-being and suffering are linked to action or inaction on the part of the Lord. But unlike individual laments, communal laments tend to stress Israel's historic relationship with the Lord, and usually seek the Lord's help against some mutual external enemy. Psalm 44 is an example of a communal lament. The group first reminds the Lord of past help that the Lord has given to Israel in the form of military victories (vv. 1–8). Next, the singers describe their present condition, in which they are suffering defeat and shame (vv. 9–16). Note especially the reference to being "scattered…among the nations" in verse 11, which suggests that this psalm was composed in the exilic period. The singers then complain against the Lord, in a very bitter and accusatory tone, that this condition of theirs is undeserved (vv. 17–22); they have not abandoned the Lord, so why has the Lord abandoned them? Finally, the singers entreat the Lord to wake up and do something about their miserable situation (vv. 23–26).

Hymns

Another common type of psalm is the hymn, in which the singers express to the Lord their praise, trust, or gratitude. Like laments, hymns might be sung by individuals or by groups. Psalm 23 is an individual hymn. In verses 1–4, the singer characterizes the Lord as a good shepherd, whom she trusts to lead her safely through life's difficulties. In verses 5–6, the singer characterizes the Lord as a gracious host, satisfying all the needs of those who "dwell in the house of the Lord"—meaning those who worship in the Temple. Some scholars take this last reference as an indication that Psalm 23 was written by a priest or a Temple functionary.

Psalm 136 is an example of a communal hymn. Since it seems to be divided into single-lined stanzas and refrains, scholars believe that the singing of this psalm was truly a group effort; the priest or elder would sing the first half of each verse, and the congregation of worshipers would sing the second half as a response. The psalm begins with a summons to all to give thanks for the Lord's steadfast love (vv. 1–3). It then recounts the Lord's praiseworthy actions at the Creation (vv. 4–9), during the Exodus (vv. 10–16), and in the conquest of Canaan (vv. 17–22). The singers recapitulate their reasons for giving thanks and praise (vv. 23–25), and close with a final summons to thanksgiving (v. 26).

Enthronement Psalms

Some Hebrew songs characterize the Lord as a king enthroned and celebrate the Lord's reign; these are called enthronement psalms. Psalm 93 begins by describing the Lord on a throne (vv. 1–2). It then characterizes the Lord's rule as control over the forces of chaos; even the waters—a typical symbol of chaos in the ancient Near East—lift up their voices to the Lord. Finally, the Lord is praised as a wise lawgiver (v. 5). Psalm 98 is another enthronement psalm. After an opening summons to worship (v. 1), the psalm describes a future period in which the Lord will reign as king over the entire world (vv. 2–3). A summons is made to all nations to praise the Lord their king (vv. 4–6), and then a similar summons is made to the things of nature (vv. 7–9); the Lord enthroned is king over the natural world as well as the human world.

Liturgical Psalms

Although many of the psalms had a liturgical use, some of them seem to have been written specifically for incorporation into the Israelites' public worship of YHWH, and are thus called liturgical psalms. Consider Psalm 24, which was probably sung during the entry of the ark of the covenant into the sanctuary— perhaps after a procession of the ark around the Temple grounds. Verses 1 through 6 would have been sung by a choir inside the Temple gates. The psalm begins with a brief doxology (a hymn of praise) to the Lord as creator (vv. 1–2). A question is then posed (v. 3): Who shall be permitted to ascend the Temple mount and stand in the inner sanctuary? The answer follows: Only those who are morally fit shall enter (vv. 4–6). Verses 7 through 10, which would have been sung by those outside the gate who were bearing the ark, call for the Temple gates to be opened so that the Lord may be admitted.

Wisdom Psalms

Some of the songs in the Book of Psalms bear more resemblance to wisdom literature than they do to any of the types of songs mentioned above; these are known as wisdom psalms. We shall discuss the characteristics of wisdom literature below. Here we shall simply consider two brief examples of wisdom psalms. Psalm 1 imparts sage advice in the form of a blessing coupled with a curse: The righteous will be blessed (vv. 1–3), while the wicked will perish (vv. 4–6). Psalm 127 is also meant to instruct its hearers. It cautions them that anxiety has no place in the life of the faithful, since only the Lord can provide security (vv. 1–2), and it advises them to regard their sons as blessings bestowed upon them by the Lord as a means to their security (vv. 3–5).

B. The Song of Songs

The Song of Songs is not really one song, but a collection of songs that celebrate erotic love—that is, sensual love between men and women. The title Song of Songs is a superlative (like Show of Shows or Holy of Holies), designating these songs as the best songs of all. The book is also known as the Canticle of Canticles (from its Latin title, *Canticum Canticorum*) and as the Song of Solomon. This book has traditionally been attributed to King Solomon, but most scholars doubt that Solomon actually wrote it. Although Solomon is mentioned in chapters 3 and 8, those references are in the third person rather than the first. Scholars believe that these poems were attributed to Solomon by an editor who wished to lend to them the authority of someone who was known for both his wisdom and his active love life.[5]

The poems in the Song of Songs are thought to have attained their final form sometime in the third century BCE, but most of the material contained in them is much more ancient. The fact that the poems use natural and agricultural images as metaphors for human sexuality suggests that the poems may even have roots in the fertility rites and songs of the Canaanite worshipers of Baal.[6] The poems' emphasis on the characters of the bride and the bridegroom may also indicate that these poems were sung aloud as part of Israelite wedding ceremonies.

Warning: Explicit Lyrics!

Compared to the rest of the songs in the Hebrew canon, the poems in the Song of Songs are quite risqué in their celebration of erotic love and sensuality. One of the literary devices used in the Song of Songs is the *wasf* (from an Arabic word meaning "description").[7] *Wasf*s were a traditional part of Arabic weddings, in which the bride would sing to the groom about the beauty of his body, and the groom would sing to the bride about the beauty of hers. The Song of Songs contains a *wasf* sung by a woman to a man (5:10–16) and one sung by a man to a woman (7:1–9); each is quite explicit in its praise of the subject's physical beauty. The poems in the Song of Songs also contain some very suggestive passages in which the lover beckons her beloved, inviting him to join her in sensual delights (4:16—5:1; 7:10–12). To the Jews of the ancient world, these poems were so explicitly erotic that debates about whether or not they should be admitted to the Hebrew canon raged until the second century CE!

What Motivated Their Canonization?

Why were these poems eventually canonized? While it is difficult to say with certainty, we can identify two precedents to which those who favored canonization of the Song of Songs may have appealed. One can be found in the Book of Hosea. As we saw in the previous chapter, Hosea took "a wife of whoredom" in order to symbolize the Lord's relationship with an unfaithful Israel (Hos 1:2–3). But the Lord also told Israel that a day would come when the Lord would take Israel as his wife forever (Hos 2:16–20). This idea in Hosea may have suggested a way of reading the love poetry in the Song of Songs *allegorically*; if the Lord thinks of Israel as his wife, then the Song of Songs can be read as a heavily symbolic celebration of the love between the bridegroom YHWH and the bride Israel.

Another reason why the Song of Songs was ultimately canonized would seem to be that its poems reflect a scripturally based understanding of sexuality as an expression of mutual care, friendship, and equality. In the Creation myths, sexuality is presented as a natural, healthy gift given to the first human beings by God (Gen 1:27–28; 2:24–25). The Song's celebration of erotic sensuality as an expression of love is in keeping with this earlier scriptural message (see especially Song 5:16b).[8]

C. Lamentations

The third collection of songs in the Writings is the Book of Lamentations, a set of five poems mourning the fall of Jerusalem to the Babylonians. Tradition has attributed this book to the prophet Jeremiah, who witnessed Jerusalem's fall, but no evidence internal to the work supports this attribution. Indeed, stylistic and thematic differences between the Book of Jeremiah and the Book of Lamentations strongly suggest that the latter is not the work of the prophet. Still, the poems' vivid accounts of the horrific events of 586 BCE (2:6, 9; 4:19) and of the conditions in Judah thereafter (2:11–12; 4:9–10) suggest that at least some parts of the Lamentations were written by someone who was an eyewitness to the siege of Jerusalem, and who remained in Judah after the city fell. To this day, many Jews recite the Lamentations annually on the ninth of Av, a day of fasting that commemorates Jerusalem's fall. (Av is the fifth month of the Hebrew sacred calendar; it falls in July–August.) This practice is thought to have originated very early in the exilic period.

Literary Form

The Lamentations are interesting in their literary form. Chapters 1 through 4 are alphabetic acrostic poems, meaning that each stanza begins with one of the twenty-two successive letters of the Hebrew alphabet. In chapters 1, 2, and 4, there is one verse per letter, yielding twenty-two verses total. In chapter 3, there are three verses per letter, yielding sixty-six verses. Chapter 5, though not arranged acrostically, also has twenty-two verses—probably for the sake of consistency. The meter of the poems (three beats in the first line, two in the second) is that which was typically used in funeral dirges, so that reciting the Lamentations is like mourning the death of the City of David.[9]

Suffering and Hope

The poems in the Book of Lamentations paint a stark picture of the anguish that the Jews felt over the destruction of their capital city and their Temple. Jerusalem is characterized as a widow, reduced from a princess to a vassal (1:1). The city itself is in ruins, and its leaders have been deported (2:9). Those who remained in Judah faced severe famine (4:4, 9) and some may have even resorted to cannibalism (4:10). Without a Davidic king (5:16a) or a Temple (referred to as Mount Zion at 5:18), the Jews' whole world seems to have been shattered. The authors of the Lamentations do not regard their situation as unjust; they explain the suffering of Jerusalem as punishment for Jerusalem's sins (1:8, 22; 4:13, 22; 5:16b) that the Lord was right to inflict (1:18; 2:17; 4:11). Still, amid their suffering and shame, the authors of the Lamentations hold out hope in the Lord's steadfast love for Israel. When Jerusalem's punishment is complete and the Lord's anger has passed, the Lord will provide for the chosen people once again (3:19–33).

II. WISDOM LITERATURE

The books of Proverbs, Ecclesiastes, and Job are unlike other books in the Tanak in that they are concerned neither with the history of Israel nor with the covenant between the Lord and the chosen people. Instead, they focus on deep questions about the human condition: What is the purpose of life? What must one do in order to achieve happiness? Is there order in the universe? Because of their interest in such philosophical questions, these books are considered wisdom literature. Wisdom literature was common throughout the ancient world, including the ancient Near East. Archaeologists have found collections of Sumerian and Babylonian proverbs that date back to 2000 BCE. The fact that most ancient cultures had some form of wisdom literature helps to explain why the Hebrew wisdom literature is not explicitly concerned with the Mosaic Covenant; the Israelite wisdom writers were participating in an international discussion, a universal search for meaning.[10] As we shall see, the Tanak's three wisdom books preserve three different perspectives on the meaning of human life.

A. Proverbs

Authorship and Date

Tradition has attributed the Book of Proverbs to King Solomon, who was known for his wisdom (1 Kgs 3:5–12; 4:29–34). While some of the wise sayings contained in the Book of Proverbs may indeed date back to Solomon, scholars believe that the book was written during the postexilic period, for a number of reasons. First, the book takes a rather derogatory tone in its remarks about monarchs (16:14; 19:12; 20:2; 25:2–7). Since the Solomonic era was ancient Israel's golden age, the tone that the Book of Proverbs takes toward monarchs suggests that its author was working in a later period of Israel's history than the reign of Solomon. Second, the book emphasizes the individual over the nation, a shift in thought characteristic of the postexilic period. Third, the book contains an alphabetic acrostic poem (31:10–31), a literary form that is thought to have emerged late in the Hebrew tradition. Fourth, although the Book of Proverbs was written in Hebrew, the author frequently used Aramaic words. This suggests that the book was written during the Persian period, because Aramaic was the official administrative language of the Persian Empire from about 500 BCE.[11]

Egyptian Influence

Some parts of the Book of Proverbs seem to have been influenced by a very ancient piece of Egyptian wisdom literature, the *Instruction of Amen-em-opet* (1000–800 BCE), which seems to have had a wide circulation in the ancient Near East. The *Instruction* takes the form of a father's advice to his son, and a number of its sayings are mirrored in the Hebrew Proverbs:[12]

Instruction of Amen-em-opet	Proverbs
Chapter 1	22:17–18
Give your ear and hear what is said, give your heart to understand it. Putting them in your heart is worthwhile.	Incline your ear and hear my words, and apply your mind to my teaching; for it will be pleasant if you keep them within you.…
Chapter 6	15:16
Better is bread when the heart is happy, than riches with sorrow.	Better is little with the fear of the LORD than great treasure and trouble with it.

Chapter 6	16:8
Better is poverty from the hand of your divine patron than wealth from a granary full of stolen grain.	Better is a little with righteousness than large income with injustice.
Chapter 6	22:28
Do not carry off the landmark.	Do not remove the ancient landmark that your ancestors set up.
Chapter 7	23:4–5
Riches…have made themselves wings like geese.	Do not wear yourself out to get rich.… When your eyes light upon it, it is gone; for suddenly it takes wings to itself, flying like an eagle toward heaven.
Chapter 18	19:21
One thing are the words said by men, Another thing is what the god does.	The human mind may devise many plans, but it is the purpose of the LORD that will be established.

Of course, the similarity between these two works does not mean that the author of the Book of Proverbs plagiarized Egyptian wisdom literature. It simply means that these types of ideas and sayings were in wide circulation in the ancient Near East. Indeed, while it is possible that the author of Proverbs had a copy of the Egyptian work, it is equally possible that both the Egyptian and the biblical proverb writers appealed to still earlier oral or written sources.

Conservatism

The main theme in the Book of Proverbs is the importance of maintaining those practices that tradition has associated with a healthy and happy life. It relates the acquisition of wealth to intelligence and hard work (10:4; 24:3–4). It stresses the importance of teaching (1:2–4; 6:20–22) and cautions against the vices of laziness (6:6–11; 24:30–34), promiscuity (5:3–10; 6:24–26), and intemperance (23:20–21). In a stylistic coupling of opposites, the Proverbs assert that fear of the Lord—that is, awe of and reverence for the Lord—will bring rewards and life, whereas disdain for the Lord will bring punishment and death (1:7, 29–33; 8:35–36; 10:2–3, 16–17, 24–25, 27). The ultimate goal of life is to achieve wisdom, for only wisdom brings true happiness (3:13–18; 8:12, 17–21). Insofar as it upholds such traditional views about how one should live a good and happy life, the Book of Proverbs may be regarded as conservative in outlook.

In addition to praising wisdom as the highest good in human life, the Book of Proverbs also characterizes wisdom as that which orders the universe, for it was by means of divine wisdom that God created the world (3:19–20; 8:22–23, 27–31). The Book of Proverbs even manifests a sort of protofeminism when it personifies wisdom not as a man, but as a woman (1:20–28; 8:1–36). Indeed, Proverbs 31:10–31 praises a good wife for her strength, her compassion, her diligence, and her wisdom—an impressive list of virtues for a woman living in a patriarchal society!

B. Ecclesiastes

Authorship and Date

The Book of Ecclesiastes takes its name from the Greek word *ekklēsiastēs*, which is a translation of the Hebrew word by which the author of this work refers to himself: *Qoheleth*. Although English editions of the Bible usually translate these terms as "teacher" or "preacher," both the Greek *ekklēsiastēs* and the Hebrew *qoheleth* literally mean something like "one who convenes (or addresses) an assembly." The fact that the author of

Ecclesiastes refers to himself as *Qoheleth* suggests that he was either a teacher or the head of a prophetic school. The book is thought to have been written in the postexilic period, sometime between the fourth and second centuries BCE, for two main reasons. First, the book is written in a very late form of biblical Hebrew, and it contains an abundance of Aramaic words and phrases. Second, the book manifests themes characteristic of Stoicism and Epicureanism, Greek philosophies founded by Zeno in the fourth century BCE and Epicurus in the third century BCE, respectively. The Stoics held that everything that occurs in the world is fated; all events—even the thoughts and actions of human beings—occur with the necessity of natural law. The Epicureans held that the best way to achieve lasting happiness was to cultivate and appreciate life's simpler pleasures. Not all scholars agree that the author of Ecclesiastes was influenced by these Greek philosophies but, if he was, it is unlikely that this would have occurred prior to the Hellenistic period, which began with the conquest of Palestine by Alexander the Great in 333 BCE.

Skepticism

Whereas the Book of Proverbs had taken a conservative approach to life, recommending the cultivation of traditional virtues, the Book of Ecclesiastes takes a skeptical approach that challenges traditional wisdom. The work begins with the pessimistic assertion that "[a]ll is vanity," that is, everything is futile (1:2). The *Qoheleth* believes that history and nature both move in an ever-recurring cycle, and this belief leads him to the (Stoic?) conclusion that all events in life are predetermined and unchangeable (1:4–9; 3:1–8, 15). This means that life has no grand meaning or purpose; whether one pursues wisdom or remains a fool, one will ultimately die and then be forgotten (1:11; 2:14–16). While he advises his readers to be reverent (5:2, 4, 7), the author ultimately takes the (Epicurean?) view that the best one can hope for in life is to eat, drink, and be merry—in other words, enjoy it while it lasts, for it will not last long! (3:9–14; 5:18; 8:15).

Note that the Book of Ecclesiastes ends with two short appendices that clearly seem to have been added by later authors.

The first (12:9–12) may have been attached by a disciple of the *Qoheleth;* the student tries to soften the master's harsh words by characterizing them as mere "goads," and by advising us not to make too much of them. The second (12:13–14) seems to have been attached by a much more orthodox editor.

C. Job

The Book of Job is both a folktale and a dramatic dialogue in poetic form. The folktale, which serves as a narrative prologue and epilogue to the poem (1:1—2:13; 42:7–17), tells of a pious man who suffers misfortunes without complaint and is then rewarded by God for his faith. This story is thought to be quite ancient; for instance, it was known to Ezekiel and his audience (Ezek 14:14, 20). Most scholars think that it was first written down in Hebrew in the early part of the first millennium (1000–800) BCE, but that it had circulated orally throughout the ancient Near East during the second millennium BCE.

Authorship and Date

The poetic dialogue (3:1—42:6) is difficult to date, though its themes suggest an origin in the exilic or postexilic periods. Some scholars have argued that the poem was written by an Edomite rather than a Jew, for several reasons. First, the story of Job seems to be set in Edom; the location of Job's homeland of Uz is unknown, but it is associated with Edom in some biblical passages (Gen 36:28; Lam 4:21). Second, the poetic dialogue itself—as opposed to the introductory verses at the tops of the chapters—does not use the name YHWH, but instead uses a host of other words for the Deity, including one that the people of southern Edom used for their god. Third, the author's Hebrew is unusual in that it is strongly influenced by both Aramaic and Arabic. While this evidence does not prove that the author of the poem was an Edomite, it is perhaps enough to show that, if the author was Jewish, he had a strong Edomitic influence in his background.[13]

The Folktale

The prologue to the Book of Job (chapters 1 and 2) begins with the Lord holding court with the other heavenly beings (literally, "sons of God"). One of these heavenly beings is Satan (Hebrew *ha-satan*, "the accuser"), whose job seems to have been to bring calamities to good people on earth in order to test their integrity.* The Lord praises Job's piety, but Satan counters that Job is pious only because the Lord has blessed him with health and wealth; take those things away, Satan argues, and Job's faith will founder. Confident that Job will remain faithful, the Lord allows Satan to test him. Satan takes away Job's livestock, his servants, and even his ten children, but Job remains faithful. Satan then obtains the Lord's permission to inflict physical suffering on Job himself. When this prose narrative continues in the epilogue (42:7–17), Job has remained faithful, and the Lord rewards him by restoring his blessings twice over.

The Poetic Dialogue

The poetic part of the Book of Job, for which the folktale is just a frame, takes the form of a dialogue between Job and his friends. This discussion is an exercise in theodicy; the question that concerns the participants is whether God allows innocent people to suffer and, if so, whether God can be considered just in doing so. Job's friends dogmatically defend the traditional doctrine of divine retribution—the idea that suffering is only inflicted on people by God as punishment for their sins. Since God only rewards and punishes justly (4:7–9), the fact that Job is suffering means that he must have sinned (11:1–6). Job disputes this tradi-

---

* In most of the references to him in the Hebrew scriptures, *ha-satan* ("the accuser" or "the adversary") is a member of the heavenly court who acts upon the Lord's instructions. This characterization is found not only in Job, but also in Zechariah 3:1 and 1 Kings 22:19–22 (though in the latter passage he is unnamed). See also Numbers 22:22 and 22:32, where the Hebrew word *satan* is used of a divine messenger. The idea of Satan as a purely malevolent being standing in opposition to God seems to have emerged late in Jewish thought, probably through the influence of the elaborate demonology of the Persians. By the time 1 Chronicles was written in the Persian period (350–250 BCE), Satan was conceived as a being who does evil of his own will (1 Chr 21:1).

tional doctrine, asserting his innocence and thus the injustice of his suffering (9:21–23). He complains that his contest with God is an unfair fight, since his opponent is unseen and omnipotent (9:11–12, 19, 32–33). Job challenges the Deity to show itself and answer to Job's charges (23:1–4). He even swears an oath of clearance, that is, a curse against himself if his claims are not true (31:1–40). When God finally responds to Job, it is by way of cross-examination: "Where were you when I laid the foundation of the earth?" (38:4); "Will you condemn me that you may be justified?" (40:8). In the end, Job admits to having spoken out of his depth, and repents (42:1–6).

What Does It Mean?

The meaning of the Book of Job is still a matter of great debate. Some take it to contain the positive message that God has evil under control (40:12–19) and that, though human beings may not always understand its workings, divine justice always prevails. Others see a darker message. At Job 42:7, God chastises Job's friends, saying to them, "My wrath is kindled against you…for you have not spoken of me what is right, as my servant Job has." But Job's friends had defended the doctrine of divine retribution, whereas Job had claimed that God allows innocent people to suffer. Some people take this passage to suggest that, in the grand scheme of things, human beings are insignificant; both good and evil can befall them, but not because God is keeping tabs on them and meting out rewards and punishments for their actions. Thus, whereas the books of Proverbs and Ecclesiastes were relatively straightforward in their views on the meaning and value of human life, the Book of Job remains mysterious—a tribute, at the very least, to the masterful artistry of its author.

8

Postexilic Writings

I. THE PERSIAN PERIOD

When their long captivity in Babylonia came to an end, the Jews passed from being subjects of the Neo-Babylonian Empire to being subjects of the Persian Empire. The Persian period lasted for two centuries, during which time those Jews who returned to Jerusalem—and those who had remained in Judah during the Exile—struggled to rebuild the city and its Temple.* Our survey of the Persian period will begin with a brief overview of the Persian Empire. We shall then examine some of the biblical books that are thought to have originated during this period.

A. The Persian Empire

Cyrus the Great

The Persians were a people who lived in southwestern Iran. For the first half of the sixth century BCE, the Persians were vassals of the Medean Empire to their north. In 559 BCE, King Cambyses I of Anshan (a subsection of Persia) was succeeded by his son, Cyrus II (the Great). By about 550, Cyrus had united the Persians and overthrown the Medes. He went on to conquer the kingdom of Lydia, an ally of the Babylonian Empire in Asia

---

* Not all the Jews who had been forced out of Judah by the Babylonians returned to Judah when Babylon fell; those who continued to live abroad are referred to as *Diaspora* Jews, from the Greek word meaning "dispersion."

Minor, and in 539 he took Babylon itself. Reversing the Babylonian policy of forced relocation, Cyrus issued a decree allowing all peoples deported by the Babylonians to return to their homelands. Thus, Cyrus brought an end to the Babylonian Exile, not only for the Jews, but for countless Lydians, Armenians, and Ionian Greeks as well.[1]

King Darius

Cyrus the Great died while leading an expedition against the Massagetae on the eastern edge of his empire (in modern Afghanistan) in 530 BCE. He was succeeded by his son Cambyses II, who secured the Persian Empire's hold over the entire Near East by conquering Egypt in 525 BCE. Three years later, Cambyses II died unexpectedly on his way back to Persia. Following his death, a group of Persian priests tried to help one of their own usurp the throne. This usurper was defeated by Darius I, a Persian nobleman who had served as a general under Cambyses II. Darius would reign for thirty-six years (522–486 BCE), during which time he expanded the Persian Empire eastward to the borders of India and westward to the borders of Greece.

Darius is credited with having developed an effective infrastructure and bureaucracy for the Persian Empire. He systematized the administration of his realm by reorganizing it into twenty territories called satrapies, each of which was ruled by three officers: (1) a political leader known as the satrap (from the Medean term *khshathrapan*, "protector of the realm"); (2) a general in charge of the Persian troops in the satrapy; and (3) a person called the "Eyes and Ears of the King," who kept tabs on the other two and reported directly to the Persian emperor. This division of power ensured that no one officer gained too much control in any part of the empire.

Darius also ensured that information could travel quickly between the capital and the satrapies by constructing roads linking all parts of his domain to each other, and by establishing an efficient mounted courier service. The Greek historian Herodotus (484–425 BCE) would later assert that these Persian mounted couriers were "stayed by neither snow nor rain nor heat nor dark-

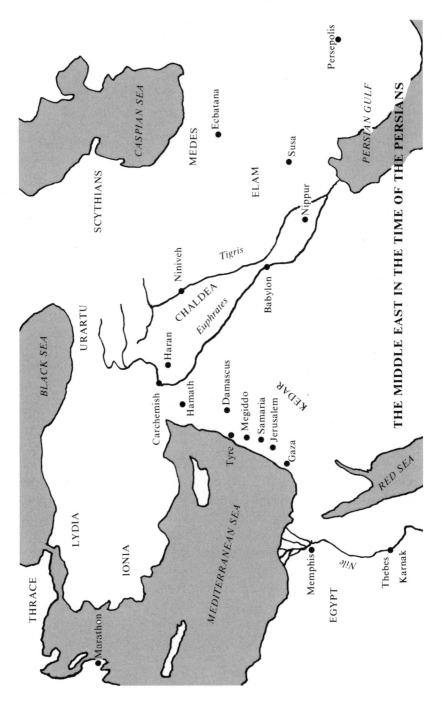

THE MIDDLE EAST IN THE TIME OF THE PERSIANS

ness from accomplishing their appointed course with all speed." Does this quotation sound vaguely familiar? That's because a paraphrase of this ancient Greek historian's description of the Persian Empire's couriers is the motto of the United States Postal Service!

Persians v. Greeks

In 499 BCE, a revolt broke out among the Greek colonies on the Ionian coast of Asia Minor, encouraged by the city-states of mainland Greece. Darius suppressed this revolt, and later sought to punish the Greeks by sending a large invasion force overland in an attempt to take Greece from the north. This campaign was repelled by the Greeks at the Battle of Marathon (490 BCE). Darius' son Xerxes I (486–464 BCE) would also attempt to conquer Greece. In 480 BCE, the Persians defeated the Spartan forces at Thermopylae and proceeded to burn Athens, but the bulk of the Persian army had to withdraw after the Athenian navy inflicted severe damage on the Persian fleet at the Battle of Salamis. The remnants of the Persian army that did remain in Greece were defeated by a combined force of Greek city-states at the Battle of Plataea in 479 BCE.

Zoroastrianism

From the time of Darius I, the official religion of the Persian Empire was Zoroastrianism, which had been founded in northern Iran by the prophet Zarathustra (*Zoroaster* in Greek) sometime between 1400 and 1000 BCE. Zoroastrianism is a monotheistic religion in that it condones the worship of one and only one god, *Ahura Mazda* (Lord Wisdom). But Zoroastrianism is dualistic in both its metaphysics and its ethics. While *Ahura Mazda* is the creator of all that is good, and thus the only being worthy of worship, he is opposed by an eternally existing source of evil, *Angra Mainyu* (Fiendish Spirit). Zoroastrianism thus regards all events in the cosmos as a struggle between the forces of good (Truth) and evil (Lie). Zoroastrian doctrines include an elaborate angelology and demonology, which are thought to have influenced Jewish thinking about angels and devils. The English word *angel*, which refers to a semidivine being, is a translation of the Greek *angelos* and the

Hebrew *mal'akh,* both of which simply meant "messenger." It was not until the postexilic period that Jewish thought clearly began to conceive of these messengers as superhuman beings, some of whom were good and some of whom were evil.[2] Jewish theology was probably also influenced by Zoroastrianism's notions of a resurrection of the dead, a final judgment, and an eternal reward or punishment for one's deeds in life, ideas that do not come into prominence in Jewish thought until the postexilic period.

Although Zoroastrianism was the official religion of the Persians, there is no evidence that the Persian Empire sought to impose its beliefs on its subject peoples. Indeed, the Persians were considerably tolerant of other faiths, and Persian kings even made prayers and sacrifices to the gods of their subjects. While such practices may have been motivated by an acknowledgment of and respect for gods other than *Ahura Mazda,* the Persian policy regarding subject peoples' religions was also utilitarian in nature; showing reverence to a subject people's deity was good public relations, and allowing subject peoples to maintain shrines and temples where monetary offerings were made was an effective means of raising tax revenues for the empire.

B. The Chronicler's History

The biblical books of 1 and 2 Chronicles, Ezra, and Nehemiah are collectively referred to as the Chronicler's History because they were originally one long book, the product of an author or group of authors known to us only as the Chronicler. Scholars date the Chronicler's History to the postexilic period, around 350–250 BCE. The work as a whole is a rewriting of the biblical narrative, from the creation of the world to the restoration of Judah after the Exile. Borrowing heavily from the Deuteronomic History, the books of 1 and 2 Chronicles retell the story of Israel up to the Exile, but they place special emphasis on the role of King David; nineteen of 1 Chronicles' twenty-nine chapters are about him. David is portrayed as having established Israel as a religious community centered on the Temple (1 Chr 21:18ff.). This emphasis is thought to reflect the Jews' postexilic life; having neither a king nor national independence, their sense of identity derived primarily from the practice of their national religion.[3]

Sheshbazzar

The books of Ezra and Nehemiah supplement the history contained in 1 and 2 Chronicles, bringing that history up to date by recounting the Jews' efforts to rebuild Jerusalem during the Restoration. The Chronicler's account of the reconstruction is somewhat muddled, in part because the sequence of events it records appears not to be chronologically ordered. The reconstruction seems to have occurred in several stages. According to the Book of Ezra, the first stage was led by Sheshbazzar in roughly 538 BCE, shortly after Cyrus the Great's emancipation of the exiles. We know very little about this Sheshbazzar. Because he is described as a prince of Judah (Ezra 1:8), some scholars think he may have been a son of Jehoiachin who is referred to elsewhere as Shenazzar (1 Chr 3:18). Leading a group of exiles, Sheshbazzar carried back to Jerusalem the Temple treasures that Nebuchadnezzar had stolen, and which Cyrus had released to him. Sheshbazzar also seems to have been appointed governor of Judah by Cyrus, and to have begun a reconstruction of the Temple (Ezra 1:7–11; 5:14–16). After these brief references to him, Sheshbazzar simply vanishes from the biblical record.[4]

Zerubbabel and Jeshua

The next stage of reconstruction occurred under the leadership of Zerubbabel and Jeshua. During the reign of Darius I, Zerubbabel was governor of Judah and Jeshua was high priest. They are credited with erecting an altar to the Lord, resuming the offering of sacrifices to YHWH, and reinstituting the celebration of feast days, even though the Temple was still under construction (Ezra 3:2–7). Indeed, work on the Temple seems to have languished during Zerubbabel's tenure, for he was still governor in 520 BCE, when the prophets Haggai and Zechariah pressed for the Temple to be completed (Hag 1:1, 14). It is not clear whether either Zerubbabel or Jeshua lived to see the Temple's completion in 515 BCE, as neither of them is mentioned in the biblical report of that completion (Ezra 6:15).[5]

Nehemiah

The Chronicler's History is silent on the next half-century or so, resuming its account of the reconstruction with the story of Nehemiah. Because much of the Book of Nehemiah is in the first person, scholars believe that the Chronicler possessed a copy of Nehemiah's memoirs, which he incorporated into his history. Nehemiah was serving the Persian king Artaxerxes I (464–423 BCE) as cupbearer—a trusted butler who poured and sampled the king's wine—when he heard that Jerusalem was vulnerable to attack because it still lacked a defensive wall. In 445 or 444 BCE (the twentieth year of Artaxerxes' reign, according to Nehemiah 1:1), Nehemiah appealed to the Persian king for permission to go to Jerusalem and refortify it, which the king granted (Neh 2:1–8). Nehemiah's efforts to rebuild Jerusalem's defenses were opposed by Sanballat (governor of Samaria), Tobiah (governor of Ammon), and Geshem (governor of the Arab tribes), all of whom surely feared that an increased imperial status for Jerusalem would mean a decreased status for themselves (Neh 2:10, 19). Nehemiah countered their objections by pointing out their lack of authority in the City of David (Neh 2:20), and his workers finished rebuilding the wall under the protection of a heavy guard (Neh 4:7–23).

Ezra

The final stage of the reconstruction was focused, not on Jerusalem's Temple or material defenses, but on its faith. It was led by Ezra, a scribe from the line of Aaron who is thought to have lived in Babylon during the reign of Artaxerxes II of Persia (404–360 BCE). The Chronicler's History portrays Ezra as having arrived in Jerusalem in 458 BCE (Ezra 7:7–10), prior to the arrival of Nehemiah in 445. However, many scholars believe that Ezra came after Nehemiah, for several reasons. First, although the books of Ezra and Nehemiah both refer to King Artaxerxes of Persia, biblical authors did not use Roman numerals (as we do) to distinguish different kings who used the same name. Second,

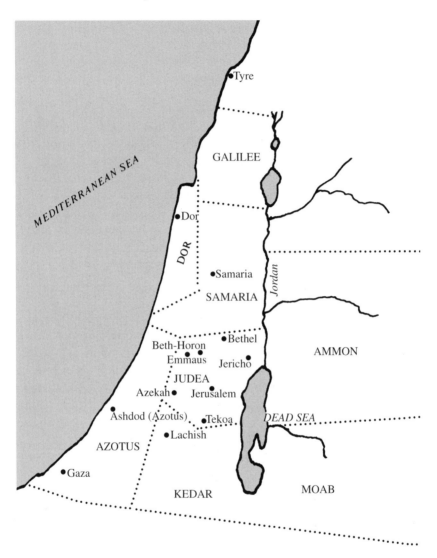

PALESTINE IN THE TIME OF EZRA AND NEHEMIAH

the high priest during Nehemiah's time was Eliashib (Neh 3:1), whereas the high priest during Ezra's time seems to have been Eliashib's grandson Jehohanan, who is loosely referred to as "Eliashib's son" at Ezra 10:6. Third, Ezra's prayer of thanksgiving suggests that Nehemiah's defensive wall had already been completed by the time Ezra arrived in Jerusalem (Ezra 9:9).[6]

Growing up in Babylonia, Ezra had devoted himself to the study of the Torah. When he reached adulthood, he sought and received a royal commission from Artaxerxes to go to Jerusalem and "make inquiries" according to the Jewish law. Indeed, Artaxerxes empowered Ezra to enforce the Jewish law and to mete out punishment to transgressors in the form of death, banishment, confiscation of goods, or imprisonment (Ezra 7). When he arrived in Jerusalem, Ezra read the Torah aloud to the people, who had to have it interpreted for them (Neh 8:5–8). It is likely that this *interpreting* was actually *translating;* the Jews living in Jerusalem may not have been able to understand the Hebrew Ezra was reading to them until Ezra's fellow scribes—whom he had brought with him from Babylonia—translated it into the now more familiar Aramaic.[7]

Indeed, the entire postexilic period seems to have been one, not just of reconstruction, but of religious reform. From the point of the view of the Chronicler, faith in YHWH had grown stronger among the Jews exiled to Babylonia, but it had weakened among the Jews who had remained in Judah. Thus, the Chronicler's characters are on a religious mission to preserve Israel's identity by reforming its religious practices. This is clear in the two issues that most occupy them. First is their concern to maintain the religious purity of the Jewish people. Note, for example, that Zerubbabel rejects an offer to help in the rebuilding of the Temple from some unnamed adversaries of Judah (Ezra 4:1–3). These "adversaries" were probably Samaritans.* The concern to preserve their identity

---

* The Samaritans lived in the territory to the north of Judah that had once been part of the northern kingdom of Israel. They practiced a form of Judaism, in that they worshiped YHWH and observed the laws of the Torah, but they were considered outcasts by most Jews, for two reasons: (1) the Samaritans regarded only the Torah as authoritative scripture, which means that they rejected the works of the Jewish prophets; and (2) they worshiped at a temple on Mount Gerizim (near the kingdom of Israel's first capital, Shechem) which, according to the Samaritan version of the Torah, is more holy than either Mount Sinai or Jerusalem.

thus seems to have engendered a certain exclusivity among the Jews of the Restoration. Similarly, both Ezra and Nehemiah rail against the problem of intermarriage, that is, the practice among Jewish men of taking foreign wives who did not convert to Judaism (Ezra 10:1–5, 10–12; Neh 13:1–3, 23–27).

A second concern stressed in the Chronicler's History is the restoration of the Jewish cult. Nehemiah 8:14–18 tells of the reinstitution of the Feast of Booths (Tabernacles), a festival of thanksgiving for the land that the Lord had given to the Israelites, bringing an end to their desert wanderings. Apparently, this holiday had not been celebrated in a long time, though Mosaic Law demanded it (see Lev 23:33–43). Nehemiah also describes the recommissioning of the Levites as servants in the Temple, the installation of singers to perform in the Temple liturgy, and the reinstitution of the Sabbath rest (13:10–22).

Theological Shifts

It is important to note the significant theological shifts that occur during the Restoration. Although the religious reforms of this period involve the reconstruction of the Temple and the reinstitution of the cult practices within it, those who brought the message of reform to Judah from their places of exile in Babylonia had learned to live as Jews *without* a Temple. They did this by focusing on the Torah and fulfilling its requirements as strictly as they could. Ezra's reading of the Torah to the people of Jerusalem is evidence of this new, Exile-inspired Judaism. Prior to the Exile, Israel understood itself as a nation whose relationship with the Lord was mediated by priests serving in the Temple. After the Exile, the Jews increasingly came to understand themselves as a Torah-based faith community. This meant that, for postexilic Jews, the primary means of maintaining and expressing their relationship with the Lord was no longer the offering of sacrifices—though this continued—but rather personal prayer and study of the scriptures. This postexilic emphasis on personal devotion was motivated by the Exile itself, which had deprived the exiled Jews access to the Temple and its sacrificial cult. It was also influenced by the work of the exilic-era prophets Jeremiah and Ezekiel, both of whom had stressed the idea that the Lord's rewards and pun-ishments would no longer be dealt to Israel as a group, but would be dealt to individuals according to their merit. Finally, the shift in emphasis from the Temple to the Torah would mean that, in the postexilic period, scribes like Ezra—that is, those who were experts on the Jewish law—would come to supplant prophets as the religious authorities of Judaism.[8]

C. Two Short Stories

Ruth

The biblical books of Ruth and Esther both relate events occurring in the lives of their title characters, and both books place those events in specific historical contexts. The Book of Ruth is set in the period of the Judges, while the Book of Esther is set in the Persian period. For reasons that we shall consider below, however, biblical scholars regard these books as fictional short stories rather than historical narratives, and they believe both were written in the postexilic period. Both books are also festival scrolls, meaning that they are read aloud as part of the celebration of specific Jewish holidays.

The Book of Ruth is a festival scroll read on the Jewish holi-day of Pentecost. Known also as the Feast of Weeks, Pentecost honors the establishment of the Sinai Covenant, and is tradition-ally celebrated fifty days (seven weeks) after the Passover holiday. The Book of Ruth tells the story of Naomi, a woman who relo-cates from Bethlehem to Moab with her husband and two sons. Once there, Naomi's sons take Moabite wives. Then, as the result of some sort of epidemic, Naomi's husband and sons all die (1:1–5). When Naomi heads back to Judah, she tells her two daughters-in-law that they may return to their fathers' houses (1:6–13). One of them does so; her name is Orpah, which means "disloyal" in Hebrew (1:14). The other is named Ruth, which means "companion." Ruth pledges her allegiance to Naomi, and even converts to Naomi's Yahwist faith (1:16–17). Back in Judah, Ruth meets and falls in love with Boaz, a kinsman of her deceased husband. Boaz "redeems" the widow Ruth—that is, rescues her from her widowhood—by marrying her according to the Levirate Law (or Law of Redemption), which dictated that a childless widow should be married by the deceased husband's closest male relative (see Deut 25:5–6). The story ends with Boaz and Ruth giving birth to Obed, the grandfather of King David (4:17–18).

Although the Book of Ruth is set in the period of the Judges (1:1), and may be based on a story that dates to that period, scholars believe that it was written in the postexilic period (around 400 BCE), for a number of reasons. First, the Hebrew in which the Book of Ruth is written was heavily influenced by the Aramaic language. As we have already noted, Aramaic influences on the Hebrew language were uncommon until the Persian period, when Aramaic was the official administrative language of the Persian Empire. Second, the author explains the custom of attestation—an ancient Israelite means of confirming a transaction by the exchange of a sandal—as though it is an obsolete practice with which the author does not expect the audience to be familiar (4:7). Third, and most important, the story recounts a marriage between a Jewish man and a Moabite woman. As we have already seen, intermarriage was a hot-button issue of the postexilic period; Ezra and Nehemiah both campaigned against it. The fact that the Book of Ruth presents a Moabite woman as a virtuous daughter-in-law, a faithful wife, and the great-grandmother of King David strongly suggests that this book was intended as an attack on postexilic efforts to prohibit intermarriage. On the other hand, the fact that Ruth converts to Judaism might be regarded as supportive of the positions of Ezra and Nehemiah, since it was the taking of wives who did *not* convert to Judaism that they regarded as ruinous. Either way, the fact that the book seems to be addressing the issue of intermarriage is strong evidence that it was written in the postexilic period. Finally, we should note that the Book of Ruth seems to have been regarded as a fictional short story rather than an historical narrative even by its ancient Jewish audience. The fact that the compilers of the Hebrew canon placed the Book of Ruth among the Kethuvim (Writings) rather than among the Former Prophets—which record the early history of Israel, including the period of the Judges—tells us that the Book of Ruth has long been regarded more as a piece of literature than as a historical record.[9]

Esther

The Book of Esther is read on the feast of *Purim*, a Jewish holiday the origin of which the Book of Esther explains. The story is set in Susa, the winter residence of the Persian kings (their main capital was at Persepolis). Esther is a Jewish woman whom the Persian King "Ahasueras" (Xerxes I) takes as his wife (1:1—2:18). Mordecai, Esther's cousin and guardian, saves the king from a plot by would-be assassins (2:19-23), but refuses to bow before the king's Agagite prime minister, Haman (3:1-2).* Rather than vent his anger on Mordecai alone, Haman plans to destroy all the Jews throughout the Persian Empire. He casts lots (*purim* in Hebrew) to determine the date of the slaughter, and convinces the Persian king that the people to be killed are outlaws who do not obey the king's laws (3:5-11). But then, in an ironic reversal of fortunes, the king rewards Mordecai for having thwarted the assassins' plot, conferring honors on him that Haman was expecting for himself (6:1-11). When Esther reveals her Jewish identity to the king and pleads for her people to be spared (7:3-6), the king orders Haman to be hanged on the very gallows that Haman had built for Mordecai (7:8-10), and then issues a new decree granting the Jews a day of slaughter against their enemies (9:5).

Like Ruth, the Book of Esther is thought to be a fictional short story rather than an historical account. Again, a number of considerations support this assessment.[10] First, there is no extra-biblical record of Xerxes I or any other Persian king having a Jewish wife; indeed, extrabiblical sources agree that the wife of Xerxes I was a Persian woman named Amestris. Second, the book seems to contain the sort of exaggeration that is characteristic of imaginative fiction, suggesting that both the author of Esther and

---

* Mordecai refuses to bow to Haman because Haman is an Agagite, that is, a descendent of the Amalekite king, Agag (see 1 Sam 15). The Amalekites were a nomadic people who lived in the Negev Desert and northern Arabia. According to the Book of Deuteronomy, the Amalekites had brutally attacked the Hebrews on their Exodus from Egypt to Canaan (see Deut 25:17-19).

her readers approached the book as literature rather than as a factual record. For instance, the king holds a banquet that lasts six months (1:4); the candidates for the position of queen receive a yearlong beauty treatment (2:12); the bribe that Haman offers the king is roughly $18 million (3:9); and Haman's gallows are eighty-three feet high (5:14). Most staggering, however, is the claim that 75,510 Gentiles were slain by the Jews in a single day (9:6–9, 16), a massacre that could hardly have escaped the notice of extrabiblical writers.

If, as scholars suspect, the Book of Esther is not an account of historical events, then why was it written? One suggestion is that it was intended specifically to explain and justify the Jewish holiday of *Purim*, for which there is no other biblical sanction. The beginnings of *Purim* are unclear, but it does seem to have been founded during the Persian period. Moreover, many scholars suspect that the Jewish holiday of *Purim* was initially a Babylonian holiday that the Jews adopted during the Babylonian Exile. This hypothesis is supported by the fact that the names of the main characters in the story are of Mesopotamian origin: Esther's name derives from *Ishtar*, the Babylonian goddess of love; Mordecai's name derives from *Marduk*, the chief deity of the Babylonian pantheon. If the Jews of the Exile did celebrate a Gentile holiday, the religious reforms of the postexilic period certainly could have motivated an effort to explain and justify that holiday as having a uniquely Jewish origin.

Because the Book of Esther stresses the importance of Jews' remaining loyal to their faith community while under the control of a pagan government, some scholars are inclined to think that it was written after the Persian period, when the Near East came to be dominated by the Greeks. To this later period we shall now turn our attention.

II. THE HELLENISTIC PERIOD

The years of Persian domination in the ancient Near East were followed by a period of Greek domination. This era is referred to as the Hellenistic period, from the word used to designate the culture of classical Greece. We shall begin with an historical overview of this period and then examine a biblical book that dates to it.

A. The Greek Conquest

Alexander the Great

In the year 336 BCE, King Philip II of Macedonia was assassinated by the chief of his bodyguard. He was succeeded by his twenty-year-old son Alexander III (the Great). Two years later, Alexander began his meteoric career by launching an assault on the Persian Empire. After winning some initial victories in Asia Minor, he took Palestine in 333 and then Egypt in 331. At the Battle of Gaugamela in 331, Alexander's forces routed the Persian army, securing the Greek conquest of the Persian Empire and forcing King Darius III to flee for his life—which was taken by his own soldiers shortly thereafter. In 327, Alexander marched on India, but the following year his battle-weary and homesick troops refused to go any farther, and Alexander was forced to abandon his Indian campaign. In the year 323 BCE, at the age of thirty-three, Alexander the Great died in Babylon. The cause of his death remains a mystery; he may have contracted malaria or cholera, or he may have been poisoned by one or more of his officers.[11]

After Alexander died, his generals fought against each other for control of the territories that Alexander had conquered. By the time the dust from these conflicts had settled, two Greeks had emerged as the new rulers of the Near East: General Ptolemy became king of Egypt and Palestine, and General Seleucus became king of Babylonia. Seleucus's kingdom also came to include Asia Minor and Syria in 301 BCE, when he defeated another of Alexander's former generals, Antigonus.

Ptolemies v. Seleucids

Thus, by the third century BCE, Judah found itself under the control of the Ptolemaic Kingdom of Egypt. The Ptolemaic kings—Ptolemy I and his successors—ruled from the city of

Alexandria, which Alexander had founded in 331. For the most part, the Ptolemies ruled their territories much as the Persians had done, allowing their subject peoples freedom of religion and a fair amount of autonomy. In Judah, this self-rule was exercised by the high priest of Jerusalem. But the militarily and economically strategic land of Palestine was coveted by the Seleucid Kingdom to the north. The Ptolemies and Seleucids fought each other for control of Palestine throughout the third century BCE; the Ptolemies managed to maintain control of the area through six separate campaigns by the Seleucids. Finally, in 199 BCE, the Seleucid king Antiochus III defeated the Ptolemies at the Battle of Paneas and annexed Palestine to the Seleucid Kingdom.[12]

Antiochus IV

Judah enjoyed fairly good relations with the Seleucid monarchs Antiochus III and his son, Seleucus IV, who ascended the throne after his father's death in 187 BCE. But in 175, Seleucus IV was murdered by his own prime minister; his younger brother, Antiochus IV, succeeded him. Antiochus's relations with the Jews started out poorly and grew steadily worse. One of his first moves was to appoint a Jew named Menelaus as high priest in Jerusalem. Menelaus was not of the Zadokite line; his appointment thus violated the Jewish tradition that the religious leader of Jerusalem should be a descendent of Zadok, the high priest under David and Solomon. Antiochus was probably unaware of this custom; he appointed Menelaus as high priest simply because Menelaus bribed him. When a delegation of Jews from Jerusalem went to Antioch, the Seleucid capital, to complain against the corruption of their new high priest, Menelaus sent another bribe to Antiochus, who then had the delegation executed.

In 169 BCE, Antiochus led his army in a failed attempt to conquer the Ptolemaic Kingdom of Egypt. On his way back to Syria, he stopped in Jerusalem and looted gold and silver from the Temple treasury in an effort to offset the costs of his military campaign. To Antiochus, this was probably a simple matter of taking what he believed rightfully belonged to him. To the Jews, it was an illegal and impious action.

Still, the worst was yet to come. In 167 BCE, Antiochus sent forces to Jerusalem who tore down the city's defensive walls and constructed a fortified position within the city called the *Akra* (Greek for citadel). The Seleucid troops then occupied this fortress, along with some pro-Antiochus Jews (including Menelaus). Antiochus also imposed a harsh new system of taxes on the Jews. Next, he prohibited all distinctively Jewish customs and ceremonies, including Temple sacrifices, festival observance, circumcision, and the Sabbath rest. Anyone who violated this prohibition was subject to death. Finally, Antiochus's soldiers erected a statue of the Greek god Zeus Olympus in the Temple sanctuary. Before this statue, on the altar that had once been YHWH's, the Seleucid soldiers then sacrificed a pig—an animal that the Jews regarded as particularly unclean (Lev 11:7; Deut 14:8).

It is worth noting that, at least initially, it was not the goal of Antiochus IV to outlaw the Jewish faith. Rather, Antiochus wished to *Hellenize* the Jews within his kingdom—that is, he wanted to encourage them to adopt the same sort of Greek customs and ideas that many other peoples in the Mediterranean world had adopted in the wake of Alexander's conquests. Some Jews themselves wished to see such a cultural shift occur in Judah, and those Jews supported Antiochus in his efforts. Most Jews, however, regarded Hellenization as a threat to the very existence of Judaism, and thus resisted Antiochus's efforts. The conflict between Antiochus IV and the Jews over the issue of Hellenization would ultimately lead to a Jewish revolt against the Seleucid Kingdom, a topic that we shall take up in the next chapter.

B. The Book of Daniel

The Book of Daniel is two quite different books in one. Chapters 1 through 6, which are thought to date to the Persian period, are a collection of hero legends about Daniel and his friends, youthful Jews living at the Babylonian court during the Exile. Throughout these stories, Daniel and his friends are portrayed as models of piety and fidelity, whose faith saves them from such dangers as a fiery furnace (ch. 5) and a lions' den (ch. 6).

Apocalyptic Literature

Chapters 7–12 of the Book of Daniel contain apocalyptic literature.[13] The English word *apocalypse* comes from the Greek word *apokaluptein*, which means "to uncover" or "to reveal." Thus, an apocalypse is an uncovering or a revelation of something. More specifically, apocalyptic literature is a report of visions that have been revealed to the author by God. These visions typically involve cataclysmic events leading to the end of the present world order and the Lord's establishment of a new world order. Scholars believe that apocalyptic literature was produced at times of crisis and persecution, and that its purpose was to give hope and consolation to the persecuted. Thus, although apocalyptic visions appear to be predictions of future events, scholars believe that the authors of apocalyptic literature were writing about their own times but setting their stories in the past, so that their commentaries are in the future tense. The authors' goal, scholars believe, was to console their contemporaries with the hopeful message that the suffering they endured was something God had foreseen and allowed to happen, but from which God would soon rescue them. This view of the nature and purpose of apocalyptic literature is supported by the fact that such literature is heavily symbolic. If apocalyptic authors were writing about contemporary people and events, then camouflaging those people and events by means of symbols would have been an effective way for the authors to protect themselves—and their work—against their persecutors.

Historical Symbols in the Book of Daniel

Chapters 7–12 of Daniel contain four apocalyptic visions that were purportedly revealed to Daniel. While the people and events to which these visions allude date back to 600 BCE, those in chapter 11 suggest that the second half of the Book of Daniel was written during Antiochus IV's persecution of the Jews. Verses 3–4 describe a "warrior king" who shall "rule with great dominion," but whose "kingdom shall be broken and divided" rather than going to his progeny. These verses probably refer to Alexander the Great, whose empire was torn apart by his generals after his death. Verses 5–6 describe conflicts between the "king of the

146

north" and the "king of the south," which represent the Seleucid and Ptolemaic kingdoms, respectively. A reference to the northern king's defeat of the southern king (vv. 15–16) would seem to refer to the Battle of Paneas, at which the Seleucids defeated the Ptolemies and gained control of Palestine. A northern king is described as "a contemptible person" who shall "obtain the kingdom through intrigue" (v. 21). This person is most likely Antiochus IV, who ascended the Seleucid throne after his older brother, Seleucus IV, was murdered; the author assumes that Antiochus IV must have been involved in his brother's untimely death. Verses 29–30 describe Antiochus IV's failed attempt to invade the Ptolemaic Kingdom; that effort had failed largely because the Ptolemies were aided by ships of the Roman navy— the word *Kittim* in verse 30 is a code word for Romans. On his way home after this failed campaign, Antiochus had looted the Jerusalem Temple; Daniel 11 refers to this event as an action "against the holy covenant" (v. 30). We are told that forces sent by the contemptible king will "profane the temple" and "set up the abomination that makes desolate" (v. 31), a reference to the Seleucid troops who occupied the Jerusalem Temple and erected within it a statue of Zeus Olympus. The "little help" that will come to those suffering this king's persecution (v. 34) probably refers to the beginnings of the Maccabean revolt, which we shall discuss in the next chapter. There even seems to be a reference to Antiochus IV's throne name, *Epiphanes* ("God manifest" in Greek), which to the Jews was a blasphemous claim to divinity (v. 36).

Dating the Book of Daniel

The many references to the Seleucid Kingdom in Daniel 11 suggest a narrow period within which the latter half of the Book of Daniel seems to have been written. This is because all the references to Antiochus IV are accurate—that is, they refer to historical events confirmed by extrabiblical sources—*except* for those that describe his death. Daniel envisions Antiochus capturing Egypt, Libya (west of Egypt), and Ethiopia (south of Egypt), then dying somewhere along the coast—perhaps in Sinai or Philistia— on his way back to Syria (11:42–45). In fact, Antiochus never conquered Egypt or its neighbors, and he died fighting the Parthians in the eastern part of his kingdom in 164 BCE. Since the author of the apocalyptic visions in Daniel seems to have been working when Antiochus's persecution of the Jews was well under way, but before Antiochus had met his death, scholars date the writing of Daniel 7—12 to the years between 167 and 164 BCE.[14]

Hope in Resurrection

The author of the apocalyptic visions in Daniel assures his readers that the suffering they have endured is in accord with God's will (11:36), and he warns them that worse is yet to come (12:1). But he also consoles his audience with the message that these catastrophic events will be followed by a resurrection and judgment of the dead, leading to eternal life for the righteous and eternal punishment for the wicked (12:2). This latter passage is incredibly significant, as most biblical scholars consider it to be the Hebrew Bible's only unequivocal statement on the concept of resurrection.* The Yahwist faith had long had a conception of some form of existence after death, as evidenced in the Hebrew Bible's many references to Sheol (Gen 37:35), also known as the Pit (Isa 38:18). But, like the Greeks' Hades, the biblical Sheol was not a place where the deceased took up a new and better form of existence, nor did a soul's going to Sheol involve any sort of judgment, reward, or punishment. Rather, Sheol was conceived as a shadowy place to which all souls—good and bad alike—descended after death (see, for example, Isa 14:9–11; Ps 6:5; 88:10–12). The fact that the theological concepts of resurrection, judgment, and afterlife seem to emerge relatively late in Judaism suggests that their emergence was, at least in part, the result of the Jews' encounters with Zoroastrianism during the Persian period.

---

* Aside from Daniel 12:2, the only other passage in the Tanak that seems to refer directly to the idea of a general resurrection of the dead is Isaiah 26:19. The correct interpretation of this latter passage, however, is a matter of debate among biblical scholars.

9

Late Second Temple Judaism

The period of Jewish history that falls between the end of Greek domination (mid-second century BCE) and the Roman destruction of the Jerusalem Temple (70 CE) is known as the late Second Temple period. Judaism as we know it today was very strongly influenced by the political, cultural, and theological events and issues of this era. In order to understand and appreciate the significance of the Second Temple period, we shall first focus our attention on major historical events having to do with the Hasmonaean Dynasty and the Roman conquest of Palestine. We shall then examine the various Jewish sects that came to prominence during this time. Along the way, we shall consider some of the apocryphal works that scholars date to the Second Temple period. The word *apocrypha* ("hidden" in Greek) was used during the Second Temple period to describe books that were considered unsuitable for public reading, that is, books that did not have a liturgical use. Today, the word is typically used to refer to books that are accepted as canonical by some religious communities but not by others. A number of books that were written during the Second Temple period have been preserved even though Palestinian Jews did not admit them into the Tanak. Some of these books are considered canonical scripture by Catholic and Orthodox Christians—who refer to such books collectively as the Deuterocanon (second canon)—but they are not considered canonical by Jews or Protestant Christians.

I. THE HASMONAEAN PERIOD

The Hasmonaean period, also known as the Maccabean period, was an era in which Judah achieved self-rule under the Jewish Hasmonaean family. Much of our information about this period comes from the apocryphal book of 1 Maccabees, an extremely valuable historical narrative that was written in Hebrew by an unknown author in roughly 100 BCE.

Mattathias ben-Hashmon

We have already seen that the Jews faced severe persecution under the Seleucid king, Antiochus IV Epiphanes. In 167 BCE, Antiochus paganized the Jerusalem Temple and outlawed such Jewish practices as circumcision, Temple sacrifice, and the Sabbath rest. In order to enforce his new policies, Antiochus sent soldiers throughout Judah whose orders were to burn Torah scrolls, force the Jews to participate in pagan sacrifices, and execute any Jews who resisted (1 Macc 1:41–64).

In that same year, a group of such soldiers arrived in the town of Modein, about fifteen miles northwest of Jerusalem, where Mattathias ben-Hashmon was the local Jewish priest. The soldiers ordered Mattathias to lead the Jews of Modein in a pagan sacrifice, but Mattathias refused. When one of Modein's Jews began to comply with the soldiers' commands, Mattathias killed him. He also killed the commander of the Seleucid troops. Mattathias and his sons then fled to the hills and began assembling a guerrilla army (1 Macc 2:1–30).

Judas the Hammer

Mattathias died in 166 BCE and was succeeded as leader of the rebels by his son Judas, whose nickname was The Hammer; he is known as Judas Maccabeus from the Latinization of the Aramaic word for hammer, *maqqaba*. Under Judas's skillful leadership, the guerrillas won a number of victories over the troops that Antiochus sent in an effort to quell the rebellion, and each victory drew more Jews into the rebel ranks (1 Macc 2:49—4:35). In 164, Judas's rebels attacked and recaptured much of Jerusalem from the Seleucid troops. Those troops still held the Akra, the citadel they had built within the city, but Judas's forces drove them out of the Temple and off of the Temple mount. Having regained their center of worship, the Jewish rebels removed the pagan statues that Antiochus's soldiers had erected there, rebuilt the altar, and resumed the offering of sacrifices to YHWH. The Jews celebrated their purification and rededication of the Temple for eight days (1 Macc 4:36–59). This event is still commemorated annually in the eight-day Jewish festival of *Hanukkah*, which means "dedication" in Hebrew.[1]

The Hasmonaean Dynasty

Judas Maccabeus continued to lead the rebels for the next four years, during which time they extended their control south into the Negev Desert, west to the seacoast, and north into Galilee. When Judas died in battle against the Seleucids in 160 BCE, he was succeeded by his brother Jonathan. Throughout most of the period in which the Hasmonaean rebels had been fighting the Seleucids, the office of high priest in Jerusalem had been vacant. But in 152 BCE, Jonathan was appointed high priest by Alexander Balas, a contender for the Seleucid throne who wished to have the military support of Jonathan and his Jewish rebels (1 Macc 10). When Jonathan died nine years later as the result of treachery by the Syrian general Trypho, he was succeeded by his brother Simon. Simon finally wrested the entire city of Jerusalem from the Seleucids and their Jewish sympathizers, and then negotiated a treaty with the Seleucids that granted Judah its independence and acknowledged Simon's authority as both high priest and political ruler (1 Macc 12—13). Thus began the Hasmonaean Dynasty— the hereditary monarchy of the descendents of Mattathias ben-Hashmon. This dynasty would rule a politically independent Jewish state—called Judea—for the next seventy years.

Over time, strife developed within the Hasmonaean Dynasty, and the infighting that resulted would ultimately contribute to the dynasty's demise. When Alexander Jannaeus, the grandson of Simon, died in 76 BCE, he was succeeded by his widow, Salome Alexandra. Alexandra ruled as queen for nine years, with her son Hyrcanus II serving as high priest. When she died in 67 BCE, armed conflict broke out between the supporters of Hyrcanus II and those of his younger brother, Aristobulus II. The latter emerged victorious; Aristobulus II became king and high priest, and Hyrcanus agreed to back down. But then a person named Antipater sought to stir up trouble between the two brothers. Antipater was the governor of Idumea, the region south of Judea previously known as Edom. He convinced Hyrcanus to appeal to the Nabataean king, Aretas III (85–62 BCE), for help in usurping the Judean throne.* In the armed struggle that ensued, both brothers would appeal to the fast-growing Roman Empire for help. This would turn out to be a drastic mistake; the involvement of Rome would bring to an end both the Hasmonaean Dynasty and Judean independence.[2]

II. THE ROMAN PERIOD

Pompey

The Roman general, Pompey, had conquered the Seleucid Empire in 64 BCE. The following year, while Pompey was campaigning in Asia Minor, the two contenders for the Judean throne both sent envoys to him, seeking his help. Pompey returned to Damascus, where he met separately with Hyrcanus, Aristobulus, and a Jewish delegation that sought to depose both brothers and transfer political control to the priests. Pompey decided not to take any immediate action, telling all sides of the dispute to cool off for a bit. But then Aristobulus gathered his troops in Alexandrium, a fortress thirty miles northeast of Jerusalem. Regarding this as a hostile move, Pompey invaded Judea. Aristobulus surrendered, but his supporters in Jerusalem, who had holed themselves up in the Temple, did not. When Pompey reached Jerusalem, Hyrcanus—still hoping that Pompey would put him on the throne—opened the

---

* The Nabataeans were an Arabic tribe whose kingdom, in the first century BCE, extended from Damascus in the north, through the Transjordan, and south into Arabia (between the Euphrates and the Red Sea).

PALESTINE IN THE TIME OF THE MACCABEES

PROVINCE OF JUDEA ••••••••

------- MAXIMUM EXTENT OF THE HASMONEAN KINGDOM

city gates to the Romans. The Romans besieged the Temple for three months, and finally drove Aristobulus's supporters out.[3]

Pompey's seizure of Jerusalem in 63 BCE marked the end of the Hasmonaean Dynasty. No longer an independent state, Judea became a tribute-paying vassal of Rome, subject to the Roman governor of Syria, whom Pompey had recently installed to rule over what had formerly been the Seleucid Kingdom. In return for his support, Pompey made Hyrcanus II high priest, but the office was stripped of any political power. He also left Antipater in charge of Idumea. When Pompey returned triumphantly to Rome, he took several hundred Judean prisoners with him as slaves, including Aristobulus II.

Julius Caesar

In 60 BCE, Pompey allied himself with two other powerful Roman generals, Julius Caesar and Marcus Crassus. This power-sharing agreement, known as the First Triumvirate, would not last. After Crassus died fighting the Parthians in 53, Pompey sought to achieve complete dictatorial control over the Roman Empire by persuading the Roman senate to remove Caesar from his position as governor of Roman Gaul. In 49, Julius Caesar led his troops across the Rubicon into Italy, where he defeated the forces of Pompey. Pompey himself fled first to Greece, then to Egypt, where he was murdered. The dictatorial power sought by Pompey was now in Caesar's hands.

Both Hyrcanus II and Antipater supported Caesar during the civil war; they even sent troops to help Caesar's forces defeat Pompey's forces in Egypt. In return, Caesar appointed Hyrcanus "Ethnarch of the Jews" and made Antipater governor of Judea. Antipater then secured the governorship of Jerusalem for his elder son Phasael, and the governorship of Galilee for his younger son Herod (the Great). Caesar would rule over the Roman Empire for only five years; he was assassinated by the Roman senators Cassius and Brutus in 44 BCE. After Caesar's death, another civil war broke out. It ended two years later, when the forces loyal to Cassius and Brutus were defeated by the forces of Antony (a military commander under Caesar) and Octavian (Caesar's grand-nephew and designated heir). Antony, in charge of the empire's eastern provinces, made Phasael and Herod joint rulers of Judea.

Augustus

In 40 BCE, Antigonus, the son of Aristobulus II, sought to restore Hasmonaean control of Judea by forming an alliance with the Parthian Empire in northwestern Persia. The Parthians invaded Syria and Judea with the support of much of the Jewish population. Phasael committed suicide and Herod fled to Rome, where he appealed to Antony and Octavian for help. Just as the Parthians were installing Antigonus as king of Judea, the Roman senate named Herod king of Judea. With Roman military support, Herod campaigned in Judea from 39 to 37, eventually defeating the Hasmonaean-Parthian alliance and securing his control of the kingdom.

Herod the Great would rule as king over Judea until his death in 4 BCE. During that time, conflict erupted in the Roman Empire between Octavian and his former ally, Antony. Octavian defeated Antony's forces at the Battle of Actium in 31 BCE. Antony and his wife, Queen Cleopatra VII of Egypt, committed suicide shortly thereafter. His victory complete, Octavian took the name *Augustus* (The Exalted One) and became the first official Roman emperor. Herod quickly pledged his allegiance to Augustus, and was rewarded by being granted lands in Samaria and the Transjordan formerly held by Antony and Cleopatra.

The Romans and the Jews

Jewish life under the Roman Empire was not wholly unbearable. A number of imperial edicts, the first of which was issued by Julius Caesar, were designed to protect the Jewish way of life. For example, Jews were exempted from compulsory service in the Roman military, since it would be impossible for them to observe their dietary laws and the Sabbath rest while serving in the legions.[4] Jews could not be summoned to appear in court on the Sabbath. The Temple tax, paid annually by all adult male Jews, was protected as sacred money, which meant that stealing it was a crime against the Roman Empire, punishable by death. Finally, while Rome's taxation of its subject peoples was heavy, the Jews were exempted from taxes that were specifically intended to fund the empire's many religious public works projects—for example, temples dedicated to emperors or pagan gods.[5]

Herod the Great

Still, most Jews resented being under the political control of yet another foreign power. Many also resented the fact that their monarch willingly collaborated with the empire. Indeed, Herod was a very loyal vassal king. When he built a port city on the Mediterranean coast, he named it Caesarea in honor of Augustus Caesar. In both Caesarea and Samaria, Herod erected Roman-style temples dedicated to the emperor. Herod also erected new buildings in Jerusalem, refortified the Hasmonaean fortress of Masada near the Dead Sea, developed new agricultural areas, and undertook a major renovation and expansion of the Jerusalem Temple—though in Greco-Roman style, with a Roman golden eagle on the gate. The heavy taxation that financed Herod's building projects, along with his subservience to Rome, made him unpopular among many Jews. The fact that Herod was an Idumean, rather than a Judean, also led some Jews to regard him as an interloper with no legitimate claim to the Judean throne.* Nor did it help that Herod often used murder and execution to stamp out any perceived or imagined threats to his power. Those who died upon Herod's command included one of his wives, a mother-in-law, a brother-in-law, and three of his own children. As Emperor Augustus is reported to have said, it was safer to be Herod's pig than Herod's son.[6]

When Herod died in 4 BCE, his kingdom was divided among his three surviving sons: Archelaus was given control of Judea, Samaria, and Idumea; Antipas was put in charge of Galilee and Perea (in the Transjordan); and Philip was given charge of Auranitis and Trachonitis (largely non-Jewish areas east of Galilee, across the Jordan River and the Sea of Galilee).

---

* The Idumeans practiced the Jewish faith, but were not ethnically Jewish. They had converted to Judaism after the Hasmonaeans conquered Idumea in the second century BCE. Whether the Idumeans converted to Judaism voluntarily or were forced to convert remains unclear, as ancient sources disagree on this point.

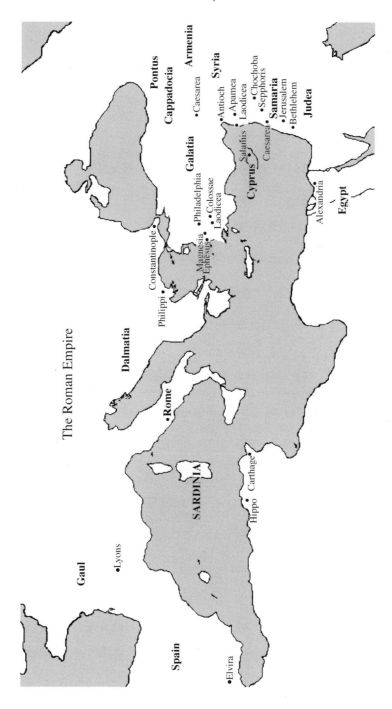

The Roman Empire

Gaul

Spain

Dalmatia

Rome

SARDINIA

Lyons

Elvira

Hippo

Carthage

Philippi

Constantinople

Magnesia
Ephesus

Philadelphia
Colossae
Laodicea

Galatia

Pontus

Cappadocia

Armenia

Antioch

Apamea
Laodicea

Syria

Caesarea

Chochoba
Sepphoris

Samaria

Jerusalem
Bethlehem

Judea

Salamis

Cyprus

Caesarea

Alexandria

Egypt

157

Frustrated by his mismanagement, the people of Judea soon rioted against Archelaus. Varus, the Roman governor of Syria, put down the uprisings and stationed an entire Roman legion— about five thousand troops, plus one hundred to two hundred cavalry—in Jerusalem. More than two thousand rioters were crucified. In 6 CE, when substantial delegations from Judea and Samaria went to Rome to complain to Augustus about Archelaus, Augustus decided that he had had enough of Archelaus's incompetence and banished him to Gaul. Judea, Samaria, and Idumea thus became part of the province of Syria, under the local supervision of a Roman *praefectus* (prefect). (The title of this office would change to *procurator* in 44 CE.) Thus, Palestinian Jews would live under the direct political control of the Roman Empire for the next sixty years.[7]

The Jewish War

The Second Temple period of Judaism reached its dramatic climax with the Jewish War of 66–73 CE, in which the Judeans took up arms against the Roman occupation forces. At first, the Judeans' guerrilla tactics were successful. But Rome, concerned about the growing Parthian Empire in Persia, could not afford to lose control of the strategically crucial Palestine. Emperor Nero sent three Roman legions under the command of General Vespasian to put down the Jewish rebellion. In 67 CE, the Romans captured Galilee. When Nero committed suicide the following year, Vespasian headed to Rome to contend for the throne, placing his son Titus in charge of the Roman forces. In 70 CE, Titus captured Jerusalem and destroyed the Temple. This Temple, which had been built during the Restoration and renovated under Herod, was the second to be razed by a foreign power. It would never be rebuilt.[8]

III. JEWISH SECTARIANISM

A number of distinct Jewish sects emerged during the Second Temple period. Much of what we know about these sects comes from the Jewish historian Josephus,* who described them as various "schools of thought" within Judaism. We shall use the term *sect* to mean a subgroup within a larger religious community that is distinguished from that larger community by a distinctive set of beliefs and/or practices.

Before we discuss the sects, two cautions are in order. First, we must be careful not to take the fact that Jewish sects existed as an indication that every Jew of the Second Temple period was a member of one sect or another. On the contrary, the majority of Jews continued to practice Judaism as they always had: observing the Mosaic Law, paying the Temple tax, and making pilgrimages to the Temple during the annual festivals of *Sukkot* (Booths), *Pesach* (Passover), and *Shavuot* (Weeks). Thus, while the Jewish sects were influential during the Second Temple period, they must be regarded as subgroups within the larger, traditional Jewish faith.

Second, it is important to bear in mind that, though they were often at odds, the various Jewish sects had much more in common with each other than they had points of disagreement. For instance, while they might disagree on how the rituals of the Temple cult should be organized and conducted, the various sects all acknowledged the importance of the Temple as the Jews' center of worship. Similarly, while the sects disagreed about how, and to what extent, the Mosaic Law should be interpreted, they nonetheless all agreed that the Torah was the ultimate law and basis for the Jewish faith. Finally, while some of the more radical sects thought that their way of practicing Judaism was the only correct way of doing so—and thus that Jews who were not members of the sect were sinners or pseudo-Jews—this was the exception rather than the rule. Most Jews of the Second Temple period, both those who were sect members and those who were not, regarded each other as Jews in the fullest sense; they simply acknowledged that there were many different ways in which one

---

* Flavius Josephus (37–100 CE) served as one of the commanders of the Jewish forces in the early stages of the Jewish War. After he was captured by Vespasian, however, Josephus changed sides and began serving the Romans as a translator and advisor, for which service he was ultimately granted Roman citizenship. After the war, Josephus wrote a number of books that he hoped would help the Romans better understand the Jews.

could practice the same Jewish faith. With these cautions in mind, let us now examine the major sects of the Second Temple period.[9]

A. The Pharisees

The word *Pharisee* derives from the Hebrew word *p'rushim*, which means "separate"; it may first have been applied to the Pharisees by other Jews as a slur. The Pharisees were the largest sect in the Second Temple period; Josephus estimated their membership at six thousand. Emerging early in the second century BCE, the Pharisees were a pietist movement composed largely of middle- and lower-class laypersons. Although the Pharisees counted some priests among their members, the leaders of the sect were secular scholars who were experts in the study of the Torah. The Pharisees believed that all Jews, as opposed to just the priests, should try to obey all the Mosaic laws regarding ritual purity. Since it was difficult for the average Jew to observe all the Mosaic laws all the time—by the Pharisees' count, the Torah contained 613 distinct laws—the Pharisees seem to have allowed relatively liberal interpretations of the Torah, provided that those interpretations were made by learned scholars. Over time, the Pharisees came to recognize two distinct sets of laws as authoritative: the written law (the Torah) and an oral law, which they called the ancestral tradition. This ancestral tradition preserved the interpretive teachings of the Pharisaic scholar-leaders, which were passed down orally from generation to generation. It included both *Halakah* (The Path), obligatory principles regarding morality and ritual purity, and *Haggadah* (Narration), or edifying stories.

The Pharisees held a number of nontraditional theological beliefs, some of which are reflected in writings that date to the Second Temple period. The Pharisees believed that, at some undisclosed time in the future, a general resurrection of the dead would occur. The dead would be judged by God for their deeds in life and then rewarded or punished in the afterlife. As we have already seen, the mention of such a resurrection and afterlife at Daniel 12:2 (written around 176–164 BCE) is the first clear statement of these ideas in the Tanak, which indicates their relatively late emergence in Jewish thought. Such ideas can also be found in 2 Maccabees, an apocryphal book written early in the first century BCE (see 7:9 and 12:44).

The Pharisees also believed in the existence of superhuman angels and devils. The emergence of such beliefs in Second Temple Judaism is evidenced in the apocryphal Book of Tobit, which most scholars date to the second century BCE. In that book, the characters Tobit, his son Tobias, and Tobias's wife Sara are all aided by the angel Raphael, who is disguised as a human being but reveals his true nature at the end. One of the feats that Raphael helps Tobias accomplish is the exorcism of the demon Asmodeus, who had killed all seven of Sara's previous husbands.

Of all of the Second Temple period sects, the Pharisees were to have the most profound impact on the formation of modern Judaism. It was their emphasis on reading and interpreting the Jewish law that would ultimately lead to the prominence of the synagogue as a place of prayer and study. After the destruction of the Second Temple by the Romans in 70 CE, the Pharisaic sect evolved into rabbinic Judaism, from which virtually all contemporary forms of Judaism descended. Like the Pharisees before them, the rabbis of post-Second Temple Judaism passed the ancestral tradition down orally from one generation to the next, devoted themselves to careful observance of the Mosaic Law, and maintained a belief in the resurrection of the dead. Around 200 CE, a rabbi named Judah the Patriarch compiled and edited a written version of the Pharisaic/rabbinic ancestral tradition called the *Mishnah* (from the Hebrew verb *shanah*, "to repeat" or "to learn"). However, scholars are unsure how much if any of the material in the *Mishnah* dates back to the Pharisees of the Second Temple period, as much of it seems to be the work of rabbis who worked in the second century CE.[10]

B. The Sadducees

The Sadducees are known to have existed as a distinct sect by the mid-second century BCE. Their name is a Greek rendering of the Hebrew word *Tzadduqim*, which derives from Zadok, the name of the high priest in the time of David and Solomon. The Sadducean sect was much smaller than the Pharisaic, as its membership was limited to aristocrats. The Sadducean sect was made up primarily of priests who served in the Temple and their relatives by blood or marriage. Because the Temple was both the center of worship, where sacrifices to YHWH were performed, and the Jews' national bank, where revenues from the Temple tax and other monetary offerings were stored, the Sadducees' involvement with the Temple made them extremely powerful. This is clear in the fact that the Sadducees tended to dominate the Sanhedrin, which was a group of advisors to the high priest. The Roman Empire allowed the Sanhedrin to act as a judicial body with jurisdiction over the Jews' internal affairs—for example, it was up to the Sanhedrin to decide cases in which a Jew was accused of a serious violation of the Jewish law such as blasphemy. Although Pharisees also served on the Sanhedrin, it was composed primarily of Sadducees.

Relative to the Pharisees, the Sadducees were conservative with regard to both politics and theology. Politically, the Sadducees were interested in maintaining the status quo. Since Rome reserved the right to appoint Jerusalem's high priest, and the high priest controlled both the Temple and the Sanhedrin, it was in the Sadducees' interests to collaborate with the Romans; for the Sadducees, appeasing Rome was a means of maintaining and protecting their positions of wealth and power. Theologically, the Sadducees regarded only the Mosaic Law recorded in the Torah as authoritative, which means that they rejected the oral law of the Pharisees as illegitimate. Because they were primarily concerned with the maintenance of the Temple and its cult, the Sadducees believed that most of the Mosaic purity laws applied only to priests and not—as the Pharisees thought—to Jewish laypersons. The Sadducees also rejected the Pharisees' beliefs in a resurrection, an afterlife, and superhuman angels and demons, on the grounds that such beliefs were not sanctioned by the Torah (see Mark 12:18; Acts 23:7–8). Finally, whereas the Pharisees believed in both free will and fate—that is, they believed that some human choices are free, whereas others are determined by God—the Sadducees rejected the idea of fate altogether. They held instead that human beings have complete freedom of will and are thus morally responsible for all of their choices. This idea is reflected in another apocryphal work, the Wisdom of Jesus ben Sirach, which dates to around 180 BCE. Writing in the tradition of wisdom literature, Jesus ben Sirach stresses human responsibility on the grounds that the Lord "created humankind in the beginning, and he left them in the power of their own free choice." Thus, whether one keeps the commandments or not is one's own doing, an exercise of one's own free will (15:11–15, 20).

The Sadducees and Pharisees alike were deeply involved with the political struggles of the Second Temple period, and the influence wielded by both sects fluctuated as a result of those struggles. From the time the Second Temple was completed in 515 BCE until the time of the Maccabean revolt, the office of high priest was held by members of the Zadokite family. When Jonathan assumed the high priesthood in 152 BCE, the Zadokites—and thus also the Sadducees, of which sect the Zadokites were members—lost control of that office to the Hasmonaean family. In the early years of the Hasmonaean Dynasty, Sadducean influence in both the Temple and the Sanhedrin waned, while Pharisaic influence grew stronger. By the time Queen Alexandra reigned (76–67 BCE), the Pharisees clearly had the upper hand. When Alexandra's son Aristobulus II contended for the throne with his brother Hyrcanus II, the Sadducees threw their support behind the former, while the Pharisees supported the latter. Aristobulus's victory brought a return to power and influence for the Sadducees, though the high priesthood remained in Hasmonaean control. Both sects were dealt a blow when, during the reign of King Herod (37–4 BCE), the Sanhedrin was disbanded. When it was reestablished in 6 CE, the Sadducees found themselves in power again, but at the cost of collaborating with a Roman prefect.

Unlike the Pharisees, the Sadducees did not survive Judaism's Second Temple period. The Roman destruction of the Second Temple deprived the Sadducees of both their power base and their role in the nation's public worship as mediators between the Jewish people and YHWH. After 70 CE, the Sadducean sect simply disappeared.

C. Radical Groups

In addition to the Pharisees and Sadducees, a number of smaller and more radical Jewish sects also emerged during the Second Temple period. Among these were the Essenes, the Qumran Community, the Zealots, and the Sicarii.

The Essenes

The Essenes were an ascetic group who sought to lead a more devout life by withdrawing from society and living in monastic communities. Their name (*Essenoi* in Greek) is problematic; since it only occurs in Greek texts, it is impossible to say what Hebrew or Aramaic word it may have been meant to transliterate. Some scholars have suggested that it might trace to the Hebrew word *Hasidim*—which means "pious ones" and was the name of a group who participated in the Maccabean revolt (see 1 Macc 2:42–44; 7:13–17)—but this is speculative at best.[11]

The Essenes held their prayers, their meals, their work, and their property in common. Only adult men could become members of the sect, and then only after a three-year probationary period. Most Essenes were celibate, though many of them seem to have taken up celibacy after having already married and fathered children. Josephus asserts that there was also a second order of Essenes that shared all the beliefs and practices of the first with the exception that, in this second order, members did marry in order to procreate.

The Essenes took the Mosaic Law very seriously and, according to Josephus, they avoided the Jerusalem Temple because they disagreed with the Temple leadership on issues of ritual purity. Unlike the Sadducees, who denied fate, and the Pharisees, who believed in both fate and free will, the Essenes believed that all things that occur in the world—including human acts of choice—are predetermined by the divine will. The Essenes also believed in an afterlife, though ancient sources disagree on how the Essenes conceived of that afterlife; Hippolytus of Rome (170–236 CE) says that they believed in bodily resurrection, whereas Josephus says that they believed only in the immortality of the soul.[12]

The Qumran Community

Another radical Jewish sect was that which maintained a monastic community at Qumran, on the northwest coast of the Dead Sea, from roughly 150 BCE until 68 CE. It was this community that produced the Dead Sea Scrolls. First discovered in 1947, the Dead Sea Scrolls are a set of 870 complete or partial manuscripts that had been hidden in caves near Qumran. Roughly one quarter of those manuscripts are biblical texts; indeed, whole or partial copies of every book of the Hebrew Bible except Esther were found at Qumran.* The other three-quarters of the manuscripts are sectarian documents (such as rules for the community), commentaries on the Hebrew scriptures, and copies of noncanonical religious books. The copies of the Hebrew scriptures found at Qumran are the oldest existing manuscripts of those scriptures; they are roughly one thousand years older than any other manuscripts of the Hebrew scriptures thus far discovered.

The Qumranites called themselves the Community or the Congregation. Their leaders are referred to in the scrolls as Sons of Zadok, presumably priests of the Zadokite line. The scrolls also make many references to the Teacher of Righteousness, who was either the founder or an early leader of the community at Qumran. Some scholars have suggested that this Teacher of Righteousness may have been the high priest in Jerusalem, or at least a de facto leader at the Temple, who was forced out when Jonathan was appointed high priest by Alexander Balas in 152 BCE. The Qumranites believed that the Teacher of Righteousness had been given a special revelation from God regarding how the scriptures should be interpreted, which was then passed on to other members of the community.

Their interpretation of the Hebrew Bible led the Qumranites to hold a number of distinctive beliefs. For example, whereas the Jerusalem Temple followed a lunar calendar, the Qumranites believed that the scriptures demanded a calendar that incorpo-

---

* Actually, no fragments of Ezra were found either. However, during the Second Temple period, the Book of Ezra was probably part of the Book of Nehemiah, of which a fragment was found at Qumran. Thus, it is very likely that Ezra was represented in the Qumran library.

rated both lunar cycles and solar cycles. The result was that the Qumranites celebrated Jewish holidays on different dates than other Jews did. The Qumranites also had well-developed eschatological beliefs. They believed that they were living in the end times, that the day of the Lord was close at hand; soon the Lord would intervene in human history to establish a new world order, whereby the wicked would be punished and the righteous exalted. One of the sectarian documents among the Dead Sea Scrolls, titled "Some Observances of the Law," asserts that "this is the End of Days when they will repent in Isra[el] for[ever...].″[13] Another scroll found at Qumran, known as the "War Rule," predicts that the End of Days will be preceded by a great battle in which the "sons of light" (the Qumranites, aided by angels) would vanquish the "sons of darkness, the army of Satan" (which would consist mostly of Romans, aided by demons). The Qumranites also believed that, near the end of time, the Lord would send *two* messiahs: one would be "of Israel," meaning a secular leader from the Davidic line, while the other would be "of Aaron"—that is, a priestly messiah.

There has been much debate among biblical scholars about who the people at Qumran were. Some scholars, most notably Lawrence Schiffman, have argued that the Qumran community was founded by or at least strongly influenced by Sadducees. Schiffman's argument is based largely on the Dead Sea Scrolls text known as "Some Observances of the Law," which is also called the Halakhic Letter because it deals primarily with ritual purity obligations. On Schiffman's interpretation, the Halakhic Letter is a copy of a letter that the members of the Qumran community sent to the high priest in Jerusalem. The letter suggests that the Qumranites had withdrawn from participation in the Temple cult because they disagreed with the Temple leadership on a number of matters regarding ritual purity. It lists twenty-two specific points of disagreement on purity issues, taking a position closer to that of the Sadducees than to that of the Pharisees. Indeed, the Qumranites appear to be even more conservative than the Sadducean Temple leadership, whom they fault for failing to observe a strict interpretation of the Mosaic purity laws. The letter seems intended to make the Temple authorities' errors clear to them, and thereby to make possible the Qumranites' return to Temple service. Thus, according to Schiffman, the Qumran community was founded by a group of Sadducees during the Hasmonaean period. Unwilling to tolerate either a non-Zadokite high priest or the growing influence of the Pharisees in the Hasmonaean Temple, a small group of Sadducees withdrew from Temple service and retreated to the desert.[14]

While Schiffman's argument is intriguing, the consensus among biblical scholars is that the Qumranites were actually members of the Essene sect. What we know about the Essenes comes primarily from three ancient sources: Josephus, the Jewish philosopher Philo of Alexandria (15 BCE–50 CE), and the Roman geographer Pliny the Elder (23–79 CE). Much of what these ancient authors assert about the Essenes parallels what we know about the Qumranites based on the Dead Sea Scrolls and archaeological findings at Qumran. Pliny asserts that there was a group of Essenes living on the western shore of the Dead Sea north of En-Gedi—that is, on the northwestern coast, which is where Qumran was located. Like the Essenes, the Qumranites underwent a two- to three-year probationary period before attaining full membership in the community. As did the Essenes, so the Qumranites held all their possessions in common, and both groups took their meals together only after bathing and saying grace.

Josephus distinguishes two orders of Essenes, one living a celibate lifestyle in isolation, the other marrying and living in society. Similarly, the Qumranites distinguished between those of their community who lived in isolation at Qumran and those living in "camps"—that is, in society. Like the Essenes, both of these Qumranite groups avoided the Jerusalem Temple because of disagreements with the Temple leadership regarding purity issues. Finally, the Qumranites believed in angels and demons, they believed in an afterlife, and they believed that all things are ruled by fate. According to our ancient sources, these are all beliefs that the Essenes held and the Sadducees explicitly rejected. Since the Dead Sea Scrolls make clear that the Qumranites held these counter-Sadducean beliefs from nearly the beginning of their time at Qumran, it is highly unlikely that the Qumran community could have been founded by Sadducees.* Thus, as Dead Sea Scrolls scholar James VanderKam has stated, "The Essene hypothesis…accounts for the totality of the evidence in a more convincing way than any of its rivals."[15]

When the Jewish War broke out in 66 CE, the Qumranites must have thought that the End of Days they were awaiting had finally arrived. The Essenes and the Qumranites alike marched out to engage the Roman forces of Vespasian in 68 CE. The Roman legions obliterated both groups.

The Zealots and the Sicarii

Two other Jewish sects of the Second Temple period were radical, not in their theological beliefs, but in their militancy. These were the Zealots and the Sicarii. According to Josephus, the Zealots agreed with the Pharisees on issues of theology. What set them apart were their political views. Unwilling to live under the rule of a foreign power, the Zealots advocated, armed for, and presumably trained for a guerrilla-style revolt against the forces of the Roman occupation. It is thought that the Zealots were mostly peasants for, though they participated in the Jewish War against Rome, their motivation seems to have been as much economic as it was political. During that war, the Zealots looted the houses of wealthy Jews, they burned down the palace of the high priest, Ananias, and they destroyed the Jerusalem palace of Agrippa II, who was the great-grandson of Herod the Great and king of the northern territories once controlled by Herod's son Philip. They also torched Jerusalem's archives, which Josephus claims was an effort to erase the debt record and thereby "to secure the support of an army of debtors and enable the poor to rise with impunity against the rich."[16]

Another militant sect of the Second Temple period was the Sicarii ("daggermen," from the Latin word for dagger, *sica*). Emerging

---

* Schiffman's argument is further complicated by the fact that the parallels he draws between Qumranite and Saducean interpretations of the Mosaic Law are based on rabbinic accounts of disagreements between the Sadducees and the Pharisees as recorded in the *Mishnah*. As noted above, most scholars believe that the material recorded in the *Mishnah* was primarily the work of rabbis who lived in the second century CE. Thus, many scholars doubt that the portrayals of Second Temple period Jewish sects in the *Mishnah* are historically accurate.

in the 40s CE, the Sicarii opposed the Roman occupation but initially focused their attention on Jews whom they deemed to be Roman collaborators. The sect's name derives from the weapon that the Sicarii typically used to assassinate pro-Roman Jews. The Sicarii fought against the Romans in the early stages of the war, but their conflicts with other Jews eventually led them to retreat to the mountaintop fortress of Masada on the Dead Sea. Although the Romans captured Jerusalem in 70 CE, bringing an end to the Zealots, the Jewish War did not officially end until the year 73 CE, when the Romans finally took Masada. According to Josephus, the approximately 960 Sicarii at Masada took their own lives just before the Romans breached Masada's walls, so as not to be killed or captured by their pagan enemy. While Josephus is not always entirely reliable, archaeological evidence at Masada suggests that his account of the Sicarii's end may be accurate.[17]

D. Hellenistic Jews

We shall close this chapter on the Second Temple period with a brief discussion of the Hellenistic Jews. Although they did not constitute a sect in the strict sense, the Hellenistic Jews would play an important role both in the formation of modern Judaism and in the emergence of the early Christian church.

In our survey of the history of Israel, we have seen a number of occasions on which the Jews were uprooted from their homeland and relocated elsewhere. This process, known as the *Diaspora* (dispersion), began with the fall of the northern kingdom of Israel to Assyria in 722 BCE. Later, when the southern kingdom of Judah fell to Nebuchadnezzar in 586 BCE, many thousands of Jews were taken to Babylon, while a smaller number fled to Egypt. When the Babylonian Exile ended, many of the exiled Jews chose to remain in their new homes rather than return to Judah. And throughout both the Persian and Hellenistic periods, many Jews migrated throughout the Near East, North Africa, and Europe. Thus, by the time Pompey marched into Jerusalem in 63 CE, there were Jewish settlements in virtually every major city of the Roman Empire.

Because the Greek domination of the Mediterranean world during the Hellenistic period had been so thorough, the cultural impact of the Greeks outlasted their political control. During the Second Temple period, although the official language of the Roman Empire was Latin, Greek was still the language of common discourse in all the lands Alexander the Great had conquered, and Hellenistic artistic and philosophical ideas were still in wide circulation. Thus, when we refer to Hellenistic Jews of the Second Temple period, we mean those Jews living in cities throughout the Roman Empire whose language and culture were shaped by the lasting influence of Hellenism.

The Septuagint

One of the most important Hellenistic Jewish communities in the Second Temple period was located in Alexandria, Egypt. The Jews in Alexandria spoke Greek either as their first language or, in at least some cases, as their only language. For this reason, the Alexandrian Jews produced the first translation of the Hebrew scriptures into Greek. This process began in the mid-third century BCE, during the reign of the Ptolemies. Over the next three centuries, the Greek translation of the Hebrew scriptures would be revised and expanded to include a number of books that never came to be part of the Hebrew Tanak. This Greek version of the Hebrew scriptures is known as the Septuagint—from the Latin word for seventy—and it is often referred to by the Roman numeral for seventy, LXX. Both the name and the abbreviation derive from a legend according to which the Septuagint was produced through the joint effort of seventy scholars. Since more Jews living in the Second Temple period spoke Greek than spoke Hebrew, the Septuagint eventually became popular with Jews throughout the Mediterranean. For the same reason, the Septuagint would become the Old Testament of the early Christian churches. This explains why the Christian Old Testament differs from the Hebrew Tanak in its content; unlike the Hebrew text that achieved canonical status among Palestinian Jews, the Septuagint contained the works now known as the Apocrypha or Deuterocanon.

4 Maccabees

The influence of Greek thought on the Hellenistic Jews is most clearly demonstrated in the apocryphal Book of 4 Maccabees. Written in Greek by an unknown author, 4 Maccabees gets its name from the fact that its author uses events related in 2 Maccabees as examples of the book's themes. Scholars date the work to sometime between 20 and 54 CE, when Cilicia, Syria, and Phoenicia formed a single province of the Roman Empire (4:2). The location of its writing is unknown, though most scholars believe that it was written either in Alexandria or in Antioch.

The Book of 4 Maccabees is a good example of Hellenistic Judaism because its author, who is clearly Jewish and concerned with the Jewish law, nonetheless approaches his topic in the Greek philosophical style. He states that the purpose of his work is to discern "whether devout reason is sovereign over the emotions" (1:1). Here the author is dealing with a question that was central to ancient Greek philosophy. Indeed, his answer to that question seems to have been influenced by the work of the ancient Greek philosopher Plato (428–348 BCE). In a work called the *Republic*, Plato had argued that an excellent human being must have four virtues: wisdom, courage, temperance (self-control), and justice. The most important of these, Plato thought, was wisdom; without knowledge to guide one's judgments and choices, the other virtues cannot be attained. Similarly, the author of 4 Maccabees states that rational judgment is the highest virtue (1:2), which rules over any emotions that are contrary to justice, courage, and self-control (1:6). As in Plato, so in 4 Maccabees, the good person is one in whom reason rules over emotions and appetites; such a person "is temperate, just, good, and courageous" (2:21–23). While it is impossible to say definitively whether the author of 4 Maccabees was directly influenced by the work of an ancient Greek philosopher, it is nonetheless clear that Greek concepts and ideas had a powerful influence on the way Hellenistic Jews thought about their faith.

Part III
THE CHRISTIAN SCRIPTURES

Jesus of Nazareth

Jesus of Nazareth was the founder of a Jewish movement that would ultimately become Christianity. He is also the main character of the New Testament. Our purpose in this chapter is to gain a sense of who Jesus was. We shall begin with the concept of the historical Jesus. We shall then discuss some of the sources to which scholars appeal in their efforts to understand Jesus. Next, we shall attempt to construct an historical account of Jesus' life. Finally, we shall consider the meaning of some of the titles that were applied to Jesus by the first Christians.

I. THE JESUS OF HISTORY AND THE CHRIST OF FAITH

Biblical scholars who study the life and work of Jesus often draw a distinction between the Jesus of history and the Christ of faith. In making this distinction, scholars do not mean to assert that there were two different persons by the name of Jesus. Rather, the distinction has to do with how one approaches and evaluates the available sources of information about Jesus.

The Historical Jesus

When scholars refer to the Jesus of history, they mean the person about whom assertions can be made by application of the empirical historical method. Scholars using that method look for information about Jesus in both biblical and extrabiblical sources, and they attempt to evaluate the reliability of those sources as objectively as possible. They also consider the relevance of findings in such disciplines as archaeology, sociology, and anthropology. The result of this kind of research is a theoretical reconstruction of the events in the life of Jesus.

The Christ of Faith

When scholars refer to the Christ of faith, they mean the person who is the object of faith and worship for members of the Christian community. More precisely, the Christ of faith is Jesus as he has been interpreted and proclaimed by Christians ever since the Christ Event. The Christ Event is the set of experiences that convinced the first Christians that Jesus of Nazareth was not just a human being, but the messianic savior whose arrival many Jews had been anticipating.[1] The account of the Christ Event that is preserved in the New Testament gospels reaches its climax in stories of Jesus appearing to his disciples after his death. Whether or not those stories are historically reliable (a topic to which we shall return in the next chapter), something happened to Jesus' disciples that convinced them that, after his death, Jesus had "entered into an entirely new form of existence, one in which he shared the power of God and in which he could share that power with others."[2] Since then, the Christ of faith has been an object of both theological reflection and worship for Christians.

The "Real" Jesus

It is important to note that, in searching for the historical Jesus, we are neither trying nor claiming to uncover the *real* Jesus, for two reasons. First, application of the empirical historical method to ancient sources can produce, at best, only a very rough sketch of any historical figure. As one biblical scholar has observed, "Historical knowing is like a sieve that catches big chunks but lets much fine stuff slip through."[3] Thus, the data that we collect about the Jesus of history will provide us with an outline of his life—when he was probably born, where he most likely lived, when and how he seems to have died, and so on—but it will tell us little about his day-to-day words or actions, and still less about his innermost thoughts.

176

Second, to claim that the Jesus of history is the *real* Jesus would be to imply that the Christ of faith is somehow artificial or imaginary, which is not the goal of the academic approach to the Bible. Scholars engaged in the search for the historical Jesus try to avoid making appeals to faith, that is, they try not to make use of interpretations and evaluations of data that presuppose a devotional approach to the Bible. But this does not mean that such scholars cannot be persons who practice the Christian faith. Rather, scholars take pains to distinguish what they may believe as Christians from what they can assert on the grounds of verifiable historical data, because it is only by doing so that objectivity can be achieved. Thus, scholars researching the historical Jesus attempt to suspend their own religious beliefs temporarily in order to ensure that their scholarly judgment will not be clouded or biased by those beliefs.

Analogy: Haile Selassie I

To make the foregoing points more clear, consider an analogous example. Haile Selassie I was the ruler of Ethiopia from 1930 to 1974. Practitioners of the Rastafarian religion believe that Selassie—whom Rastafarians call by his throne name, Ras Tafari—was divine. That is, they believe that Selassie was the Deity—whom Rastafarians call Jah—living on the earth in human form. Now it is possible for a Rastafarian to engage in theological reflection upon and interpretation of the data about Haile Selassie's life. But a Rastafarian could also distinguish between the Selassie of history and the Tafari of faith. If a Rastafarian wished to construct an historical account of the life of Haile Selassie, she would not have to abandon her beliefs about the Tafari of faith, nor would she have to deny that what she believes on faith about Ras Tafari also applies to the historical figure of Selassie. She would, however, have to be careful not to let her personal belief in the divinity of Ras Tafari influence how she evaluates the reliability of historical data about Haile Selassie. So it is with scholars who conduct research on the historical Jesus; having drawn a distinction between the Jesus of history and the Christ of faith, their goal is to gain an understanding of the former that neither presupposes nor depends upon beliefs about the latter. Once this goal is attained, they may then turn to the theological task of interpreting data about the Jesus of history in terms of Christian beliefs regarding the Christ of faith, and vice versa.

Why Search for the Historical Jesus?

Some biblical scholars argue that there is little to be gained by making a distinction between the Jesus of history and the Christ of faith. Those who take such a position often do so because they have observed how easily that distinction can be taken to ridiculous extremes. Indeed, there have been scholars who, in their search for information about the historical Jesus, have begun with an unjustified bias against the data provided by the Christian scriptures. They hold that, because the documents of the New Testament were written by Christians for Christians, this means that those documents preserve only the theological beliefs of the first Christians, not historical facts. When scholars of this view go looking for the historical Jesus, they end up producing reconstructions of his life according to which (a) the Jesus of history bears little or no resemblance to the Christ of faith, or even to the subject of the New Testament gospels, and/or (b) the Jesus of history is forced into a mold that those scholars think he should fit: cynical philosopher, radical social reformer, and so on. Such accounts of the Jesus of history are problematic, in two ways. First, any account of the historical Jesus must somehow connect the words and deeds of Jesus to the theological beliefs that Jesus' followers came to hold. As one scholar has noted, "[W]e cannot pare the gospel material down to a nontheological core, and then proclaim that we have found Jesus, since Jesus himself was a theologian."[4] Second, when we limit our understanding of Jesus to what the empirical historical method can tell us about his life, we fail to grasp the significance that Jesus has for the Christian community. To those who practice the Christian faith, the *real* Jesus is not an historical figure as reconstructed by scholars. To Christians, the *real* Jesus is the person whom they regard as having been raised from the dead, as living, and as enthroned at the right hand of God; he is the person whose continued existence is "manifested in the powerful presence of the Holy Spirit among believers."[5] In other words, the Jesus whom Christians worship as divine is not an ancient historical figure, but a person who Christians believe is alive and present to them in a mysterious and powerful way. Thus, scholarly reconstructions of the life of the historical Jesus cannot undermine the basic tenets of Christianity, nor should they be intended to do so.

The foregoing paragraph makes clear why it is important not to overemphasize the distinction between the Jesus of history and the Christ of faith. Nonetheless, the search for information about the historical Jesus can and should play a valuable role, not only in an academic understanding of the Bible, but also in an understanding of Christian belief. For Christians believe that their claims about the Christ of faith—that he was the anticipated Messiah, that he was raised from the dead, that others can achieve salvation through him, and so on—also apply to the historical figure of Jesus. As the theologian Thomas Rausch has argued, this means that Christians' understanding of the Christ of faith must be "grounded in the words and deeds of the Jesus of history." If it is not—if no connection can be drawn between the historical figure of Jesus and the beliefs that constitute Christianity—then Christianity would seem to be merely an "ideological construction...[that is,] a mere mythologization of the founder of Christianity."[6] If Christians are to maintain that the Jesus of history and the Christ of faith are one and the same person, it must be possible for Christian theologians to establish some sort of relationship between things that the earthly Jesus said and did, on the one hand, and things that Christians believe about Jesus, on the other. A historical account of the life of Jesus can help them to establish such a relationship. With this in mind, we shall now examine the sources available to scholars in their search for the Jesus of history.

II. SOURCES ON THE HISTORICAL JESUS

A. Extrabiblical Sources

Josephus

Extrabiblical sources of information on the life of Jesus are few in number and small on details. One such source is the *Antiquities of the Jews* by Josephus.[7] In that work, Josephus makes a reference to James, whom he describes as "the brother of Jesus-who-is-called-Messiah *[Christos]*" (20.9.1). This description indicates that Josephus thought of Jesus, not as the anticipated Jewish savior, but as a messianic pretender. Another passage in the *Antiquities* also makes reference to Jesus. The version of this passage that has been passed down to modernity reads as follows:

> At this time there appeared Jesus, a wise man, if indeed one should call him a man. For he was a doer of startling deeds, a teacher of people who receive the truth with pleasure. And he gained a following both among many Jews and among many of Greek origin. He was the Messiah *[Christos]*. And when Pilate, because of an accusation made by the leading men among us, condemned him to the cross, those who had loved him previously did not cease to do so. For he appeared to them on the third day, living again, just as the divine prophets had spoken these and countless other wondrous things about him. And up until this very day the tribe of Christians, named after him, has not died out (18.3.3).

Note that, in the version of this passage that has been passed down to us, Josephus makes three explicitly Christian claims: (1) Jesus was the anticipated Jewish savior *(Christos)*; (2) Jesus appeared to his disciples after his death; and (3) Jesus fulfilled the prophecies of the Jewish scriptures. Because Josephus refers to Jesus as "Jesus-who-is-called-Christ" later in the same work, and because it is known that Josephus never converted to Christianity

Jesus of Nazareth

Damascus

•Sidon
•Sarepta

•Tyre   •Caesarea Philippi

Chorazin•
•Capernaum •   •Bethsaida
Gennesaret• *Sea of Galilee*
Cana •   •Gerasa
Nazareth• Tiberius
•Nain   •Pella
•Caesarea

MEDITERRANEAN SEA

•
Samaria/Sebaste

• Joppa   R. Jordan
• Lydda

•Emmaus

•Ashkelon
Jerusalem•
Bethlehem •   *Dead Sea*

•Hebron

Masada •

Beersheba •

• Sodom

• Gomorrah

MAP IN THE TIME OF JESUS

but remained a Jew his entire life, most scholars agree that the explicitly Christian claims in this passage must have been added by Christian editors at some point in its transmission—probably between the third and sixth centuries. Biblical scholar John P. Meier has offered the following reconstruction of the passage as it may have been worded in the original text of Josephus:

> At this time there appeared Jesus, a wise man. For he was a doer of startling deeds, a teacher of people who receive the truth with pleasure. And he gained a following both among many Jews and among many of Greek origin. And when Pilate, because of an accusation made by the leading men among us, condemned him to the cross, those who had loved him previously did not cease to do so. And up until this very day the tribe of Christians (named after him) has not died out.

Even if we suppose, with Meier, that the original version of this passage from Josephus made no explicitly Christian claims, both of the references to Jesus in the *Antiquities* nonetheless give us valuable information about the Jesus of history. First, Josephus concurs with the New Testament that Jesus was a first-century Palestinian Jew who was crucified by order of the Roman prefect Pontius Pilate. Second, Josephus refers to Jesus as a "wise man" who performed "startling deeds" and had a following; he thus confirms that Jesus engaged in a public ministry and had disciples. Third, the fact that Josephus regards Jesus as a messianic pretender tells us that, either during or after Jesus' lifetime, Jesus came to be regarded by at least some of his followers as the Messiah, the savior whom many Jews had been anticipating.

Tacitus

Another extrabiblical reference to Jesus can be found in the *Annals* of the Roman historian Publius Cornelius Tacitus (55–120 CE). In his discussion of the great fire of Rome in 64 CE, Tacitus tells us that Emperor Nero sought to blame the fire on Christians. He then explains,

[Christians take their name] from Christus, who was executed by sentence of the procurator Pontius Pilate when Tiberius was emperor. That checked the pernicious superstition for a short time, but it broke out afresh—not only in Judea, where the plague first arose, but in Rome itself, where all the horrible and shameful things in the world collect and find a home (15.44).[8]

Tacitus thus confirms three pieces of information about Jesus that we have already found in Josephus, namely, that Jesus existed, that he had a following, and that he was condemned to death by Pontius Pilate. Note that Tacitus seems to think that Christus was the name of the founder of Christianity; he does not recognize that the Greek word *Christos* was a title that Christians applied to Jesus. Moreover, as F. F. Bruce points out, the fact that his tone toward Christianity is blatantly derogatory suggests that Tacitus probably did not consult Christians for his information about Jesus. Thus, Tacitus may have obtained his information from some sort of official police record that was written at the time of Jesus' death and preserved in imperial archives.[9]

B. Biblical Sources

Since the extrabiblical sources of information about Jesus are so limited, scholars seeking to reconstruct the life of the historical Jesus must turn to the biblical accounts preserved in the New Testament gospels. Here they run into a problem. The general consensus among biblical scholars is that there were three stages in the development of the gospel tradition. The first stage consisted of the original words and deeds of Jesus. Then, after Jesus' death, his apostles proclaimed him as Messiah by means of an oral tradition in which Jesus' words and deeds were passed on by word of mouth. Finally, when those apostles who had been contemporaries of Jesus began to die, their teachings were compiled into written form by the authors of the gospels, who were Christians writing for their fellow Christians.[10] Thus, the problem with consulting the gospels for information about the Jesus of history is that the gospels are not, and were not intended to be, historical accounts or biographies in our modern sense of those terms. Instead, they are the end product of a long process of theological reflection, an interpretation of the life of Jesus by those who believed in the Christ of faith. While the gospels do contain historical information about the experiences of the first Christians, they also contain theological interpretations of those experiences. A scholar seeking the historical Jesus must not confuse such theological interpretations with objective historical data.

Authenticating Criteria

In order to overcome this problem, biblical scholars attempting to reconstruct the life of the historical Jesus must read the gospels critically. They do so by measuring the words and deeds that the gospels attribute to Jesus against a set of authenticating criteria.[11] The more clearly a saying or action attributed to Jesus satisfies one or more of these criteria, the more likely it is that the saying or action traces to the historical Jesus. Some of the more commonly applied authenticating criteria are as follows:

1. *Multiple Attestation:* Is the saying or action mentioned in multiple independent sources? The more independent sources there are that attest to a saying or action, the more probable it is that that saying or action traces to the historical Jesus.* For example, it can be argued that Jesus probably shared a last meal with his closest disciples, during which he interpreted the bread and wine as symbolizing his own body and blood. This event is attested in both the Gospel of Mark (14:22–25; Matthew and Luke borrow and build upon Mark's version) and in Paul (1 Cor 11:24–26).[12]

---

* For reasons we shall see in the next chapter, the gospels of Matthew, Mark, and Luke are not considered entirely independent sources. Thus, the fact that a particular saying or action is attributed to Jesus in two or three of these gospels does not necessarily increase the likelihood that the saying or action is historical. However, if a saying or action is attributed to Jesus in at least one of those three gospels, *and* in the Gospel of John, *and/or* in the letters of Paul—which, having been written prior to the four New Testament gospels, are independent of them—then its historical likelihood is increased.

2. Dissimilarity: Is the saying or action dissimilar from typical ways of thinking and acting at that time? A gospel passage may satisfy the criterion of dissimilarity in two ways. First, a saying or action satisfies the criterion of dissimilarity if it would have been *embarrassing* to the early Christian church—by, for instance, being contrary to the early church's teachings. The fact that a given saying or action attributed to Jesus might have been embarrassing to the early church is good reason to think that it was not simply an embellishment on the part of the author, as the authors of the gospels would not have been likely to embellish a story in ways that were contrary to their own beliefs or those of their intended audience. Second, a saying or action may satisfy the criterion of dissimilarity if it is *innovative,* that is, if it breaks with the accepted beliefs and customs of Second Temple Judaism and is thus unlikely to have been part of the first Christians' way of thinking. One example of a saying of Jesus that satisfies the criterion of dissimilarity as innovation is Jesus' prohibition of divorce (Mark 10:2–12; 1 Cor 7:10). Such a prohibition would have been innovative in the culture in which Jesus and his disciples lived, for the Sinai Covenant had permitted divorce (Deut 24:1–4).[13]

3. Short Form: Where different versions of a saying or action are preserved in various sources, the shorter form is the most likely to trace to the historical Jesus. This is because writers who are borrowing from other sources tend much more often to embellish the material than to reduce it. For instance, Matthew attributes to Jesus a blessing on the poor in spirit (that is, the meek): "Blessed are the poor in spirit, for theirs is the kingdom of heaven" (5:3). Luke attributes a similar saying to Jesus but, in Luke's version, the blessing is addressed to those who are literally impoverished: "Blessed are you who are poor, for yours is the kingdom of God" (6:20). As part of this discourse, Luke also attributes to Jesus a curse on the rich, which was not part of Matthew's version: "But woe to you who are rich, for you have received your consolation" (6:24). Given the differences between these two accounts, scholars are inclined to regard Matthew's version as closer to what the historical Jesus might have said; it is likely that the author of Luke interpreted and embellished the saying in a way that suited one of his particular concerns as an author, namely, that Christians should care for the poor.

4. *Coherence:* Is the saying or action attributed to Jesus consistent with other sayings and actions traceable to the Jesus of history, and with the early history of the Christian church? Do our reconstructions of the life of Jesus and of the emergence of Christianity make sense of each other? Obviously, this criterion can only be applied once some claims about the historical Jesus or the early church have been established with a high degree of historical probability. But once some claims have been so established, this criterion can help scholars to gauge which sayings or actions might trace to the historical Jesus and which seem more likely to be the result of interpretation on the part of the gospel authors. For example, scholars are skeptical of the assertion in Mark that Jesus "declared all foods clean"—meaning that Jesus told his followers that they need not observe the dietary laws of the Sinai Covenant (7:19). Virtually all biblical scholars agree that the question of whether Christians needed to observe the laws found in the Torah—including the dietary laws—was fiercely debated in the first few decades after the death of Jesus. Evidence that this was a divisive issue is well documented in letters attributed to Paul (Gal 2:11–12; Rom 3:28; 6:14; Col 2:16–17, 20–22) and in the Book of Acts (10:9–17; 15:1–21). But if, as Mark claims, the historical Jesus had asserted that his followers need not observe the dietary restrictions of the Torah, then why would his followers have been deeply divided over whether or not they should observe those laws? The strong evidence that members of the early church struggled with this issue makes it highly unlikely that the historical Jesus "declared all foods clean."[14]

5. *Rejection and Execution:* Because extrabiblical sources confirm the biblical claim that Jesus was executed as a criminal by the Roman prefect of Judea, those sayings or actions attributed to Jesus that might have been interpreted as threatening by the authorities of his day must be considered, at least initially, as having a certain degree of historical plausibility. For this reason, many scholars believe that some historical fact lies behind the gospel accounts of Jesus' action in the Temple (more on this below).

186

These authenticating criteria provide scholars with a means of trying to separate the gospels' historical data from their theological interpretations and embellishments. If a saying or action attributed to Jesus satisfies one or more of these criteria, then scholars have reason to think that the saying or action may trace to the historical Jesus himself—as opposed to being an author's interpretation of events. Of course, like all historians, scholars researching the Jesus of history deal not in certainties, but in levels of probability. The available evidence cannot *prove* that the historical Jesus did or did not say this or do that; instead, the evidence can help to place a given saying or action attributed to Jesus on a scale from highly probable to highly improbable. Thus, the more authenticating criteria a saying or action satisfies, the more reason scholars have to regard that saying or action as historically grounded.

III. LIFE OF THE HISTORICAL JESUS

The Basics

Having surveyed the sources of information about the Jesus of history, we are now in a position to begin a sketch of his life.[15] Even if we limit ourselves to the information provided by extrabiblical sources and our general knowledge of the period, we can make a number of claims about Jesus that possess a very high degree of historical probability. We can say that Jesus was a Palestinian Jew who lived during the reign of Emperor Tiberius (14–37 CE). His Greek name *Iesous* derives from the Hebrew name *Yeshua* (YHWH saves), a common Jewish name in the Second Temple period. He definitely would have spoken Aramaic, but he may have spoken Hebrew as well, and perhaps even some Greek. He was clearly a preacher who had followers. During his ministry, Jesus came to be regarded as a healer and a worker of wonders. In this he was not alone; many people were regarded as miracle workers in the Near East of the Second Temple period. Jesus said or did something of which the authorities in Judea disapproved. He was executed by crucifixion on the order of Pontius

Pilate, who was the Roman prefect of Judea, Samaria, and Idumea from 26–36 CE. At some point, Jesus' followers began to claim that Jesus was the savior whose coming they had been anticipating. Whether his followers made this claim during or only after Jesus' lifetime, or whether Jesus ever made such a claim about himself, the extrabiblical sources do not tell us.

If we now incorporate data provided by the New Testament, we can flesh out the foregoing sketch considerably. Even on a fairly conservative application of the authenticating criteria to the gospels, we can say a number of things about the historical Jesus that, though not historically certain, are highly probable.

Early Life and Baptism

Many scholars believe that Jesus was born around 6–4 BCE, the last years in the reign of Herod the Great, because the infancy narratives in Matthew and Luke—which seem to be independent of each other—both mention Herod at the beginning of the story (Matt 2:1; Luke 1:5). Jesus seems to have grown up in the Galilean city of Nazareth, and his ministry was for the most part based in Capernaum, a fishing village on the Sea of Galilee. He did not undertake his ministry until his late twenties or early thirties, shortly after his baptism by John the Baptist. The historical existence of John the Baptist is confirmed by Josephus. Moreover, scholars regard the gospels' assertions that Jesus was baptized by John as satisfying the criterion of dissimilarity, as that event would probably have been a point of embarrassment for the early church. Since John was baptizing people as a sign of repentance for their sins, Jesus' submitting to baptism suggests that he had sins and was in need of repentance, an idea inconsistent with early Christian theology (see 2 Cor 5:21; Heb 4:15; 1 Pet 2:22; 1 John 3:5).

Message and Following

Jesus' disciples included women, which was innovative for the time; first-century Pharisaic masters had followers/pupils, but they were all men.[16] The fact that the gospels attribute to Jesus numerous debates with scribes and Pharisees suggests that Jesus not only knew Hebrew, but was well versed in the Hebrew scriptures; indeed, he may even have been literate. The gospels, Acts, and Paul all attest that Jesus commissioned twelve of his disciples for special duties (though these sources are not entirely in agreement regarding those disciples' names). One of these duties included helping Jesus to spread his message. Jesus' message was probably theocentric, that is, God-centered: Jesus spoke not about himself, but about God. More specifically, Jesus preached about what he called the kingdom of God. This kingdom of which Jesus spoke was not a place, but an event; it referred to God's power entering into the world in a radically new way. Thus, the term might better be translated as the *reign* of God. Jesus seems to have regarded this reign of God both as something that was already happening in the present (Matt 12:28; Luke 17:20–21) and also as something to be expected—perhaps in its fullest form—in the very near future (Mark 1:15; 9:1; Matt 6:10; Luke 21:31). In addition to his disciples, Jesus also seems to have associated with those who were generally scorned by society at large, such as prostitutes and tax collectors. His basic message to everyone seems to have been one of compassion; he stressed that the kingdom of God was open to all, but that entry into it required "radical obedience to God and selfless love toward other people."[17]

Jesus was unlike other religious authorities of his day. He could not claim authority based on his position in Jewish society, as the priests could do. Nor did he claim to have received special training in the interpretation of the Jewish law, as the leaders of the Pharisees could claim. Rather, Jesus taught on his own personal authority; to Jesus and his disciples, Jesus' saying something was reason enough for his listeners to believe that it was true.[18] He seems to have both addressed and referred to YHWH as *Abba*, the Aramaic term by which children addressed their male parent—it can be translated as "Father" or even "Daddy." He also seems to have made frequent use of the word *amen*, a Hebrew word meaning "so be it" or "certainly"; indeed, he often began sentences with it (see, for example, Mark 10:15, 29; Matt 5:18; John 1:51; in all these passages, the word *amen* is translated in the NRSV Bible as "truly"). Many scholars think that both Jesus' use of *Abba* and his use of *amen* satisfy the criterion of dissimilarity, because both would have been innovative at the time.

Action in the Temple

Matthew, Mark, and Luke are probably correct in their assertions that, toward the end of his ministry, Jesus performed a dramatic action at the Jerusalem Temple in the days leading up to the Passover festival, an action that brought him to the attention of the local authorities. He may have prophesied that the Temple would be destroyed or, more likely, that it would soon be replaced by a new and better Temple of God's own making.[19] Perceiving this action as some sort of threat, and anxious to maintain control over the large crowds that had assembled in Jerusalem for the festival, the high priest had Jesus arrested. The gospels are probably correct that a member of Jesus' handpicked inner circle arranged for Jesus to be captured by the authorities, as this event seems to satisfy the criterion of dissimilarity by being an embarrassment to the early church.

Condemnation and Execution

After his arrest, Jesus probably had a hearing before the high priest (and perhaps his counselors, the Sanhedrin), at which Jesus was condemned on a charge of blasphemy. Blasphemy was a capital offense under Jewish law, but the Romans had stripped the Jews of the right to administer the death penalty when they assumed direct control of Judea in 6 CE. Thus, Jesus was handed over for another hearing before Pilate. At this latter hearing, Jesus would have been charged with something like sedition—the only sort of charge on which Pilate could or would have condemned him, since crimes against the Jewish law were the jurisdiction of the Sanhedrin, not the Roman prefect. Jesus was crucified in 29–33 CE. The *titulus* (charge sheet) attached to Jesus' cross probably read *Iesus Nazarenus Rex Iudaeorum* (Jesus of Nazareth, King of the Jews), for this suggests that he was condemned by the Roman prefect for having been a false claimant to the Jewish throne—that is, for having challenged the Roman emperor's authority over Judea (John 19:19; compare Matt 27:37; Mark 15:26; Luke 23:38).

So ends our theoretical reconstruction of the life of the historical Jesus. You will note that this reconstruction makes no mention of Jesus' resurrection from the dead, the climax of the gospel accounts of his life. This is not because the gospel accounts of the resurrection do not satisfy the criteria of authenticity. It is because resurrection is a transhistorical event, an act of God that occurs outside of the spatiotemporal world of human experience and thus beyond the scope of empirical history. If the resurrection occurred, it was not the earthly Jesus whom the disciples experienced as having been raised from the dead; the Jesus the disciples experienced was the Jesus they believed to have been glorified, exalted, and seated at the right hand of God. Still, although the empirical historical method cannot comment on claims about transhistorical events, it can affirm that a number of people had some sort of experience that convinced them that Jesus had come back from the dead, and that this idea itself was radically innovative. While some Jews of the Second Temple period had come to believe that there would be a general resurrection of the dead at the end of time, the idea that one person should be raised from the dead before the end of time was unprecedented in Jewish thought. The empirical historical method can also affirm that, however incredible the first Christians' beliefs might have been, the first Christians as a whole were neither stupid nor insane, as is evident in the fact that they were capable of propagating their new movement with great success.

IV. TITLES APPLIED TO JESUS

We shall close our discussion of Jesus of Nazareth by examining three of the titles that are applied to him in the New Testament. It is important to note that, though the early Christian church certainly applied these titles to Jesus after his death, and some of Jesus' disciples may have done so during Jesus' lifetime, we cannot be at all certain whether the historical Jesus ever used these terms to describe himself.

Messiah

One of the titles applied to Jesus by his disciples is messiah. The English word *messiah* and the Greek word *christos* ("Christ" in English) are both translations of the Hebrew word *mashiah* (anointed). Thus, when early Christians described Jesus as *mashiah* or *christos*, they were identifying him as an anointed one. To understand precisely what that meant to Jews in the Second Temple period, we must look at the biblical development of the concept of *mashiah*.[20]

The earliest biblical uses of the term *mashiah* were linked to the ceremony by which priests and kings were sworn into office. In Exodus, the Lord instructs Moses to consecrate Aaron and his sons as priests by anointing them with oil (28:41; 29:7). In 1 Samuel, Saul becomes Israel's first king when he is anointed by Samuel (10:1). Later, David refers to King Saul as "the Lord's anointed" (24:6). And in 1 Kings, the high priest Zadok makes Solomon king by anointing him with oil (1:39). On one and only one occasion, a non-Jewish king is even referred to as *mashiah*: In the work of Second Isaiah, King Cyrus the Great of Persia is described as the anointed one of the Lord who will free the Jews from their Babylonian captivity (Isa 45:1).

Over time, the term *mashiah* came to take on deeper theological significance. In the tumultuous period leading up to the Babylonian Exile, the prophets linked the idea of *mashiah* to their hope that the Lord would provide them with a better king than the ones they had seen recently, who seemed to be leading Judah into ruin. Thinking back to the Davidic Covenant, in which the Lord had promised that David's kingdom and dynasty would be everlasting (2 Sam 7:11–16), the prophets began to anticipate the coming of an ideal king from the line of David who would reestablish the glory of Israel, subdue all of Israel's enemies, and inaugurate an era of unprecedented peace (Isa 9:6–7; 11:1–16; Jer 23:5–6; Mic 5:1–5). This idea persisted into the Restoration (Zech 9:9).

In the Second Temple period, the idea of the coming Davidic *mashiah* also began to take on eschatological features. Influenced by the apocalyptic passages in the book of Daniel (7:13–14, 18, 22) and by the prophets (Isa 2:2–4; 32:16–20; 65:17–25; Amos

9:11–15), some Jews came to associate the messiah with the day of the Lord. According to the eschatological thought of such Jews, the day of the Lord would be preceded by the persecution of martyrs, whose suffering would serve as a sacrificial atonement for the sins of Israel (see 4 Macc 1:11; 6:28–29; 17:22). When the day of the Lord arrived, YHWH would intervene in human history by sending the anointed one to establish a new world order; then and only then would the wicked be punished, the righteous exalted, and lasting peace enjoyed.

Thus, to many of the Jews who lived during the lifetime of the historical Jesus, the notion of *mashiah* carried with it, at the very least, connotations of military conquest and political power. To some of those Jews, it also had eschatological connotations; if the messiah was in their midst, then the end of the era and the Lord's establishment of a new world order were near at hand.

Son of God

The New Testament also refers to Jesus as the Son of God.[21] While its usage in the Christian scriptures seems intended to imply that Jesus was in some way divine, this is not how the expression was typically understood by Jews in the Second Temple period.

The title Son of God appears a number of times in the Tanak. In some cases, it is used to refer to semidivine beings who inhabit the heavenly realm along with the Deity (Gen 6:1–4; Job 1:6; 2:1). But it is also used to refer to human beings. Thus, the people of Israel are sometimes described as the son or sons of God, as in Exodus 4:22: "Thus says the LORD: Israel is my firstborn son." (See also Deut 14:1; 32:5, 19; Hos 11:1; Jer 31:9). The title was also used to describe Israel's kings, as in 2 Samuel 7:14; here the Lord asserts, with regard to David, "I will be a father to him, and he shall be a son to me." (See also Ps 2:7; 89:26.) In these passages, the characterization of particular people as sons of God was clearly not meant to imply that those people were more than human—that they had been born by supernatural means or that they possessed superhuman powers. Rather, it was used to stress the idea that the persons so described had an especially close relationship with the Lord, like that which often exists between fathers and sons. That such an interpretation of the title Son of God was still operative in the first century CE is clear in the assertion of Paul that "all who are led by the Spirit of God are children [literally, *sons*] of God" (Rom 8:14). When Paul says this, he does not mean that all Christians have the divine status that the New Testament attributes to Jesus. Rather, he means that Christians' faith brings them into an intimate relationship with God.

It is impossible to know whether the title Son of God was applied to the historical Jesus during his lifetime. If it was, then those who used it probably intended it to mean that Jesus was on very intimate terms with God, as human sons are usually understood to be on intimate terms with their human fathers. Of course, if this is how it was used of Jesus, it would mean that his followers regarded him as special; they took Jesus to be able to discern the will of God, and they took God to be responsive to Jesus' prayers. By the time the gospels were written, however, Christians had come to think of Jesus as being more than just a human being; they had come to think of Jesus as having a divine origin. This is the meaning that Son of God will have in the gospels.

Son of Man

A third title applied to Jesus in the gospels is the enigmatic Son of Man.[22] This title also occurs in the Hebrew scriptures. Ezekiel uses the expression "son of man" (*ben adam* in Hebrew) some ninety times; it is the title by which the Lord addresses the prophet. Since this usage seems intended to contrast the prophet's human frailty with the Lord's power, the NRSV translates *ben adam* as "mortal" in Ezekiel. The title also seems to have been used in the Second Temple period as a polite substitute for the first person singular pronoun. Since the Aramaic expression for a man (*bar enas*) literally meant "son of [a] man," a man could use it to refer to himself in situations calling for deference or humility—in much the same way that a person might humble herself before a monarch by referring to herself, not as "I," but as "your subject." Still, neither of these uses seems to capture the meaning that early Christians intended when they described Jesus as the Son of Man. To gain a sense of that meaning, we shall consider two texts: Daniel and 1 Enoch.

In the apocalyptic chapters of the Book of Daniel, written during the Seleucid persecution of 167–164 BCE, the Son of Man is linked to the anticipated messiah. One of the apocalyptic visions that describes the coming of the ideal king begins, "I saw one like a son of man coming with the clouds of heaven" (7:13). Thus, anyone familiar with the Book of Daniel, as most Jews of the Second Temple period were, could have interpreted Son of Man as being a messianic title.

That the Son of Man had eschatological connotations is also suggested by the pseudepigraphic book of *1 Enoch.** Though it is attributed to a descendent of Adam (see Genesis 5:1–24), most scholars believe that *1 Enoch* was written in the second or first century BCE. In chapter 48 of that work, the author describes an apocalyptic vision in which "that Son of Man was given a name, in the presence of the Lord of the Spirits, the Before-Time; even before the creation of the sun and the moon, before the creation of the stars, he was given a name in the presence of the Lord of Spirits." In the same chapter, this Son of Man is described as "the Chosen One" and as the "light of the Gentiles" who shall be worshiped by all the peoples of the world, and he is identified with the messiah. In chapter 51, the author describes a future time when all of the dead will be resurrected: "Sheol [the underworld] will return all the deposits which she had received and hell will give back all that which it owes." When this general resurrection occurs, the Chosen One described above will sit in judgment over the dead, separating the righteous from the wicked. Thus, to the author of *1 Enoch*, the Son of Man is a messianic figure who has existed since the beginning of time, and who is waiting to come in judgment at the end of time.

There is one problem with citing *1 Enoch* as having established a precedent for thinking of the Son of Man in eschatological terms,

---

* The word *Pseudepigrapha* (which means "written under a false name" in Greek) is used to refer to a number of Jewish writings, produced between roughly 200 BCE and 200 CE, that (a) are similar to books of the Hebrew scriptures in their style and subject matter, (b) were never included in either the Jewish or Christian canons of scriptures, and (c) are falsely attributed to famous persons, usually characters of the Tanak (for example, the Apocalypse of Abraham, the Testament of Solomon, the Vision of Ezra).

a precedent that might have led the first Christians to apply this title to Jesus. While most scholars are confident that four of the five main sections of *1 Enoch* were written in the last two centuries BCE, the remaining section—in which we find the above references to the Son of Man as an eschatological figure—is a bit more difficult to date with confidence. This is because the oldest existing copy of *1 Enoch* is one that was found among the Dead Sea Scrolls, and this copy lacks the section containing references to the Son of Man. Thus, it is possible that the section of *1 Enoch* containing Son of Man references was added sometime after the Jewish War of 66–73 CE, when the community at Qumran was wiped out by the Romans. If this is the case, then those references may have been influenced by early Christian theology, and not the other way around. Still, it is possible that the Qumran community simply had an incomplete copy of *1 Enoch;* the original author of *1 Enoch,* working in the second or first century BCE, could have developed an eschatological conception of the Son of Man based on the imagery already provided by the Book of Daniel.

Although the evidence is inconclusive as to whether the historical Jesus used any of the above titles to describe himself, it is clear that the early Christians applied those titles to him, perhaps even during his own lifetime. As we shall see when we look at the gospels, the early Christian church would come to hold beliefs about the nature and purpose of the messiah that were very different from those held by its Jewish contemporaries. But given what we know about the development of such concepts as the messiah and the Son of Man, we can conclude the following. To the majority of Jews living in the Second Temple period, an assertion that Jesus was the Messiah or the Son of Man would have meant that Jesus was the long-awaited Davidic king who would crush Israel's enemies and usher in a new age of glory for the chosen people. If such titles were used of Jesus during his lifetime, it may have been the eschatological connotations of those titles that brought him to the attention of the Jewish authorities, who charged him with blasphemy. Likewise, it may have been the political connotations of those titles that ultimately led to Jesus' execution as an enemy of the Roman Empire.

11

The Gospels

The English word *gospel* derives from the Anglo-Saxon word *god-spel*, a translation of the Greek word that the gospel writers used to describe their own work: *euaggelion* (good tidings).[1] The gospels constitute a distinct genre of biblical literature, namely, the proclamation of the good news of salvation for human beings through Jesus the Messiah. As such proclamations of salvation, the gospels produced by the early Christian church are theological works written in light of the Christ Event. While there were many gospels produced in the century or two after the death of Jesus, the four preserved in the New Testament (Matthew, Mark, Luke, and John) were deemed by the early church to be the ones that best reflected the testimony of Jesus' first disciples. We shall begin our investigation of the gospels with a discussion of what is known as the Synoptic problem, and of one means by which biblical scholars have tried to solve that problem.

I. THE SYNOPTIC GOSPELS

The first three of the New Testament gospels (Matthew, Mark, and Luke) are known as the Synoptic Gospels, from a Greek word that means "seeing together." This is because they share a common view of the events they report.[2] For instance, their basic structure and chronology are similar: All three gospels begin the story of Jesus' ministry with his baptism by John the Baptist and his temptation in the wilderness; they then report on the events of Jesus' ministry in Galilee; and they all record one journey of Jesus and his

197

disciples to Jerusalem, which culminates in the final week of Jesus' life. The Synoptic Gospels also share a large number of parallel passages, many of which are virtually identical in their wording. To cite just a few of many examples, compare the following:

Passage	Matthew	Mark	Luke
Jesus' statement regarding his true relatives	12:46–50	3:31–35	8:19–21
Jesus' description of discipleship	16:24–28	8:34—9:1	9:23–27
Jesus' response to the question on taxation	22:15–22	12:13–17	20:20–26
Jesus crucified between two criminals	27:38	15:27	23:33

The three Synoptic Gospels have many more features in common with each other than any of them has in common with the Fourth Gospel. John's structure and chronology are different from those shared by the Synoptic Gospels. For example, in John, Jesus' action in the Temple occurs at the beginning of his ministry (2:12–22), whereas the Synoptics have it occurring toward the end of his ministry (Matt 21:11–17; Mark 11:15–19; Luke 19:45–48). While the Synoptics all report that the ministry of Jesus began after the imprisonment of John the Baptist (Matt 4:12–17; Mark 1:14–15; Luke 3:19–20; 4:14–15), the Fourth Gospel reports that Jesus' ministry overlapped with the Baptist's (3:22–24). Whereas the Synoptics record only one visit to Jerusalem by Jesus during his ministry, John records five (2:13; 5:1; 7:2–10; 10:22–23; 11:55—12:15). In the Synoptics, Jesus is crucified on the first full day of the Passover festival; in John, Jesus dies on the day of preparation for Passover, before the festival has actually begun. The content of John is also considerably different from that in the Synoptics. John omits much of the material that the Synoptics share in common, such as Jesus' baptism, the parables, the exorcisms, and the Last Supper. John also contains material that is lacking in the Synoptics, such as the miracle at Cana (2:1–11), the story of Jesus' encounter with a Samaritan woman (4:1–42), and the raising of

Lazarus from the dead (11:1–44). In the Synoptics, Jesus' teaching emphasizes the kingdom of God; in John, Jesus discusses the kingdom only once (3:3–5).

The Synoptic Problem

The striking similarities between Matthew, Mark, and Luke—and their differences from John—have given rise to what biblical scholars call the Synoptic problem. This term is not meant to imply a problem with the gospels themselves; to assert that there is a Synoptic problem is not to assert that there is something wrong with the gospels. Rather, the problem posed by the Synoptic Gospels is simply the question of how to explain their similarities. If three of the four New Testament gospels resemble each other much more closely than any of them resembles the fourth, there must be some reason why this is the case. Thus, the Synoptic problem challenges scholars to give an account of how the Synoptic Gospels were written that will make sense of the parallels between them.

The Four Source Hypothesis

While a number of theories have been offered as potential solutions to the Synoptic problem, the one most widely accepted by biblical scholars is the Four Source Hypothesis. According to this theory, the author of the Gospel of Matthew and the author of the Gospel of Luke each had independent access to, and made use of, the Gospel of Mark. That the authors of Matthew and Luke used Mark as a source is suggested by the fact that virtually all the material in Mark is duplicated in both Matthew and Luke. That the authors of Matthew and Luke had *independent* access to Mark—as opposed to one of them getting his Markan material from the other—is suggested by the fact that, when one of these two gospels disagrees with Mark in chronology, language, or details, the other does not. If only the author of Matthew had used Mark as a source, and then the author of Luke had simply read Matthew, then any changes that Matthew made to Mark would be preserved in Luke. Similarly, if only the author of Luke had had access to Mark, and then the author of Matthew had used

Luke as a source, then any changes that Luke made to Mark would be preserved in Matthew. Since the changes that Matthew and Luke make to the Markan account are independent of each other, it seems that the authors of Matthew and Luke each had their own copies of the Gospel of Mark.

The Four Source Hypothesis also posits the existence of an additional source to which both Matthew and Luke had access, but which no longer exists. Called Q (from *Quelle*, "source" in German), this hypothetical source is proposed as a way of explaining why Matthew and Luke share material that is absent from Mark. Roughly one-third of the material that constitutes the Book of Matthew parallels one quarter of the material that constitutes the Book of Luke, but this material has no parallel in Mark. Since this material mostly reports things Jesus is purported to have said, the Q source is thought to have been a collection of Jesus' sayings; a number of such collections were in circulation in the early church (see, for instance, the noncanonical Gospel of Thomas). Those scholars who posit the existence of the Q source have not reached an agreement as to whether it was a written collection of Jesus' sayings or merely an oral tradition.

Finally, each of the gospels of Matthew and Luke contains material that is unique to that gospel. For example, only Luke contains the parables of the good Samaritan (10:29–37) and the prodigal son (15:11–32), while only Matthew contains the parables of the hidden treasure (13:44), the pearl of great value (13:45–46), and the laborers in the vineyard (20:1–16). For this reason, the Four Source Hypothesis supposes that the authors of Matthew and Luke each made use of oral and/or written materials to which the other did not have access. These are designated M (the source of material unique to Matthew) and L (the source of material unique to Luke).

Thus, the Four Source Hypothesis accounts for both the major similarities and the minor differences between the Synoptic Gospels, and it does so by explaining the production of the gospels of Matthew and Luke in terms of the four sources to which their authors appealed: (1) the Gospel of Mark, to which the authors of Matthew and Luke both had access; (2) the Q source, to which the authors of Matthew and Luke both had access; (3) the M source, to which only the author of Matthew had access; and (4) the L source, to which only the author of Luke had access.

Bearing the Four Source Hypothesis in mind, let us now examine the New Testament gospels. With regard to each book, we shall first discuss scholarly opinion about the work's authorship and date, and then we shall consider some of that particular book's themes.

II. MARK

A. Authorship and Date

If the Four Source Hypothesis is correct, then Mark was the first of the Synoptic Gospels to be written.[3] Strictly speaking, the Gospel of Mark—like all the New Testament gospels—is an anonymous work, since its author never identifies himself by name in the text. A tradition dating to the first half of the second century CE attributes the work to John Mark, a companion of the apostle Paul (Acts 12:25) and an associate of the apostle Peter (1 Pet 5:13). While John Mark may have been the author, there is no indubitable evidence of this. Most scholars believe that the Gospel was written in Greek by a Hellenistic Jew who had converted to Christianity. His having been Jewish is clear in his familiarity with the Aramaic language and with Jewish customs. His Hellenism is suggested by his occasional use of Latin words. The rather bizarre route recorded at 7:31 also suggests that the author was personally unfamiliar with Palestinian geography, and thus that he lived in one of the communities of the Jewish Diaspora. Wherever the author may have lived, the book's intended audience was clearly a group of Gentile Christians; the author took pains to explain the meaning of Aramaic words (5:41; 7:11, 34; 15:22, 34) and Jewish customs (7:3-4; 14:12; 15:42) with which his audience would not be familiar.

Dating the Gospel of Mark is difficult. As we noted in the previous chapter, scholars believe that the recording of gospels in written form was the third and final stage in the development of the gospel tradition. Between the life of Jesus and the writing of the gospels, there almost certainly would have been a period in which Jesus' words and deeds were preserved and transmitted by means of an oral tradition. For the first Christians believed that the second coming of Jesus and the arrival of the kingdom of God in its fullest sense were imminent (Mark 1:15; 9:1), and thus they would have felt a sense of urgency in their efforts to spread their message. The need to commit Jesus' story to writing probably did not arise until those who had been eyewitnesses to Jesus' ministry began to die. This hypothesis alone would place the writing of Mark in the latter half of the first century CE, at the earliest. A more precise date is suggested by Jesus' statements about the Temple in chapter 13. Here, Jesus predicts that the Temple will fall (v. 2). Compared to the precision with which Jesus describes that event in Luke (21:5–6, 20–24), Mark's vagueness about when the Temple will fall (v. 32) suggests that, at the time Mark was being written, Jerusalem's capture by the Romans may have been fore-seeable, but it had not yet occurred. On the other hand, Mark's Jesus also warns his listeners to beware of false messiahs who will come at the time of suffering (vv. 21–23), explaining that his own return will come later (v. 24–27). This latter set of passages suggests that Mark was written at a time when the Temple had already fallen, but when Christians were still eagerly awaiting the new age. Thus, the passages in chapter 13 suggest a tentative date for the Gospel of Mark in the years between 66 and 73 CE. For the sake of simplicity, most scholars date Mark to 70 CE.

B. Key Themes

Imminence of the Kingdom

In Mark's account of the life of Jesus, there are three themes that stand out as receiving special emphasis. One is the immi-nence of the kingdom of God. When Jesus begins his ministry in Mark, it is with an announcement, "The time is fulfilled, and the kingdom of God has come near" (1:15). Throughout the first eight chapters of Mark, the author focuses as much on Jesus' actions as on his words; the nearness of the kingdom of God, the new age to be ushered in by the Messiah, is evident in the power and authority with which Jesus exorcises demons (1:23–27; 5:1–13) and heals infirmities (1:40–42; 2:3–12). Indeed, chapters 1—8 of Mark record no less than seventeen miracle stories. This whirlwind of miraculous activity seems intended to show that the very nature of the world is undergoing a radical change; evil and sickness are yielding to goodness and well-being. The imminence of the kingdom is even emphasized stylistically. The author creates a sense of urgency in the ministry of Jesus by repeated use of the word *immediately*; it occurs forty times in Mark's sixteen chapters. The kingdom is so near at hand that Jesus and his disciples do not have a moment to waste!

The Messianic Secret

A second theme emphasized in Mark is the secrecy with which Jesus tries to engage in his ministry. When Mark's Jesus exorcises demons, those demons recognize him as divine, but Jesus orders them not to reveal his identity (1:25, 34; 3:11–12). When he heals the sick, Jesus commands both the healed and those who witnessed the healing to remain silent about it (1:43–44; 5:43; 7:36). And when Jesus' closest disciples identify him as the Messiah for whom they have been waiting, Jesus orders them to tell no one (8:30; 9:9). This concern that Mark's Jesus shows to conceal his identity as the Messiah is referred to as the messianic secret.

The Suffering Servant

The third and most important theme in Mark is its characterization of the Messiah as a suffering servant. In order fully to appreciate this idea, we must consider the fact that most of Jesus' followers probably conceived of the anticipated Messiah in the same way that the majority of other Jews did—namely, as a divinely chosen political leader who would overthrow the Romans and liberate Judea. For this reason, Jesus' disciples must have experienced a shocking and humiliating sense of defeat when Jesus was executed as a criminal by the Romans. In his interpretation of the Christ Event, the author of the Gospel of Mark came to think of Jesus' ignominious death as a necessary part of

God's plan for the salvation of human beings; the Messiah *had* to suffer and die in order for the kingdom of God to be inaugurated. Thus, the author of Mark blends two ideas that prior Jewish thought had kept distinct: the eschatological Son of Man and the suffering servant of Isaiah 53. Second Isaiah had described a righteous servant of the Lord who would save others by suffering and dying for their sins. The author of Mark implies that this is precisely the role of the Messiah; the Son of Man came not to restore political freedom to Judea, but to free people from the burden of their sins by suffering and dying for them.

The idea of the suffering servant is most clear in Mark's three passion predictions—the three passages in which Jesus predicts his own suffering and death at the hands of the authorities (8:31–33; 9:30–32; 10:33–34). In all three, Jesus stresses that the Son of Man will suffer, die, and rise again. In the third, Jesus describes the suffering of the Son of Man in detail: "[T]he Gentiles...will mock him, and spit upon him, and flog him, and kill him." No one familiar with the Hebrew scriptures could fail to recognize in this passage an echo of Isaiah 53, which describes a servant "despised and rejected by others;...oppressed, and... afflicted...like a lamb that is led to the slaughter." Thus, in light of their belief that Jesus had risen from the dead, the early Christians came to think of the crucifixion of Jesus not as a defeat at the hands of earthly powers, but as a divinely willed act of sacrifice on the part of the Messiah. When the author of Mark captured this idea by linking the Son of Man to the suffering servant of Isaiah, he introduced a way of thinking about the Messiah that was unprecedented in Jewish thought.

III. MATTHEW

A. Authorship and Date

From about the year 130 CE, the Gospel that appears first in the New Testament canon has been attributed to Matthew, a tax collector and one of the twelve members of Jesus' inner circle; he is mentioned at Matthew 9:9, and he is referred to by the name

Levi at Mark 2:14 and Luke 5:27. As with Mark, evidence internal to the Book of Matthew is inconclusive regarding the identity of the work's author. We shall see below, however, that scholars have good reason to believe the author was a Jewish Christian.[4]

According to the Four Source Hypothesis, the author of the Book of Matthew borrowed material from Mark. This means that the Gospel of Matthew would have been written sometime after 70 CE, when Mark is thought to have been written. While there is no consensus among scholars as to a precise date, a number of reasons exist for dating the Gospel of Matthew to the years between 85 and 90 CE. These include (1) the Gospel's hostility toward the Pharisees, whose teachings had come to dominate Judaism by 85–90 (see, for example, 15:1–9; 23:2–7, 13–15, 23–33); (2) indications that the second coming of the Christ, which Christians had been expecting, had been delayed (24:48; 25:5); and (3) apparent references to the persecution of Christians by secular authorities, something that was uncommon until late in the first century (5:11; 10:18; 25:36, 39).

While it is impossible to say with certainty where the Gospel of Matthew was written, some scholars believe that it may have originated in the Syrian city of Antioch, for two reasons. One is that the first author who seems to have used material from the Gospel of Matthew in his own writings was Ignatius, the bishop of the Christian church at Antioch who died in roughly 110 CE. A second is Matthew's stress on both the universality of the Christian message and its continuity with Judaism, which suggests that the author's intended audience was a church undergoing the transition from being a largely Jewish community to one that was largely Gentile. Such would have been the case in the Christian church at Antioch in the late first century CE.

B. Key Themes

Scriptures Fulfilled

One of the reasons why scholars believe that Matthew was written by a Jewish Christian is that it emphasizes the idea that Jesus is the fulfillment of the Jewish scriptures. The Gospel begins with a genealogy that links Jesus (through Joseph) to David and to Abraham (1:1–17). This opening is significant, as it sets the tone for the whole Gospel. By linking Jesus to King David, the author implies that Jesus is the messianic fulfillment of the Davidic Covenant, God's promise to David that the Davidic kingdom would be everlasting. By linking Jesus to Abraham, the author suggests that Jesus is also the blessing to all nations that God had promised to bring about through Abraham's descendents. Thus, Matthew begins by stressing both the Jewish roots and the universal significance of Jesus as the Messiah.

The Gospel of Matthew also draws explicit connections between the events it reports and the words of the Hebrew prophets. Unlike Mark, Matthew begins with a birth narrative. According to Matthew, Jesus' mother Mary conceived him while still a virgin, in fulfillment of the prophecy at Isaiah 7:14. Mary gives birth to Jesus in Bethlehem, in fulfillment of the prophecy at Micah 5:2. Mary's husband Joseph, on the instructions of an angel, takes Mary and the infant Jesus to Egypt, in fulfillment of the prophecy at Hosea 11:1, and so on. Matthew's first four chapters alone contain no less than eleven references to prophetic passages of the Septuagint that Jesus is said to have fulfilled. Such references can be found throughout the Gospel.

Church Authority

As noted above, many scholars believe that the Gospel of Matthew was written for a church community that was undergoing demographic changes. This is partly because the author of Matthew seems particularly concerned with issues of authority and management within the Christian church. Matthew is the only Gospel to report an episode in which Jesus invests Simon-Peter with special authority. After Simon (who was also called Peter) identifies Jesus as the Messiah, Jesus says to him, "[Y]ou are Peter, and on this rock I will build my church." There is a bit of a play on words here, since the Greek name *Petros* derives from *petra* ("rock" in Greek); both translate the Aramaic word for rock, *kepha*, which could also be used as a man's name. Jesus continues: "I will give you the keys of the kingdom of heaven, and whatever you bind on earth will be bound in heaven, and whatever you loose on earth will be loosed in heaven" (16:16–19). Whatever his reasons, the author of Matthew wanted to make clear that Jesus intended Peter to have authority over the Christian church. Matthew's concern for church issues is also evident at 18:15–20, where Jesus gives instruction to his followers on how disputes between church members should be settled.

Jesus' Teaching

Matthew stresses the words of Jesus more than did Mark. In Matthew, Jesus' preaching is divided into five great discourses (chapters 5—7, 10, 13, 18, 23—25), probably so as to parallel the five books of the Torah; Jesus is presented as a new lawgiver in the tradition of Moses. A number of the sermons that Matthew records are unique to that Gospel. Among these are the parables of the kingdom (13:36–52), in which Jesus compares the coming kingdom of God to such things as a buried treasure chest and a fishing net. In some of these parables, the kingdom of God is described in eschatological terms. This eschatological vein also runs through some of the other sayings of Jesus that only Matthew records, such as the parable of the unmerciful servant (18:23–35) and the description of the last judgment (25:31–46).

Internalization of the Law

Another important aspect of the Gospel of Matthew is Jesus' approach to the Jewish law. As we noted above, the author of Matthew was concerned to show that Christianity is consistent with—indeed, is the continuation and fulfillment of—the Jewish faith. But this meant taking a position on the status of the Jewish law. Did those Jews who converted to Christianity still have to observe the laws of the Mosaic Covenant? What about Gentiles who wished to convert to Christianity; did they have to become Jews in order to become Christians? In an effort to address such questions, the author of Matthew reports sayings of Jesus that stress that the law should be *internalized;* being a follower of Jesus means not just following a set of rules, but bringing one's whole being into harmony with the spirit of those rules. Thus, Matthew's

Jesus asserts that he has come, not to abolish the law, but to fulfill it (5:17). He cites the law's prohibition of murder, but then says that even those who are angry with or who insult others are liable to judgment and punishment (5:38–42). In reference to the *lex talionis* of Leviticus 25:17–21, which had required the taking of an eye for an eye and a tooth for a tooth, Jesus tells his followers instead to suffer evil gladly, and to love not just their friends but even their enemies (5:38–48). The author of Matthew seems to recognize that this is a radical and controversial interpretation of the Jewish law; while Matthew's Jesus preaches love and forgiveness to his followers, he also declares that he has "not come to bring peace, but a sword" that will pit family members and loved ones against each other (10:34–39).

God Is with Us

Finally, the author of Matthew sought to assure his audience that being a Christian and following a new interpretation of the Jewish law did not mean cutting oneself off from the God of Abraham, Isaac, and Jacob. On the contrary, Jesus is the fulfillment of the Jewish law because YHWH is with the followers of Jesus through the person of Jesus. This idea frames the Gospel of Matthew. It occurs at the beginning, where Jesus is identified as *Emmanuel*, a Hebrew name meaning "God is with us" (1:23). It also occurs at the end, in the final words of the resurrected Jesus to his disciples: "I am with you always, to the end of the age" (28:20).

IV. LUKE

A. Authorship and Date

Like Mark and Matthew, the Gospel of Luke is anonymous insofar as its author never names himself.[5] The tradition attributing it to Luke, a physician and an associate of the apostle Paul (Col 4:14; Phlm 24; 2 Tim 4:11), dates to at least 200 CE. Many scholars believe that this tradition may be accurate. In the prologue to the Gospel of Luke, the author makes clear that he is a subapostolic (second-generation) Christian; he does not claim to have been a witness to the events of Jesus' life, but says instead that he has access both to accounts handed down orally by eye-witnesses and to written versions of those accounts (1:1–2). The polished, literary Greek in which this Gospel is written suggests that its author was either a Gentile or a Hellenistic Jewish Christian, and that he was well-educated—as a physician would have been. It is impossible to say when Luke was written, but its clear dependence on Mark and its detailed predictions of the fall of Jerusalem (19:41–44; 21:5–6, 20–24) indicate a date sometime after 70 CE. Most scholars date it around the same time as Matthew, namely, 85–90 CE.

The author of Luke was also the author of the Acts of the Apostles; how scholars know this will be discussed in the next chapter. Initially, the Book of Luke and the Book of Acts were a two-volume treatise on the origin and spread of Christianity. The author of Luke-Acts seems to have taken as his goal the completion of salvation history, that is, the story of how God brings about the redemption of human beings—a story that was begun in the Hebrew scriptures. The Tanak told the story of God's chosen people, Israel. But from the Christian point of view, that story was incomplete; some of the promises that YHWH had made to Israel—an everlasting Davidic kingdom, a blessing to all nations—were not fulfilled in the Tanak. Thus, the author of Luke-Acts continues the story, first by telling of the Davidic Messiah whom God had sent (in the Gospel of Luke), and then by chronicling the spread of Christianity from its Jewish origins to the rest of the world (in Acts). As we look at some of the features of the Gospel of Luke, it is important to bear in mind this project that its author had in view.

B. Key Themes

The Universal Significance of Jesus

One key aspect of the Gospel of Luke is the way in which its author stresses the universal importance of Jesus. Whereas Mark and Matthew portray Jesus as bringing a message primarily to his fellow Jews, Luke characterizes Jesus as having come to save all human beings, Jewish and Gentile alike. Indeed, Luke both begins and ends the story of Jesus with this message (2:10; 24:47). One way in which the author of Luke stresses the universal significance of Jesus is by means of a genealogy. As we noted above, Matthew begins with a genealogy that links Jesus to David and Abraham, key figures in the story of Israel. But Luke's genealogy traces the lineage of Jesus all the way back to Adam (3:23–38). By linking Jesus to the first human being, the author of Luke links him to all of Adam's descendents—that is, all human beings. Another way in which Luke stresses the universality of the Gospel is by placing the events of Jesus' life in the context of world history—which, in the Near East of the New Testament period, was the history of the Roman Empire. Thus, Luke begins the birth narrative of Jesus by identifying the rulers of the time: Augustus was emperor of Rome, and Quirinius was governor of the Roman province of Syria (2:1–2). Again, when Luke reports on the ministry of John the Baptist, it places the events it will narrate in a larger context by dating them to "the fifteenth year of the reign of Emperor Tiberius [26–27 CE], when Pontius Pilate was governor of Judea, and Herod [Antipas] was ruler of Galilee..." (3:1). By these means, the author of Luke sets the events he recounts, not merely in the small world of Palestine, but in the much larger world of the Roman Empire.

Gentile Inclusion

Luke also stresses the universality of the Gospel in its portrayal of the teachings of Jesus. In Mark and Matthew, Jesus appears to be somewhat ambivalent toward the Gentiles (see Mark 7:24–30; Matt 10:5–6; 15:24–26; 28:19). Luke's account, on the other hand, seems crafted to emphasize the inclusion of Gentiles in Jesus' salvific work. Consider, for example, the parable of the good Samaritan (10:29–37), in which a Jewish priest and a Levite both refrain from helping a stranger in need, whereas a Samaritan shows the stranger mercy and kindness. Similar themes of inclusiveness can be found in Simeon's prayer (2:32), the parable of the great dinner (14:16–24), and the story of the ten lepers

PALESTINE
UNDER
EARLY PROCURATORS

Tetrarchy of Herod Antipas
Tetrarchy of Philip
Under Pontius Pilate
Decapolis
Fortresses

Sidon
ITURAEA
ABILENE
Damascus
Mt. Hermon
PHOENICIA
SYRIA
Tyre
Caesarea Philippi
TETRARCHY OF PHILIP
Gischala
GALILEE
Sea of Galilee
Raphana
Tiberias
Hippos
Kanatha
Nazareth
Dion
Mediterranean Sea
Gadara
Abila
Caesarea
Scythopolis
Pella
SAMARIA
DECAPOLIS
Sebaste
Gerasa
Shechem
River Jordan
Joppa
PEREA
Philadelphia
Jamnia
JUDEA
Jericho
Jerusalem
Qumran
Azotus
Bethlehem
Ascalon
Herodium
Machaerus
Dead
Gaza
Hebron
Sea
IDUMEA
Masada
N A B A T E A

0   30
Miles

(17:11–19). But perhaps the most telling passage in this regard is Luke's account of the rejection of Jesus in his hometown of Nazareth (4:16–30). Here, Jesus reads a passage from Isaiah in the synagogue, and is well received: "All spoke well of him and were amazed at the gracious words that came from his mouth." But soon the Jews in the synagogue become enraged, drive Jesus out of town, and even try to kill him. What brought about this sudden and drastic change? Jesus had called attention to occasions on which the prophets Elijah and Elisha used their divinely given powers, not to help Jews, but to help Gentiles (a Sidonian and a Syrian, respectively; see 1 Kgs 17:8–16; 2 Kgs 5:1–14).

Social Justice

A third feature of the Gospel of Luke is its emphasis on issues of social justice. For instance, Luke seems more concerned with the role and status of women than do the other gospels. This is evident in the attention that it gives to Mary, the mother of Jesus, and Elizabeth, the mother of John the Baptist, in the birth and infancy narratives of the Gospel's opening chapters. Again, the story of Mary and Martha suggests that, in the Christian view of things, a woman's place is not in the kitchen, but alongside Jesus in the kingdom of God (10:38–42). The author of Luke is also especially concerned for the plight of the poor. Consider, for example, references to the hungry and the needy in the song of Mary (1:52–53) and in the preaching of John the Baptist (3:10–11). The passage that Jesus reads in the synagogue at Nazareth says, "[T]he Lord…has anointed me to bring good news to the poor" (4:18). While Matthew and Luke both record a blessing on the poor (Matt 5:3; Luke 6:20), only Luke adds a curse on the rich (6:24–25). The parable of Lazarus and the rich man shows a concern that the needs of the poor should be met, and suggests that those who could have met them but failed to do so will be punished (16:19–31). Luke's Jesus even tells his followers, "[N]one of you can become my disciple if you do not give up all your possessions" (14:33). While this is most likely a bit of stylistic hyperbole on the part of Luke's author—as is 14:26, just above—it suggests that the inequitable distribution of wealth was something that the author of Luke found to be inconsistent with the basic message of Jesus.

V. JOHN

A. Authorship and Date

Although the author of the Gospel of John does not identify himself by name, the Gospel does contain cryptic references to an unnamed "disciple whom Jesus loved" (21:20; see also 13:23; 19:26; 21:7). Presumably, this beloved disciple is the same unnamed person described by the Gospel as "the disciple who is testifying to these things and has written them" (21:24).[6] While a tradition dating to late in the second century CE identifies this beloved disciple with the apostle John, a son of Zebedee and one of the twelve members of Jesus' inner circle, the Gospel of John itself never makes such an identification. Moreover, extrabiblical sources suggest that John the apostle was martyred prior to 70 CE, which is earlier than the Gospel of John is thought to have been written. The Gospel itself even hints that the beloved disciple may have died before his testimony was recorded in writing (21:21–23). It is entirely possible, however, that a disciple of Jesus named John founded a Christian church—usually referred to as the Johannine Community or the Johannine School—and that members of this church community preserved his teachings and committed them to writing.

The author of the Gospel of John was familiar with some of the same stories about Jesus that were known to the authors of the Synoptic Gospels. For instance, John agrees with the Synoptics that Jesus healed the sick, multiplied loaves of bread, performed a dramatic action in the Temple, was crucified, and appeared to his disciples after his death. However, the differences between John and the Synoptic Gospels are so great that scholars have no reason to think that the author of John was familiar with any of the Synoptic Gospels; rather, the author of John seems to have appealed to an independent set of oral and/or written traditions about Jesus. Thus, dating the Gospel of John is very difficult, since the dates that most scholars accept for the Synoptic Gospels do not help us in trying to fix a date for John. Still, most scholars date the Gospel of John to the last decade of the first century (90–100 CE). There are two main reasons for this.

First, evidence internal to the Gospel of John suggests that it was written, at least in its final form, only after the split between Judaism and Christianity was nearly or fully complete. For example, John contains three passages that seem to refer to Jewish Christians being put out of the Jewish synagogues (9:22; 12:42; 16:2). It is also contains passages that condemn *the Jews* in very harsh terms (see, for example, 8:39–47). Such passages suggest that, by the time the Gospel of John was written, Christianity was no longer regarded as a movement within Judaism, but as something distinct from Judaism. Since the complete separation between Judaism and Christianity seems not to have occurred until late in the first century, 90–100 CE is a likely date for the writing of the Gospel of John.

The second reason why most scholars date John to the end of the first century has to do with that Gospel's theological sophistication, which scholars regard as an indication that some length of time had passed between the writing of the first gospels and the writing of John. This theological sophistication shall be the main topic in our discussion of the Gospel of John.

B. John's Christology

The theology that the author of John weaves into his account of the life of Jesus is regarded as sophisticated because its Christology is much more fully developed than that found in the Synoptic Gospels. Christology is the branch of Christian theology devoted to understanding the person and work of Jesus. It is primarily concerned with questions regarding Jesus' nature (Was he human? Divine? Both?) and his self-understanding (Was he fully conscious of his own mission and destiny?). When one looks at the gospels in the order in which they are thought to have been written, one sees a pattern of development in the Christology of the early Christian church. The Gospel of Mark is said to have an *adoptionist* Christology. Mark tells us nothing about Jesus' early life, and Jesus is not identified ("adopted") as the Son of God until his baptism. The gospels of Matthew and Luke are said to have a *conception* Christology; in the infancy narratives of these gospels, Jesus is identified as the Son of God from the time of his conception by the virgin Mary. The Gospel of John, on the other hand, has a *pre-existence* Christology: Jesus is identified as a divine being who existed prior to the creation of the world.

Jesus as Word

The sophistication of John's Christology is nowhere more evident than in the prologue with which the Gospel begins:

> In the beginning was the Word, and the Word was with God, and the Word was God. He was in the beginning with God. All things came into being through him, and without him not one thing came into being. What has come into being in him was life, and the life was the light of all people. The light shines in the darkness, and the darkness did not overcome it.... And the Word became flesh and lived among us, and we have seen his glory, the glory as of a father's only son, full of grace and truth (1:1–5, 14).

In order to appreciate this prologue fully, some background is necessary. The Greek term that has been translated as "Word" here is *logos*. While *logos* was used in Greek to mean "word," "speech," or "account," it also had philosophical uses. The ancient Greek philosopher Heraclitus (540–480 BCE) had used *logos* to refer to the intelligent principle that he believed to be responsible for organizing the universe. Later, the Stoics (a Greek philosophical school founded by Zeno in the fourth century BCE) would use *logos* as a term for the divine nature that they held to govern all things with rational necessity.

The word *logos* was also used by the Jewish philosopher and theologian Philo of Alexandria (15 BCE–50 CE). In his philosophical interpretations of the Hebrew scriptures, Philo used the term *logos* to refer to the divine manifestation by which God comes into contact with the created world. It is in this sense that

God *speaks* things into being in the first Creation story: "Then God said, 'Let there be light'; and there was light" (Gen 1:3). Philo's characterization of the *logos* was influenced by Jewish wisdom literature. The Book of Proverbs asserts, "The Lord by wisdom founded the earth" (3:19), and it even gives this divine wisdom her own voice: "The Lord created me at the beginning of his work, the first of his acts of long ago. Ages ago I was set up, at the first, before the beginning of the earth.... [When the Lord created the world,] I was beside him, like a master worker" (Prov 8:22–23, 30). For Philo, then, the word *logos* referred to the divine wisdom by which the Lord created all things.

Thus, when the author of John asserts that "the Word became flesh and lived among us" (1:14), he is identifying Jesus with ancient Greek and Jewish conceptions of the divine. But he is also manifesting a well-developed Christology. When John asserts that the *logos* (= Jesus) was "[i]n the beginning," he asserts that Jesus—like God—is an eternal being. When he asserts that the *logos* was "with God," he describes Jesus as a person standing in a relationship to God—that is, as a person distinct from God. When he asserts that the *logos* "was God," he asserts that Jesus is divine; Jesus is somehow both distinct from God and also identical to God at the same time. And when he asserts, "All things came into being through" the *logos*, he is asserting that Jesus was the agent of divine creation. Thus, from its very first verses, the Gospel of John presents a much more fully developed characterization of the nature and status of Jesus than we find in the Synoptic Gospels.

Things Said about Jesus

The evidence of a well-developed Christology in John is not limited to the prologue. It can also be found in the things that Jesus and his disciples say in the Johannine account. In the first chapter alone, John the Baptist and others identify Jesus as the Lamb of God, the Son of God, the Messiah, and the King of Israel; all this before Jesus' ministry has even begun! Whereas, in the Synoptic Gospels, Jesus' disciples confess that Jesus is the Messiah and the Son of God, John has one of the disciples hail the risen Jesus as "My Lord and my God!" (20:28).

216

Jesus' Sayings

The Gospel of John also attributes sayings to Jesus that portray him as being much more conscious of his own nature and mission than he had seemed in the Synoptic Gospels. In the Synoptics, Jesus' teaching was focused on God and the kingdom of God. In the Gospel of John, on the other hand, Jesus speaks primarily about himself. This is most clear in the many sayings of Jesus that contain the words "I am." Most of these sayings are predicated, for example: "I am the bread of life" (6:35); "I am the light of the world" (8:12); "I am the good shepherd...[who] lays down his life for the sheep" (10:11); "I am the resurrection and the life" (11:25). Even more powerful, however, are the unpredicated "I am" sayings, such as the one at 8:58: "Very truly, I tell you, before Abraham was, I am" (see also 8:24, 28; 13:19). The Greek expression that John uses for "I am" here, *egō eimi*, is the same expression that the authors of the Septuagint had used to translate the Hebrew expressions "I am YHWH" (Exod 6:7) and "I am he" (Isa 43:10).[7] To Jews who knew their Deity by the name YHWH, a name they considered too holy to utter aloud, such a statement on the part of Jesus could easily sound like a claim to divinity. When we compare such sayings in John to the messianic secret in Mark (which is paralleled in Matthew and Luke), we can see that John portrays Jesus as being more conscious of—and more forthcoming about—his own status and mission than he was in the Synoptic Gospels.

Jesus' Actions

Finally, the sophisticated Christology that informs the Gospel of John may be seen in Jesus' actions. In the Synoptic Gospels, Jesus usually performs miracles out of compassion for those who are suffering, and sometimes even declines to take personal credit for them (Mark 5:34; Matt 17:19–20). In John, however, Jesus' miracles are characterized as "signs...[which] revealed his glory" (2:11). In other words, John portrays Jesus' miracles as incentives to faith in Jesus' divinity. When his disciples doubt him, Jesus says to them, "Believe me that I am in the Father and the Father is in me; but if you do not, then believe me because of the works themselves" (14:11). Again, the Synoptics had portrayed Jesus' ministry as something that would precede and usher in the kingdom of God; his miracles were signs that the kingdom was close at hand, and his death and resurrection would inaugurate the kingdom and ultimately bring about salvation for all people. John, on the other hand, characterizes salvation as something that is already achieved in the very existence of Jesus: "[A]nyone who hears my word and believes him who sent me has eternal life, and does not come under judgment, but has passed from death to life" (5:24). Since the Christology at work in the Gospel of John regards Jesus as an eternally divine being, that Gospel characterizes the salvation brought by Jesus, not as a future good to be anticipated, but as a present reality.

VI. ON THE RESURRECTION

In the previous chapter we noted that resurrection is not something on which scholars studying the historical Jesus can comment; as a transhistorical event, resurrection lies outside the domain of empirical history. With this in mind, it is interesting to observe that none of the four New Testament gospels claims to offer an eyewitness account of the resurrection of Jesus, either. Instead, they describe the *effects* of the resurrection as evidence that the resurrection must have occurred. These effects take two forms: (1) accounts of Jesus' tomb being found empty; and (2) accounts of the resurrected Jesus appearing to his disciples.

Empty Tomb Stories

Many scholars, though certainly not all, would argue that the gospel accounts of the empty tomb possess a high degree of historical reliability, for two reasons. First, in all four gospels, it is women who discover that the tomb is empty and report this finding to the other disciples. The significance of this commonality lies in the fact that, generally speaking, women were not regarded as credible witnesses in the ancient world. Indeed, the gospels themselves suggest that the other disciples did not believe the women's testimony, and thus went to see the tomb for themselves (Mark 16:11; Luke 24:9–11). Since the discovery of the empty tomb by women would have been much less compelling to the gospel writers' contemporary audiences than a similar discovery by men, the gospel accounts involving women would seem to satisfy the criterion of dissimilarity. The admission that women made the crucial discovery would surely have been an embarrassment that the gospel writers could have easily avoided; the fact that they preserved this account thus lends it credibility.

A second reason why many scholars regard the empty tomb stories as reliable lies in Matthew's suggestion that those who first challenged the claim that Jesus had risen from the dead seem not to have questioned the emptiness of Jesus' tomb. According to Matthew, a guard was posted at the tomb to make sure that Jesus' disciples did not steal his body, and this same guard was later bribed by the authorities to spread the lie that the body had in fact been stolen (27:62–66; 28:11–15). Whether this account is historically reliable or not, it draws our attention to an important fact: The disciples of Jesus would not have been able to proclaim that Jesus had risen from the dead if Jesus' corpse still lay intact in the tomb. Since confirming that the tomb was empty would have been an easy thing to do, it probably was done by those interested in discrediting the disciples' claims.[8]

Appearance Stories

Of course, even if the gospel accounts of the empty tomb are historically reliable, they are ambiguous as evidence of the resurrection. There are many ways by which a tomb might be emptied of its contents, and most of them do not involve an act of God! This is why the gospel accounts of the empty tomb are complemented by stories in which the resurrected Jesus appears to his disciples. Given the theological concerns of the gospel writers, few scholars would be inclined to regard any individual appearance story as historically probable. Even if they did, they would have to acknowledge that it was not the earthly Jesus whom the disciples experienced; the Jesus the disciples experienced was the Jesus they believed to have been glorified, exalted, and seated at the right

hand of God. This distinction is supported by the gospels themselves, which suggest that the risen Christ was not recognizable to
those who had known the earthly Jesus (see Mark 16:12; Luke
24:15–16; John 20:14–15; 21:4).*

Still, even if the gospels' appearance accounts cannot be
regarded as having a high degree of historical reliability, many
scholars would be willing to assert that *something* happened to
convince Jesus' disciples that he had risen from the dead. They
would support this assertion by citing two facts. First, many Jews
of the Second Temple period did not believe in the concept of resurrection. Second, those Jews of the Second Temple period who
did believe in resurrection conceived of a *general* resurrection—of
all the dead at once—that would occur at the end of time, along
with the last judgment. Thus, the Christians' claim to have had
some experience that convinced them that Jesus had been raised
from the dead could be seen as satisfying the criterion of dissimilarity because, at the time, it was innovative; the idea that a single person should be resurrected from the dead prior to the end
of time was unprecedented in Jewish eschatological thought. The
fact this claim was made about a person who had died a disgraceful criminal's death at the hands of a secular power only
adds to the claim's originality.†

---

* The idea that the risen Christ was so different from the earthly Jesus as to be
unrecognizable to those who had known the earthly Jesus is also indirectly supported by Paul. Speaking, presumably, from his own experience of the risen
Christ, Paul asserts that, when the time comes for all the dead to be resurrected,
human beings will no longer have perishable, physical bodies of flesh and
blood, but imperishable "spiritual" bodies (1 Cor 15: 42–53).

† Jesus' death would have been regarded as disgraceful by most Jews because the
Book of Deuteronomy proclaims that "anyone hung on a tree is under God's curse"
(21:23). That the first Christians thought of crucifixion as comparable to hanging
on a tree is made clear at Acts 5:30: "The God of our ancestors raised up Jesus,
whom you had killed by hanging him on a tree." (See also Gal 3:13; 1 Pet 2:24.)

12

Acts of the Apostles

I. AUTHORSHIP

Luke-Acts

As noted in the previous chapter, virtually all biblical scholars agree that the Book of Acts was written by the same author who wrote the Gospel of Luke. In addition to similarities in vocabulary and literary style, the two books contain internal evidence suggesting that Acts was written as a sequel to the story recounted in Luke. The opening verse of Acts refers back to "the first book," in which was reported "all that Jesus did and taught." Moreover, both Luke and Acts are addressed to the "most excellent Theophilus" (Luke 1:3; Acts 1:1). Because he has a Greek name, it is believed that this Theophilus was a Gentile, but nothing else in known about him. He may have been a Gentile Christian who commissioned the writing of Luke-Acts, or he may have been a well-placed Roman whom the author wished to win over to Christianity by means of the two books. The latter suggestion is supported by the fact that the Book of Acts seems designed to make Christianity palatable to Gentiles, as evidenced in the book's occasional hostility toward the Jews (7:51–53; 21:27; 23:12; 28:23–31) and its characterization of Roman officials as sympathetic toward Christians (18:12–16; 26:30–32).[1]

Historical Context

As did the author of the Gospel of Luke, so the author of the Book of Acts shows a concern to situate the story he is telling in the larger context of world history. He links the spread of Christianity outside Jerusalem to the persecution of Christians within that city (8:1–8); he mentions the famine that befell Palestine in 46 CE, noting that it occurred during the reign of Emperor Claudius (11:28); and he reports the death of King Herod Agrippa I in 44 CE (12:20–23). As in Luke, the author's goal in Acts is to stress that the significance of the events he relates is not limited to the geographic location of those events. In the worldview of Luke-Acts, Palestine is merely the stage on which a much larger, divinely willed drama unfolds.

Emphasis on the Spirit

The Book of Acts also shares Luke's interest in the Holy Spirit. The Gospel of Luke emphasizes the role of the Holy Spirit more than the other gospels do (see Luke 1:15, 35, 41, 67; 2:25–27; 3:16, 22; 4:1). Similarly, the Holy Spirit plays a major role in the events recorded in Acts. The Book of Acts opens with the resurrected Jesus telling his disciples that they "will be baptized with the Holy Spirit" (1:5), and that they "will receive power when the Holy Spirit has come upon [them]" (1:8). This promise is quickly made good; at the feast of Pentecost, the Holy Spirit descends in the form of fire and touches the disciples, enabling them to speak in many different languages (2:1–4). In the speech that follows, Peter tells his audience that, if they repent and are baptized as Christians, then they "will receive the gift of the Holy Spirit" (2:38).

Thus, strong stylistic and thematic evidence tells us that the Book of Acts is the work of the same author who wrote the Gospel of Luke. In this light, it is significant that a number of sections in Acts are written from the first person plural perspective (16:10–17; 20:5—21:18; 27:1—28:16). These sections seem to be firsthand accounts of someone who was traveling with Paul. They thus add some strength to the argument that the author of Luke-Acts was the physician mentioned in letters attributed to Paul (Col 4:14; Phlm 24; 2 Tim 4:11).

II. THEMES

The author of Luke-Acts saw his two-volume work as a continuation of the salvation history that began in the Jewish scriptures. The Hebrew Torah (Law) and Neviim (Prophets) had recounted God's involvement with human beings from the Creation through the Babylonian Exile. (The third part of the Tanak—the Kethuvim—had not yet been fully canonized.) The Gospel of Luke continued this saga by telling of the life, death, and resurrection of Jesus. The Book of Acts is meant to complete the story by chronicling the history of the early Christian church. Just as the Gospel of Luke had reported that Jesus' ministry began with Jesus' baptism by John and an appearance of the Holy Spirit (3:21–22), so the Book of Acts reports that the Christian church began with the baptism of the apostles by the fire of the Holy Spirit at Pentecost, seven weeks after Jesus' death on the previous Passover (2:1–4).

History of the Earliest Church

The major theme of the book of Acts is the origin and spread of the Christian church from its base in Jerusalem outward to "all Judea and Samaria, and to the ends of the earth" (1:8). This theme governs the whole organization of the Book of Acts. After a brief introduction (1:1–26), the book proceeds in three stages: (1) stories about the Christian church in Jerusalem (2:1—8:3); (2) stories of Christian missionary work in Judea and Samaria (8:4—12:24); (3) stories of Paul's missionary activity in Asia Minor, Greece, and ultimately Rome (12:25—28:31).[2] The author of Acts has thus laid the work out in such a way that the geographical setting of the events it relates parallels the ever-widening scope of the early church's efforts to spread the gospel. As the setting of Acts moves from Jerusalem to the very center of the Roman Empire, so the missionary efforts of the first Christians shift away from their fellow Jews and toward the Gentile world.

Apostolic Speeches

The Book of Acts is so called because it records the works performed by the apostles in their efforts to spread the good news of salvation through Jesus the Christ. These works, which the Book of Acts offers as demonstrations of the power and authority of the apostles, typically take the form of healings performed in the name of Jesus (3:1–10; 9:32–35, 36–43; 14:8–10). But in addition to such works, the Book of Acts also records a number of speeches made by the apostles; indeed, these speeches constitute roughly one-third of the material in the book. The speeches recorded in Acts generally divide into two types: kerygmatic and apologetic.[3] In the kerygmatic speeches—from the Greek word *kerygma* (preaching or proclamation)—the apostles set forth the basic message of salvation. Such speeches usually include a number of key points: (1) Jesus' death fulfilled the Jewish scriptures; (2) Jesus has been raised from the dead and exalted as the Messiah; (3) Jesus' life and teaching have been validated by the acts that the Holy Spirit has brought about through the apostles; (4) the coming of the Holy Spirit through Jesus means that the new age is at hand; (5) those who hear these things should repent so as to be saved at the final judgment. For examples of kerygmatic speeches in Acts, consider those of Peter at 2:14–39 and 10:24–43 and that of Paul at 13:16–41.

The apologetic speeches take their name from the Greek word *apologia*, which means "defense"; in these speeches, the apostles offer a defense of themselves or their message. In some cases, the apostles must defend the gospel against Jews who regard it with hostility (7:2–53). In other cases, the apostles must defend themselves—their character and/or authority—either against their fellow Christians (20:18–35), or against Jewish authorities (26:1–23), or against Roman authorities (24:10–21).

Minor Themes

The Book of Acts also contains a number of minor themes. One is a concern for the poor, a thematic consistency between the Gospel of Luke and the Book of Acts. The author of Acts reports that members of the first Christian church in Jerusalem practiced a primitive form of economic communism; they held all their property in common, and proceeds from the communal purse—which the church leadership controlled—were used to provide for

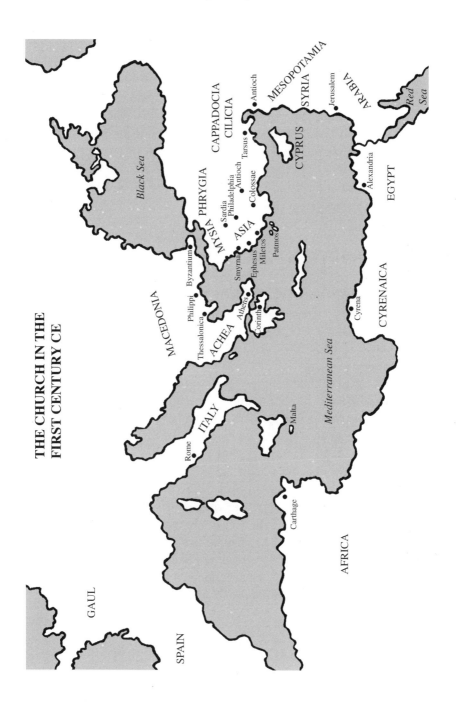

THE CHURCH IN THE
FIRST CENTURY CE

the needy (2:44–45; 4:32–35). When Palestine was suffering famine, the Christians in Antioch took up collections that they sent as relief to their fellow Christians in Judea (11:27–30). The Book of Acts also stresses the piety of the first Christians. We are told that the Jerusalem Christians were regular visitors to the Temple, and that they gathered together to pray (2:46; 3:1; 12:12). Finally, while the main theme of the Book of Acts is the spread of the gospel by the apostles, the book retains an element of the divine will operating in human affairs; see, for instance, the story of Ananias and Sapphira (5:1–11) and the explanation of Herod Agrippa's death (12:20–23).

III. APOSTLES AND THE EARLY CHURCH

The English word *apostle* derives from the Greek word *apostolos*, which means "one who is sent." While people often use the word to refer exclusively to the twelve disciples who made up Jesus' inner circle ("the Twelve"), the New Testament uses the word to refer to any persons who were personally commissioned by Jesus to spread the gospel. The number of such persons is unknown, but it is known to have included more than the Twelve. For example, Jesus' brother James was both an apostle (Gal 1:19) and a leader of the Jerusalem church (Gal 2:9; Acts 21:18), even though the gospels portray Jesus' family as having been somewhat hostile toward his ministry (Mark 3:21; 6:4; John 7:5). Paul never met Jesus during Jesus' lifetime, but he was an apostle because he received a commission in an experience of the risen Christ (Acts 9:1–19). Paul himself also distinguishes between "the twelve" apostles and "all the apostles" (1 Cor 15:5, 7). The number of apostles may actually have been quite large; the Gospel of Luke reports that, during his ministry, Jesus commissioned seventy of his disciples to spread the word that the kingdom of God was near at hand (Luke 10:1–9).[4]

The Twelve

One of the first acts of the apostles recorded in the Book of Acts was to fill the slot vacated in the Twelve by the death of Judas

Iscariot. (How Judas died is problematic; Matthew 27:5 reports that he hung himself, while Acts 1:18 records a more natural, though somewhat bizarre, death.) Having determined that Judas's replacement should be one of the disciples who had been with Jesus from the time of his baptism by John, the remaining eleven members of the Twelve prayed and cast lots to decide whether Joseph Barsabbas or Matthias should be chosen. The lots favored Matthias, who was added to the eleven (1:21–26). After this detailed account of the election of Matthias to the Twelve, Matthias is never mentioned again—either in Acts or anywhere else in the New Testament. So why would the author of the Book of Acts go to the trouble of recording this event? The answer is important to our discussion of the early Christian church. For, while there were perhaps many apostles in the early church, the Twelve were regarded from the beginning as possessing special authority. When Jesus had selected a small group of apostles to constitute his inner circle, the number that he had settled on was not arbitrary; the twelve apostles he chose were to be judges over the twelve tribes of Israel in the new age (Matt 19:28; Luke 22:30). Thus, the position vacated by Judas had to be filled in order for all twelve tribes to be represented in the leadership of the early church.

The Way

The special authority that the first Christians recognized the Twelve as possessing made them the de facto leaders of the early Christian church in Jerusalem. It is important to understand that the people who constituted this first Christian community were all Jews. They were still actively practicing their Jewish faith and making regular visits to the Temple (2:46; 3:1). Indeed, during the first few years of the Christian church, that church's members did not even call themselves Christians. Rather, they referred to their movement as the Way (Acts 9:2; 19:9, 23; 24:14, 22), while their fellow Jews referred to them as Nazarenes (Acts 24:5). The term *Christian* derives from the Greek *Christianoi* (Christ people), which was first applied to them by Gentiles in Antioch (Acts 11:26).[5] As we shall see, the fact that the first Christians still considered themselves to be Jews, and considered their faith to be simply a new form of Judaism, would soon give rise to conflict within the early church.

Through their early work at spreading the gospel, the apostles of the Christian community in Jerusalem began drawing other Jews into their ranks. These new members included Pharisees (15:5) and even priests (6:7). It was probably not until the number of Jewish Christians in Jerusalem had grown significantly that tensions between them and the non-Christian Jews, particularly the Sadducees, began to rise. Acts tells us of the arrest and imprisonment of apostles (5:18) and—shortly thereafter—the stoning of the first Christian martyr, Stephen (7:54–60). After Stephen's death, Acts reports that "severe persecution began against the church in Jerusalem" (8:1).

Hellenists and Hebrews

The exact nature of this persecution—at whom it was directed, who carried it out, and so on—is not entirely clear, but scholars believe that it may have had to do with differences between two groups of Jews: Hellenists and Hebrews.[6] The author of Acts introduces these terms at 6:1 without any explanation; he simply reports a dispute between two groups within the Jerusalem church, whom he calls the Hellenists and the Hebrews, regarding the distribution of food to widows—the former complaining that their widows were being neglected. It seems that the first Christian community, like the Jewish population of Jerusalem as a whole, was divided between Greek-speaking, Diaspora-born Jews (Hellenists) and Aramaic-speaking, Palestinian-born Jews (Hebrews). Although the main differences between the two groups were linguistic and cultural, there were probably political and theological differences as well. The Hellenists were Jews who had been influenced by the language and culture of the Greeks, which means that, relative to the Hebrews, their political and religious views were probably fairly liberal.

The Seven

When the dispute over the distribution of charity to widows arose, the Twelve decided to appoint seven men, chosen by the community, to oversee that distribution. The Greek names of those seven men suggest that they were Hellenists, and at least one of them (Nicolaus) was from Syrian Antioch (6:1–6). Most scholars believe that these seven men were probably the recognized leaders of the Hellenistic contingent within the Jerusalem church, just as the Twelve were the leaders of the Hebrew contingent. That the Hellenists had a more liberal outlook than did the Hebrews, including the Twelve, is clear in the next part of the story that the author of Acts relates. Stephen, one of the seven leaders of the Hellenistic Christians, engages in an argument with Jews at a synagogue. Acts makes clear that the synagogue in question was one frequented by Hellenists, the members of which were Diaspora Jews from such cities as Cyrene, Libya, and Alexandria, Egypt. Apparently Stephen's preaching was too liberal even for his fellow Hellenists, who accused him of speaking blasphemously against the Temple and the Jewish law (6:8–15).

According to the historian F. F. Bruce, there is evidence of a belief among some first-century Jews that, when the anticipated Messiah finally came, there would no longer be any need to observe the Mosaic laws regarding ritual and dietary purity. This view was probably more common among Hellenists than among Hebrews, and it seems to have been part of Stephen's preaching. The apologetic speech that Stephen makes at his indictment before the Sanhedrin includes a clear attack on the Temple cult: "[T]he Most High does not dwell in houses made with human hands" (7:48). The stoning of Stephen that follows appears to have been the act of an outraged and unruly mob; it could not have been a formal execution, since Rome did not permit the Sanhedrin to inflict capital punishment. It is after Stephen's death that the "severe persecution" against the Jerusalem church began. While the author of Acts does not say so explicitly, this persecution was probably directed primarily at the Hellenistic Christians who shared Stephen's way of thinking. For instance, we are told that "all except the apostles were scattered throughout the countryside of Judea and Samaria" (8:1). Since the author here seems to be using the term *apostles* to refer to the Twelve, all of whom were Hebrews, this suggests that it was only the Hellenistic Jewish Christians who were forced to flee Jerusalem. We are also told that it was Philip, one of the seven elected leaders of the Hellenists, who immediately began to proclaim the gospel in Samaria (8:5).*

Taking the Gospel to the Gentiles

Thus, the author of Acts links the spread of Christianity outside Jerusalem to the persecution of Hellenistic Jewish Christians by Jewish authorities—most of whom were Hebrews—within Jerusalem. This missionary work, which was begun in Samaria by the Hellenists, meets with the approval of the Twelve in Jerusalem (8:14-25). The early church's effort to take the gospel to the Gentiles is given dramatic form in two stories. First is the conversion of Saul (Paul), a former persecutor of Christians, of whom the Lord says, "[H]e is an instrument whom I have chosen to bring my name before the Gentiles" (9:15). Second is the story of Peter's conversion of Cornelius, a Roman centurion living in Caesarea, following a vision from which Peter learns that "God shows no partiality, but in every nation anyone who fears him and does what is right is acceptable to him" (10:34).

Acts tells us that some of the Christians who were forced to flee Jerusalem brought their message to the Syrian city of Antioch, where they found an audience among both Jews and "Greeks" (Gentiles) (11:19-20). Before long, the Christian church in Antioch was so well established that it was able to finance missionary journeys by two of its leaders, Barnabas and Paul (13:1-3). Ultimately, the success with which the early church was winning Gentile converts gave rise to controversy. Remember that the first members of the Christian community in Jerusalem had all been Jews, and that most of them had continued to practice their Jewish faith even after they had become Christians. This means that, in its early stages, the Christian church was comprised of Jews who still sacrificed at the Temple and obeyed the Mosaic Law. But once the Christians began preaching their message of

---

* That the first persecution of Christians was directed primarily at Hellenistic Jewish Christians is also suggested at Acts 9:29, where we are told that "the Hellenists were attempting to kill" the recently converted Paul. Why would the Hellenistic members of the Jerusalem church, in particular, have such murderous inclinations? Probably because it was those Hellenistic Jewish Christians whom Paul had been persecuting prior to his conversion.

salvation to non-Jews, a troubling question arose: Did one have to be a Jew in order to be a Christian? If so, then all the Gentiles who were being converted to Christianity would have to obey the Torah's dietary and ritual purity laws, and the males among them would have to undergo circumcision.

It seems that a conflict arose between the churches at Antioch and Jerusalem with regard to this issue. The Antiochene Christians were actively converting Gentiles to Christianity, and they were not demanding that those Gentiles convert to Judaism. But the more conservative church in Jerusalem, especially its Pharisee contingent, argued that any Gentile converts to the Way must "be circumcised and ordered to keep the law of Moses" (15:5). This view reflects the fact that most of the first Christians considered themselves to be Jews and continued to obey the Jewish law. But it also reflects concerns among those first Jewish Christians about the possibility of converting people who lacked the necessary background to the gospel that Judaism provided. The assertions that Jesus of Nazareth was the anticipated Davidic Messiah, and that the kingdom of God was at hand, were both intelligible to Jews because Jews understood what such terms as *messiah* and *kingdom of God* meant. But could a Gentile make sense of those assertions? If not, then the Gentiles could not truly be converted to Christianity, for they would not really understand the ideas to which they were committing themselves.[7]

The Jerusalem Conference

The controversy surrounding the conversion of Gentiles became so serious that, in 49 or 50 CE, a meeting was held in Jerusalem between the Twelve and a delegation from Antioch led by Barnabas and Paul (15:2). At this Jerusalem Conference it was decided that Gentile converts to Christianity need not undergo circumcision or obey all the purity and dietary laws of the Torah. Instead, Gentile Christians would only be required to observe three specific laws (15:20). First, Gentile Christians were to abstain from "things polluted by idols," meaning that they were not to eat the flesh of animals that had been sacrificed to pagan deities. Second, they were to abstain from "fornication." Since abstention from extramarital sexual relations seems to have been required of any Christian (Jewish or Gentile), the original wording of this provision may have been more specific; it may have required Gentile Christians to obey the Jewish marriage code recorded at Leviticus 18:6–18. Third, Gentile Christians were to conform to the Torah's prohibition of blood (Lev 17:10–13), meaning that they were not to eat animals from which the blood had not been completely drained. The justification for this third requirement may have been that the Lord had prohibited the ingestion of blood to Noah and his descendents—that is, all human beings—after the flood (Gen 9:4).

Thus, the Jerusalem Conference resolved the issue of Gentile conversion. In demanding that Gentile converts to the Christian faith observe laws forbidding certain dietary and sexual practices that were particularly offensive to Jews, and thus also to Jewish Christians, the early church leadership made it easier for Jewish Christians to come together with Gentile Christians. More significantly, however, the decision reached at the Jerusalem Conference brought an end to the idea that Christianity was merely a submovement within Judaism, and it facilitated what would prove to be a rapid spread of Christianity throughout the Gentile world of the Roman Empire.

13

The Pauline Epistles

While Jesus is the most important figure in the New Testament, the apostle Paul is clearly the second most important. Eighteen of the twenty-eight chapters in the book of Acts are about him, and thirteen New Testament letters are attributed to him. In all, roughly half the material that constitutes the New Testament deals with Paul either directly or indirectly. Paul's prominence in the New Testament canon reflects the fact that his authority was recognized very early in the history of the Christian church. By the time that 2 Peter was written in the late first century or early second century CE, at least some of Paul's letters had already attained the status of scripture among Christians (see 2 Pet 3:15–17).

Our discussion of Paul will begin with a sketch of his life and some comments on the letter as a literary form. We shall then briefly examine each of the Pauline epistles.

I. LIFE OF PAUL

Paul was probably born sometime in the first decade CE. His place of birth was Tarsus, a Roman seaport in Cilicia (southeastern Asia Minor). A bit of background is required in order to appreciate the significance of Paul's birthplace. Back in 171 BCE, the Seleucid king, Antiochus IV Epiphanes, had sought to bring Palestinian Jews to Tarsus in an effort to promote business there. As an incentive, he offered Greek citizenship to those Jews who relocated. After the city of Tarsus fell under Roman control in 64 BCE, Roman citizenship was extended to its inhabitants. Thus, Paul's being born in Tarsus was significant because it meant that, unlike most of the earliest Jewish Christians, Paul was a citizen of the Roman Empire. This may be part of the reason why Paul tended to use his Latin name, *Paulus*, rather than his Jewish name, Saul.[1]

As a young man, Paul seems to have learned the trade of tent making, perhaps from his father (Acts 18:3). Although he was born and probably spent much of his early life in a Hellenistic city, where most of the Jews would have been Hellenists, Paul describes himself and his family as belonging to the more conservative Hebrews (2 Cor 11:22; Phil 3:5). Indeed, Paul was a devout Jew; in his own words, he was "zealous for the traditions of [his] ancestors" (Gal 1:14). As a young man he went to Jerusalem to receive religious training under the Pharisaic master Gamaliel (Acts 22:3). Paul seems to have been more conservative than his teacher; whereas Gamaliel—like most Pharisees—opposed the persecution of the followers of Jesus (Acts 5:34–39), Paul became an active participant in that persecution (Acts 8:3; 1 Cor 15:9; Gal 1:13).[2]

Around the year 35 CE, Paul was en route to Damascus, hoping to discover and arrest any disciples of Jesus among the Jews in that city. Along the way, Paul had a profound experience of the risen Christ, which promptly led to Paul's conversion to Christianity. This conversion experience is recounted three times in the Book of Acts (9:1–19; 22:1–21; 26:1–23) and Paul refers to it many times in his own writings (for example, 1 Cor 9:1; 15:8; Gal 1:15ff.). After his conversion, Paul retreated to the desert for a period of time. Eventually, he journeyed to Jerusalem and met with Peter and James. He then spent some time back in Cilicia, probably in his hometown of Tarsus (Gal 1:17–21).

Much of the rest of Paul's life was devoted to missionary work. Through that work, which stretched over three distinct journeys, Paul spread the gospel and established Christian churches in Asia Minor, Cyprus, Macedonia, and Greece. In roughly 57 CE, Paul was arrested by the Roman authorities in Jerusalem after his preaching there stirred his Jewish audience into a frenzy (Acts 22:22–24). He then spent two years in prison in Caesarea. When the Roman procurator Festus proposed that Paul be returned to Jerusalem for trial, Paul invoked his right as a Roman citizen to plead his case before the emperor (Acts 25:1–12). He was transferred to Rome, where he spent two years under house arrest waiting for his case to be called (Acts 28:30). What happened next is unknown, as Paul's death is recorded neither in the New Testament nor in extrabiblical sources. Most scholars believe that, in the mid-to-late seventh decade CE, Paul was condemned and executed under Emperor Nero (54–68 CE).

II. LETTERS AS LITERATURE

Of the twenty-seven books of the New Testament, twenty-one are letters attributed to apostles of the early Christian church. Known as epistles—from the Greek word *epistole* (message)— these letters constitute a distinct literary form in the Bible. As we shall see, many of them are thought to predate the four New Testament gospels.

Letter Form

The epistles that have been preserved as books in the New Testament all adhere to the general form in which letters were written during the Roman period. In other words, Paul and the other apostles organized their letters in the same way as did other literate people throughout the Roman Empire. The typical letter of the period is divided into a number of distinct parts.[3] It begins with a greeting that identifies both the letter's sender and its intended recipient. The fact that the recipient in the letters attributed to Paul is usually a whole church congregation means that most of Paul's letters were not private communications but public documents, which Paul expected to be read and shared by everyone in the community to which he wrote. The greeting is followed by a thanksgiving, in which the sender of the letter expresses thanks for the well-being of the recipient. When this section is lacking in a letter, as in Paul's Letter to the Galatians, it is a fairly strong indicator that the sender is angry with the recipient. The thanksgiving is followed by the letter's body, in which the author's main concerns are addressed. After the body, the letter usually has a brief closing section that includes greetings to acquaintances on the recipient's end, a benediction, and the sender's signature. The signature was especially important when a letter was not handwritten by its author, but dictated to a scribe; see, for example, Galatians 6:11 and 2 Thessalonians 3:17. One feature common to the apostolic epistles that was *not* typical of other letters of the period is the insertion of a section between the letter's body and its closing. Called a paraenesis—from the Greek verb *parainein* (to advise)—this section contains moral exhortations that urge the letter's recipients to live righteously.

Authenticity

Although thirteen of the epistles in the New Testament are attributed to the apostle Paul, many scholars doubt that Paul himself actually wrote all of them. Of those thirteen letters, seven are undisputedly Pauline; virtually all scholars agree that they were indeed written by Paul himself. These are 1 Thessalonians, 1 and 2 Corinthians, Galatians, Romans, Philippians, and Philemon. For reasons having to do with vocabulary, literary style, and theology, scholars dispute the Pauline authorship of the other six letters that are attributed to Paul. In other words, scholarly opinion is divided with regard to 2 Thessalonians, Colossians, Ephesians, 1 and 2 Timothy, and Titus. Some scholars argue that Paul himself wrote these letters, but others argue that he did not.

It is important to bear in mind that, in disputing the Pauline authorship of some of the epistles that are attributed to Paul, scholars are not questioning whether those epistles carry Paul's apostolic *authority*. On the contrary, scholars agree that even those letters that seem least likely to have been written by Paul are nonetheless authoritative. They would suggest, however, that the Pauline authority of a letter need not depend upon Pauline authorship, since disciples who worked closely with Paul could have written letters that carried the spirit and authority of the apostle himself. Thus, those letters that are explicitly attributed to Paul, but which scholars believe Paul himself did not actually write, are referred to as Deuteropauline letters, meaning that they are Pauline, but in a secondary sense—by way of inspiration and authority rather than actual authorship.

III. THE EPISTLES

We shall here review the New Testament epistles that are attributed to the apostle Paul. With regard to each letter, we shall comment on both its context and its main themes.

A. 1 and 2 Thessalonians

Thessalonica was the leading city of the Roman province of Macedonia, and the site of a Christian church founded by Paul and his companions Silas (Silvanus) and Timothy during Paul's second missionary journey (Acts 15:40—16:5; 17:1-9). Because riotous Jews there had forced Paul and his companions to flee Thessalonica hastily, he later sent Timothy back to check up on the young church (1 Thess 3:1-5).

Paul's First Letter to the Thessalonians is most likely the oldest document in the New Testament, although some scholars believe that his Letter to the Galatians may be even older (see below). Paul wrote 1 Thessalonians in roughly 50 CE from the city of Corinth, where Timothy had just rejoined him following his visit to Thessalonica. While the news about the Thessalonian church was generally good, Timothy also reported two problems that Paul felt the need to address. One was that someone in Thessalonica had been speaking against Paul, challenging his authority and character. The other was that the Thessalonians were very concerned about the *parousia*. The Greek word *parousia* (presence) was used to refer to a visit by an important figure; early Christians adopted it as a word for the second coming of the Christ on the day of judgment. It seems the Thessalonians were worried that, if some members of their congregation died before the second coming, those members would not join the Christ in paradise. Apparently, Paul had not told the Thessalonians what they should believe would happen to those in their community who died before Jesus returned. This reflects an important fact about the first generation of Christians, including Paul: They believed that Jesus would return very soon—at least within their

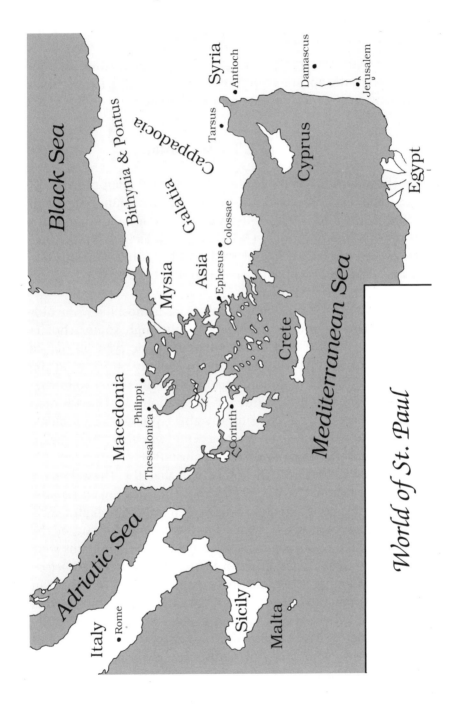

World of St. Paul

Black Sea

Bithynia & Pontus

Cappadocia

Galatia

Mysia

Asia

Ephesus
Colossae

Crete

Macedonia

Philippi

Thessalonica

Corinth

Mediterranean Sea

Adriatic Sea

Italy

Rome

Sicily

Malta

Syria

Antioch

Tarsus

Cyprus

Damascus

Jerusalem

Egypt

own lifetimes—possibly because Jesus himself had preached that his return would be imminent (Luke 9:27; Matt 16:28).[4]

Paul begins his First Letter to the Thessalonians by expressing his thankfulness for their loyalty and faith (1:2, 3, 6–8). He defends his character against those who have been denouncing him, first by refuting the allegations against him (2:3–8), then by reminding the Thessalonians that he and his companions had taken pains not to be a financial burden while among them (2:9–12). He stresses his great affection for the Thessalonians (2:17–20; 3:7–9). Finally, he assures them that, when the *parousia* arrives, the Christ will raise the dead first, and then take the living up into heaven (4:13–18).

In 2 Thessalonians, Paul is again writing from Corinth.* Paul has learned of a forged letter, claiming to be from Paul himself, that the Thessalonians have received (2:2). This spurious letter has somehow convinced the Thessalonian Christians that the *parousia*—here called the day of the Lord—was either imminent or already at hand, leading some of them to give up whatever sort of work they had previously been doing. Thus, in his second letter to them, Paul seeks to assure the Thessalonians that the day of judgment is not yet upon them. To this end, he offers a list of apocalyptic signs by which the Thessalonians may know when the end is truly near (2:1–7). He also endeavors to jar the Thessalonians out of their idleness, telling them that anyone among them who is unwilling to work should not be allowed to eat (3:6–13).

B. 1 and 2 Corinthians

Corinth was a major Greek seaport on the isthmus between the Adriatic Sea and the Aegean Sea. Like many cities heavily frequented by sailors, it was a hard-living town, replete with bars and prostitutes. Paul arrived in Corinth around 50 CE and stayed

---

* As we noted above, some scholars doubt that Paul wrote 2 Thessalonians. Because their reasons for doing so are highly technical—having to do with subtle shifts in linguistic usage, literary style, and theology—we shall not try to enumerate those reasons here. Instead, we shall regard 2 Thessalonians as authentically Pauline.

for eighteen months (Acts 18:11), during which time he founded a Christian church.

Although the New Testament presents us with two letters from Paul to the church in Corinth, internal evidence suggests that 1 and 2 Corinthians are actually a compilation of several letters that were strung together by later editors. For instance, Paul's tone toward his audience changes abruptly at 2 Corinthians 10; whereas Paul is friendly toward the Corinthians in chapters one through nine, he seems suddenly hostile toward them in chapters ten through thirteen. Again, 2 Corinthians 6:14—7:1 seems out of place; the thought begun at 6:13 continues at 7:2, as if the digressive material in between has been inserted where it does not belong.

Based on these and other internal clues, various scholars have attempted to reconstruct the correspondence between Paul and the church at Corinth. Because most of the available evidence is ambiguous, many different reconstructions are possible. Most of these reconstructions posit that 1 and 2 Corinthians together contain parts of at least three distinct letters; some claim that they contain parts of as many as seven letters. We shall here consider one plausible reconstruction of Paul's correspondence with the Corinthian church, according to which Paul sent five distinct letters to Corinth.[5]

Letter A (the Lost Letter on Immorality)

We know that the epistle that is called the First Letter of Paul to the Corinthians is not, in fact, the first letter that Paul wrote to the Christians at Corinth. This is because 1 Corinthians contains a reference to a previous letter Paul had written to them, in which he advised them "not to associate with sexually immoral persons" (5:9). This first letter of Paul to the Corinthian church, which we shall call Letter A, would have been written sometime between 51 and 54 CE. Apparently, the Corinthian Christians misunderstood Letter A to mean that they should not associate with any of their pagan neighbors, for in his next letter (Letter B = 1 Corinthians) Paul corrects this misinterpretation; his point was simply that the Christians in Corinth should not associate with members of their own congregation who fail to adhere to the moral standards of Christianity (1 Cor 5:9–13).

Although Letter A no longer exists, many scholars have argued that a fragment of it is preserved at 2 Corinthians 6:14—7:1. In this passage, which digresses rather awkwardly from the thought that precedes and follows it (6:13; 7:2), Paul exhorts the Christians in Corinth to avoid both the bodily and the spiritual defilement that comes from associating with pagans. Thus, there seems to be an affinity between this passage and the topic of Letter A. However, there are two important reasons for doubting that 2 Corinthians 6:14—7:1 is a fragment of Letter A. First, this passage so strongly advises Christians to separate themselves from non-Christians that Paul's later attempt to correct the Corinthians' misunderstanding of Letter A (at 1 Cor 5:9–13) seems not so much a reinterpretation of the position taken in 2 Corinthians 6:14—7:1 as a *reversal* of that position. Second, many scholars question whether Paul actually wrote the verses at 2 Corinthians 6:14—7:1. This brief passage contains eight words that do not occur in any of the undisputedly Pauline letters, and the words in this passage that Paul does use elsewhere are used with a different meaning here. For example, if 2 Corinthians 6:14—7:1 really is a fragment of Letter A, then Paul is here using the term *unbelievers* to refer to Christians who are engaged in immoral activities. This would mark a serious change in usage; in Paul's other letters, this term is consistently used to refer to non-Christians. Thus, the strange passage at 2 Corinthians 6:14—7:1 remains an enigma. If Paul wrote it, then why are there so many non-Pauline features concentrated in such a few short verses? If Paul did not write it, then why did he—or a later editor—insert it here so abruptly, without making any effort to adapt it to the context?

Letter B (= 1 Corinthians)

In 54 CE, Paul received word that the church in Corinth had divided into hostile factions (1 Cor 1:11–12). He also received a letter from members of the Corinthian church who wanted him to answer some questions about theology (1 Cor 7:1). Paul responds to both issues in his second letter to the Corinthian church, which is preserved in the New Testament canon as 1 Corinthians, and which we shall call Letter B. In response to the Corinthians' factionalism, Paul stresses the idea that all Christians are unified by their faith in Christ—that is, by their trust in the gospel message and their willingness to live the sort of life that Jesus had indicated (1:10–17). Since the factions seem to have been based on church members' pledging themselves to particular apostles (1:12), Paul draws a sharp contrast between claims to intellectual superiority—which some apostles, or their followers, might have been making—and the true wisdom that comes only through the gospel (1:22–25; 2:1–8; 3:18–20; 4:8–10). Paul also addresses the Corinthians' questions regarding theological issues, including marriage and celibacy (ch. 7), the Lord's Supper (ch. 11), the spiritual gifts (ch. 13), and the resurrection of the dead (ch. 15).

Letter C (the Lost Tearful Letter)

In Letter B, Paul had mentioned that he was sending his companion Timothy to visit the Corinthian church and had urged the Corinthians to receive him warmly (1 Cor 4:17; 16:10–11). Sometime in the following year (55 CE), Timothy rejoined Paul and reported some troubling news about the Corinthian church. Apparently, an individual in Corinth had slandered Paul. Statements in Paul's fourth letter to the Corinthians (Letter D = 2 Corinthians 1–9) make clear that Paul went to Corinth personally to try to deal with this situation, but that his efforts were unsuccessful; Paul describes this visit as having been "painful" (2 Cor 2:1; see also 2 Cor 12:14; 13:1–3). After this failed attempt to reconcile with the Corinthians in person, Paul wrote them a letter "out of much distress and anguish of heart and with many tears" (2 Cor 2:3–4). This third letter of Paul to the Corinthian church, which we shall call Letter C, has been lost; we know of it only because of references Paul makes to it in a later epistle.

Although the offense that had prompted the writing of the tearful Letter C had been a personal attack on Paul, the apostle's primary concern in that letter was the effect of this incident on the whole Corinthian congregation (2 Cor 2:5). Perhaps their unwillingness to discipline the offender had put their fidelity to Paul's apostolic authority in question. Paul clearly thought that the members of a church congregation and their founding apostle stand or fall together (see 1 Cor 12:26; 2 Cor 11:29). Unlike the painful visit Paul had made to Corinth, the tearful letter seems to have had the desired effect; the Corinthian congregation did eventually discipline the offender (2 Cor 2:6), which proved both the Corinthian Christians' obedience to Paul (2 Cor 2:9) and their remorse (2 Cor 7:8-12).

Letter D (= 2 Corinthians 1—9)

Later in the year 55 CE, Paul received a report about the Corinthian church from his companion Titus (2 Cor 7:6-7), who told him how faithfully the Corinthian congregation had responded to the tearful Letter C. Paul thus writes a fourth epistle to the church at Corinth. This fourth letter, which we shall call Letter D, is preserved in the New Testament canon as 2 Corinthians 1—9. In this letter, Paul celebrates his reconciliation with the Corinthian Christians by stressing both his affection for them and his confidence in their fidelity (see especially 2 Cor 7:2-16). He assures them that they are part of a new covenant with the Lord (2 Cor 3:2-6), part of a new creation achieved through the sacrificial death and resurrection of Jesus (2 Cor 5:14-21). Since the ugliness of the incident addressed in Letter C is now behind them, Paul urges the Corinthians to forgive the person whose offense had prompted that letter, and to welcome that person back into the fold (2 Cor 2:5-8). Paul also exhorts the Corinthians to reaffirm their faithfulness to the gospel and to his own apostolic authority, which they can do in part by helping Titus, whom Paul is sending to them to take up a collection for those suffering famine in Jerusalem (2 Cor 8—9).

Letter E (= 2 Corinthians 10—13)

In 56 CE, Paul received very disturbing news about events in Corinth. It seems that false apostles working in Corinth had denounced Paul and attempted—with some success—to assume control over the Corinthian church. Paul was aware that there were rival apostles at work in Corinth when he wrote Letter D, for he alluded to them in that letter (2 Cor 2:17; 3:1; 5:11–12). At that time, Paul seems to have thought that these other apostles did not pose a significant threat. Between 55 and 56 CE, however, the situation in Corinth had deteriorated significantly. Thus, Paul was forced to write a very strongly worded letter to the Corinthian church. This fifth letter, which we shall call Letter E, is preserved in the New Testament as 2 Corinthians 10—13.

Because of the frustration and outrage Paul felt over this new situation in Corinth, Letter E is uncharacteristically bitter in its tone. Paul both defends himself and attacks those who have led the Corinthians astray, whom he sardonically refers to as "super-apostles" (2 Cor 11:5). He denies his opponents' accusations that he is boastful (2 Cor 10:7–8, 13–14), that he is weak (2 Cor 10:10–11), and that he has taken advantage of the Corinthians financially (2 Cor 11:7–11). In order to defend his authority as an apostle, Paul makes a "Fool's Speech" in which he mimics the boasting of his opponents (2 Cor 11:1—12:13). In contrast to his opponents, however, Paul ironically boasts only of his own weakness (2 Cor 11:30; 12:5). He denounces his rivals as false apostles (2 Cor 11:13) and suggests that they are actually ministers of Satan (2 Cor 11:12–15). But he also has choice words for the Corinthian Christians themselves, whom he chastises for having been foolish enough to listen to such impostors (2 Cor 11:1–6, 19–21).

Given the harsh tone of Letter E, many scholars have identified it with the tearful letter Paul mentions at 2 Corinthians 2:3–4. That is, they argue that the tearful letter—which we have been calling the lost Letter C—was not lost, but that it was preserved as 2 Corinthians 10—13. This, of course, would mean that the writing of 2 Corinthians 10—13 predated the writing of Letter D (2 Corinthians 1—9), and that the reconciliation celebrated in Letter D was a resolution of the problems addressed in 2 Corinthians 10—13. However, there are compelling reasons for thinking that this identification of 2 Corinthians 10—13 with the tearful letter is mistaken. For example, Paul's references to the tearful letter indicate that the situation addressed in that letter involved an offense committed by an individual Corinthian (2 Cor 2:3–11; 7:8–12), whereas Letter E is clearly concerned with a group of false apostles. Again, Paul asserts that he wrote the tearful letter *instead of* making another painful visit to Corinth (2 Cor 1:23—2:4), but Letter E is expressly intended to prepare the Corinthians for an impending third visit that Paul planned to make to Corinth (2 Cor 10:2; 12:14, 20-21; 13:1-2, 10). Finally, when Paul expresses his satisfaction regarding the response that his tearful letter elicited among the Corinthians (2 Cor 2:5-8; 7:5-13), he says nothing to indicate that the problems that had been resolved were those at issue in Letter E. Thus, it is most likely the case that the tearful letter and Letter E (2 Corinthians 10—13) were different epistles, each of which addressed a distinct situation in Corinth.

C. Galatians

Galatia was not a city, but a Roman province in central and southern Asia Minor. Paul's Letter to the Galatians, written sometime between 48 and 52 CE, is addressed to an unspecified number of churches (1:2). These churches were probably located in the southern part of the province, which Paul had visited on his first missionary journey (Acts 13:4—14:28).

The "Judaizers"

Paul's letter to the churches of Galatia was occasioned by the preaching of Judaizers—Jewish Christians (probably from Judea) who were teaching the Gentile Christians in Galatia that conversion to Christianity required conversion to Judaism as well. According to these Judaizers, the Galatian Christians could only attain salvation if they obeyed the Mosaic Law (2:16; 3:2; 5:4), underwent circumcision (5:2-3; 6:12), and observed the Jewish feast days (4:10).

The fact that Paul's Letter to the Galatians lacks a thanksgiving section shows that he is enraged by their willingness to submit to the Judaizers' demands. Once again, Paul must take pains to defend his authority as an apostle. To this end, he explains that he received his apostolic commission directly from the risen Christ (1:11-17). He also recounts a visit to Jerusalem in which his missionary work among the Gentiles had received the blessing of Peter, James, and John (2:1–10). Here Paul seems to be describing the Jerusalem Conference (Acts 15), which took place around 49–50 CE. If so, then Paul's Letter to the Galatians probably dates to 51 or 52 CE. On the other hand, Paul could be describing a visit he made to Jerusalem prior to the Jerusalem Conference, in which case the Letter to the Galatians may have been written as early as 48 CE—making it the earliest work of the New Testament. The question regarding this letter's date is complicated by a story that Paul relates in which Peter visits Antioch and—under pressure from the "circumcision faction" (the Judaizers)—withdraws from table fellowship with the Gentile Christians there (2:11–14). The problem that faces scholars trying to date the Letter to the Galatians is to decide whether such an event would have occurred after the Jerusalem Conference, which had clearly settled the issue of Gentile conversion in Paul's favor. Of course, the date of Peter's visit to Antioch is irrelevant to Paul's purpose in recounting it; Paul uses the story to stress the legitimacy of his own apostolic authority, pointing out that he was able to challenge the head of the Jerusalem church to his very face.

Justification through Faith

In order to counter the claims made by the Judaizers, Paul insists that human beings are "justified" (accepted) by God not through their obedience to the Jewish law, but by their faith in Christ (2:15–16; 3:19–26; 5:2–6). Indeed, if obedience to the law were enough to secure salvation, then no messiah was needed, and "Christ died for nothing" (2:21). He also offers an allegorical account of the births of Abraham's sons Ishmael (son of the slave Hagar) and Isaac (son of the free woman Sarah), arguing that these two births represent two different covenants with God (4:22–31). The point of the allegory is that obedience to the law is like a form of slavery, for those who are under the law merely do what they are commanded to do, whereas faith in Christ is freedom, for those who have faith do what is good out of love (5:13–14).

D. Philippians

Philippi was a city in eastern Macedonia where Paul had founded the first Christian church on the continent of Europe (Acts 16:12–40). Paul wrote to the Philippian church from prison (1:7, 13–14, 16–17), but the location and date of his imprisonment are a matter of some debate. The Book of Acts records three incarcerations of Paul: one at Philippi (16:23); one at Caesarea (23:23); and one at Rome (28:16). Many scholars believe that Paul was probably also imprisoned at Ephesus, though the evidence for this imprisonment is indirect (see 1 Cor 15:30–32; 2 Cor 1:8). In Philippians 1:13 Paul mentions the imperial guard—possibly a reference to the praetorian guard, which was the personal bodyguard of the Roman emperor. At 4:22, he sends greetings from Christians who are serving—presumably as slaves—in "the emperor's household." These two passages might suggest that Paul wrote the Letter to the Philippians from Rome sometime during the last two years of his life. However, the Latin word *praetorium*, which is translated as "praetorian guard" in the RSV and as "imperial guard" in the NRSV, was also used to refer to the official residence of the Roman governor of a region. Such a residence probably existed in Ephesus. Similarly, the reference to slaves of the emperor's household could simply mean imperial slaves, who served at Roman installations throughout the empire. Moreover, since we know that Paul intended to head for Spain after his time in Rome (Rom 15:28), his assertions that he would visit Philippi if and when his current incarceration ended (1:26; 2:24) suggest that this letter was not written from Rome. If Paul did write to the Philippians from Ephesus rather than from Rome, then this epistle probably dates to 56–57 CE.[6]

The central theme of Paul's Letter to the Philippians is his joy in the gospel, which has not been fazed in the least by his own sufferings. Indeed, he uses the words *joy* and *rejoice* more times in this epistle than in any other. Rather than bemoaning his situation, Paul delights in the good that he believes his own imprisonment is achieving; even while in jail, Paul is spreading the gospel and converting people to Christianity (1:12–14). He believes that he will be delivered, but he also makes clear that he would be happy to sacrifice his life for Christ and thereby join him (1:18b–24; 2:17–18).

The abrupt shift in the topic of discussion at 3:1b suggests to some scholars that the Epistle to the Philippians may originally have been two distinct letters. The passages that follow this shift return to a theme we have already seen in Paul, namely, warnings against Judaizers who would "mutilate the flesh" by demanding circumcision of Gentile Christians (3:2).[7]

E. Philemon

Philemon is the only undisputedly Pauline epistle addressed to an individual rather than to a group of people.[8] Philemon was a wealthy resident of Colossae (see Col 4:9) whom Paul had converted to Christianity (v. 19). Paul writes to Philemon regarding Onesimus, a slave belonging to Philemon. The situation that occasioned the writing of this letter is debated, as the verses hinting at that situation (11, 15–16) are somewhat ambiguous. Some scholars believe Onesimus had run away from his master and met up with Paul while making his escape. Others think it more likely that Onesimus was simply in some sort of trouble with his master, and that he sought out Paul—his master's friend and mentor—in the hope that Paul would intercede on Onesimus's behalf. Whatever situation brought Onesimus to Paul, it is clear that, in the time they have spent together, Paul has converted Onesimus to Christianity (v. 10), and is now sending him back to his master (v. 12). Because Roman law allowed severe punishment of slaves—including death, in the case of runaways—and because Onesimus may have stolen something from Philemon (v. 18), Onesimus had much to fear in returning to his master. Thus, Paul appeals to Philemon to be merciful to his slave. Given his authority over the churches he has founded, Paul makes clear that he could simply order Philemon not to punish Onesimus (v. 8). But instead, Paul exhorts Philemon to accept Onesimus as a fellow Christian (v. 16), and he suggests that Philemon should "do even more" (v. 21)—presumably, that he should set Onesimus free.

In this letter, Paul twice mentions that he is writing from prison (vv. 1, 9), but he does not specify where he is imprisoned. While scholars have traditionally placed the writing of the Letter to Philemon in Rome toward the end of Paul's life, many scholars now think it is more likely that Philemon was written during Paul's imprisonment in Ephesus (56–57 CE), for two reasons. First, Ephesus and Colossae were both in Asia Minor, which means that Colossae was significantly closer to Ephesus than it was to Rome. It is thus much more likely that a slave from Colossae could have made his way to Ephesus than that he could have reached Rome. Second, Paul's writing to Philemon from Ephesus makes sense of his suggestion that he will come to visit Philemon once his incarceration ends (v. 22), whereas this suggestion is difficult to reconcile with Paul's declared intention to head from Rome to Spain (Rom 15:28).

F. Romans

The Roman Church

Unlike the other churches to which Paul wrote, the Christian church at Rome was one that he had neither founded nor—at the time he wrote his Epistle to the Romans—even visited. While the origins of the Roman church are a mystery, we can infer a bit about its history. In his biography of Emperor Claudius, the second-century Roman historian Suetonius tells us that, in 49 CE, Claudius expelled the Jews from Rome: "Because the Jews of Rome were indulging in constant riots at the instigation of Chrestus, he [Claudius] expelled them from the city" (*Claudius,* 25:4). It is not clear exactly what these riots were about; given the description of a riot in Ephesus that we find in Acts 19, it is possible that many of the rioters themselves were not sure what the riots were about! Many scholars, however, suspect that the riots of which Suetonius speaks may have begun as conflicts in Rome's synagogues between Jews who were preaching the Christian gospel and Jews who denied that Jesus was the Messiah. Whatever the cause of the expulsion, the result was that both Jews and Jewish Christians—who were indistinguishable to Romans—were forced out of the city. When the Jews began returning to Rome upon the death of Claudius in 54 CE, the Christians among them returned to a church led wholly by Gentile Christians.[9] That there were tensions between the Jewish and Gentile members of the Roman church is clear in the letter that Paul wrote to them.

Paul's Purpose

Scholars date Paul's Epistle to the Romans to the latter part of the sixth decade CE, and most believe that he wrote it from the city of Corinth. The goal of the letter is pragmatic. After a brief trip to Jerusalem to deliver relief funds to the victims of famine in Judea (funds that he had been collecting from the churches he visited), Paul hoped to embark on a missionary journey to Spain. Since his route to Spain would take him through Rome, his Letter to the Romans is intended to enlist the Roman church's moral and financial support for that journey (15:22–32).

Because his goal is to win the support of a church with which he is not personally acquainted, Paul uses his Epistle to the Romans as a sort of résumé; he tries to establish his credentials as an apostle and a missionary by clearly stating his views on a number of important issues. The epistle that resulted from this effort is Paul's longest, most mature, and most developed theological statement.

Common Need for Salvation

One of the themes of his Epistle to the Romans, an indication of the Jewish-Gentile tensions in the Roman church at the time, is Paul's insistence that all human beings stand in need of salvation. Paul states this theme at 1:16–17: "[T]he gospel…is the power of God for salvation to everyone who has faith, to the Jew first and also to the Greek. For in it the righteousness of God is revealed through faith for faith." Both Jews and "Greeks" (Gentiles) stand in need of salvation because all human beings, Jewish and Gentile alike, are under the power of sin (3:9–20). Salvation is available to both Jews and Gentiles (2:9–11), but neither can attain it through observance of the Jewish law. Rather, justification comes only by the grace of God, which both elicits and supports faith in Jesus Christ (3:21–25, 28–30). When one receives God's justifying grace, one is liberated from one's slavery to sin and is free to live righteously (6:1–7, 15–16).

The Jewish Question

Another topic that Paul addresses in his Letter to the Romans, an issue that was pressing not only to the Roman church but to all early Christians, is known as the Jewish question: What would become of those Jews who had not converted to Christianity? This question troubled early Christians because they recognized that Christianity had begun as a Jewish movement, that Jesus himself was a Jew, and that the God whom Jesus had addressed as his Father was also the God of Abraham, Isaac, and Jacob. If salvation came only through faith that Jesus was the risen Christ, which the majority of Jews did not believe, did that mean that God had forsaken the chosen people?

Paul's response to the Jewish question is both thoughtful and sensitive. First, he stresses that the revelation of God through Jesus in no way supplants the revelation of God in the Hebrew scriptures; any and all promises that God made to the Jewish people in those scriptures still hold (3:1–4). The reason why most Jews did not accept Jesus as the Messiah, he explains, had to do with the nature of their Judaism; their long observance of the Mosaic Law led them to think that salvation could come through works rather than through faith (9:30–33). Still, he warns the Gentiles not to think that they are somehow superior to the Jews; were it not for the Jewish root, there would be no Gentile Christian branch (11:13–18). Ultimately, Paul's conclusion is that God has not rejected the chosen people (11:1–2); God has temporarily hardened their hearts so that the message of Christianity might spread beyond Israel to the Gentiles, but eventually all of Israel will be saved as well (11:25–29).

The Body of Christ

Finally, in the paraenesis section of his Epistle to the Romans, Paul reinforces the themes discussed above by urging the Christians in Rome toward unity and mutual support. He creates a memorable image of the Christian church as the body of Christ; just as a human body has many different parts, each of which serves its own important purpose, so the church has many different kinds of people with many different roles to play, but they are

251

all unified by their faith (12:3–8). Mindful of his own persecution at secular hands, and perhaps also mindful of Claudius's expulsion of the Roman Jews, Paul exhorts the Roman Christians to accept the authority of those whom God has deemed fitting to hold power over them. Do good, he seems to say, and one need fear nothing from authorities either secular or divine (13:1–10).

G. Colossians and Ephesians

Ephesus was a major city in Asia Minor where, on his third missionary journey, Paul had preached for some twenty-seven months (Acts 19). Colossae was a small town not far from Ephesus, which Paul seems never to have visited (Col 2:1–2).

Authenticity Questioned

Biblical scholars are divided on whether Paul himself actually wrote the epistles to the Colossians and the Ephesians. Pauline authorship of the Letter to the Ephesians is questioned on the grounds that the author of Ephesians clearly seems to have used the Letter to the Colossians as a source; of Ephesians' 155 verses, seventy-three of them contain phrases used in Colossians. Since Paul was not in the habit of reusing his own material, the dependence of Ephesians on Colossians suggests that the former was the work of someone other than Paul.[10]

Many scholars also regard the Letter to the Colossians as Deuteropauline, for a number of reasons.[11] One has to do with vocabulary; the Epistle to the Colossians contains thirty-four words that occur nowhere else in the New Testament, and an additional twenty-eight words that do not occur in any of the undisputedly Pauline epistles. Another reason has to do with literary style; the Epistle to the Colossians lacks the rhetorical elegance of the undisputedly Pauline texts. Most important, however, are a number of subtle yet significant theological shifts that occur in the Letter to the Colossians. First, whereas Paul's other works emphasize the kingdom of God, Colossians speaks of the kingdom of the Son (1:13), a shift from a theocentric (God-centered) emphasis to a christocentric (Christ-centered) emphasis—at least with regard to how the kingdom is characterized. Second, whereas Romans had developed the metaphor of the church as the (whole) body of Christ, Colossians stresses that Christ is the head and that the church is (the rest of) the body (1:18; 2:18–19). Third, the undisputedly Pauline letters tend toward a form of adoptionist Christology, in that they typically stress the idea that Jesus was exalted to the status of Messiah *by means of* his resurrection. For instance, Paul asserts in Romans that Jesus "was declared to be Son of God...by resurrection from the dead" (1:4), and in Philippians he asserts that, after Jesus' death on the cross, God "highly exalted him and gave him the name that is above every other name" (2:8–9). In contrast, Colossians 1:15–20 presents a well-developed preexistence Christology reminiscent of the prologue to the Gospel of John: "[Jesus] is the image of the invisible God, the firstborn of all creation; for in him all things in heaven and on earth were created."* Finally, the author of the Epistle to the Colossians portrays Paul's own suffering for the gospel as "completing what is lacking in Christ's afflictions" (1:22–26). The idea here seems to be that Jesus' sacrifice was somehow insufficient, and that Paul's own suffering completes the work that Jesus had begun in order to achieve the salvation of human beings. Although Paul suffered often for the gospel, in none of his other letters did Paul ever suggest that Jesus' work was incomplete or that his own suffering had salvific value. Thus, this third shift in Pauline theology suggests to many scholars that the Letter to the Colossians was written by a disciple of Paul after Paul's death, as a reflection on the apostle's martyrdom. While none of the foregoing points taken by itself would clearly tell against Pauline authorship, all of them taken together have made many scholars doubt that the Epistle to the Colossians is the work of the apostle himself.

---

* The fact that Colossians seems to manifest a preexistence Christology does not, in itself, entail that Paul did not write it. For some passages in undisputedly Pauline letters suggest that Paul thought of Jesus as preexistent; see, for example, 2 Corinthians 8:9 and Philippians 2:6. The correct interpretation of such passages is a matter of much debate. The important point here is that, even if Paul did think of Jesus as preexistent, his letters typically focus on Jesus' exalted status at the *present* time—the time between Jesus' resurrection from the dead and his anticipated return. Thus, Colossians' stress on Jesus as the firstborn agent of creation is, at the very least, uncharacteristic of Paul.

Syncretism

The main purpose of the Epistle to the Colossians is to warn the Christians in Colossae against the dangers of syncretism, that is, the blending of faiths. It seems that some of the Christians in Colossae had been merging their Christian beliefs with the beliefs of both pagan religions (2:8) and Judaizers (2:11). The result was a warped version of Christianity according to which Christ's sacrifice was not enough to secure human beings' salvation; Christians thus had to practice asceticism and engage in mysterious rites in order to help angelic forces defeat demonic forces (2:16–19, 20–21). In response to this problem, the Epistle to the Colossians stresses the preeminence of Christ; as the first-born of all creation, Christ has power and authority over all things (1:15–17). Thus, nothing is needed for salvation but faith in Christ, to whom all things answer and through whom all people are free (3:1–4, 11).

The Trinity

The Epistle to the Ephesians reiterates Colossians' theme of the preeminence of Christ (1:20–23). But it also stresses the idea that Jews and Gentiles are reconciled through Christ; by making salvation available to all, the death and resurrection of Jesus achieved the divine will by uniting the chosen people with the rest of the nations (2:11–16; 3:6). The Letter to the Ephesians also makes a number of references to what would later come to be known as the Trinity. The Trinity is a Christian conception of the Deity that acknowledges, based on scriptural evidence, that there are personal relationships within that Deity. Thus, the Trinity is God conceived as three distinct Persons—the Father, the Son, and the Holy Spirit—sharing one and the same divine nature. While the word *Trinity* is not used in the New Testament, Paul seems to have had this idea in mind at 2 Corinthians 13:14, where he writes: "The grace of the Lord Jesus Christ, the love of God, and the communion of the Holy Spirit be with all of you." Similarly, in three different passages, the Epistle to the Ephesians seems to distinguish three distinct manifestations of the Deity (2:17–20; 3:14–17; 4:4–6).

H. The Pastoral Epistles: 1 and 2 Timothy and Titus

The Latin word *pastor* means "shepherd." The letters 1 and 2 Timothy and Titus are known as the pastoral epistles because they are primarily concerned with the well-being of church leaders and of the "flocks" to which they tend. Each of the three pastoral epistles purports to be a letter from Paul to an associate who is serving as Paul's delegate in a local church community; Timothy is Paul's representative in Ephesus and Titus is Paul's representative in Crete.[12]

One of the issues of concern in the pastoral epistles is the spread of false teachings within the church. It seems that a number of people had been led to believe that Christianity demanded a severe form of asceticism, and were thus abstaining from sexual relations, certain kinds of food, and alcohol (1 Tim 4:3; 5:23; Titus 1:15). Some Christians may also have fallen under the influence of proto-Gnosticism. To make clear what this means, we need to say a few words about Gnosticism.

Gnosticism

Gnosticism was a set of closely related religious movements that emerged in their fullest form in the second century CE, but which seem to have originated in the first century CE. The practitioners of Gnosticism—known as Gnostics—believed that the material world is evil, but that human souls are divine. Thus, Gnostics held that human beings' salvation could be achieved only through the possession of secret knowledge (*gnosis* in Greek) that would liberate their souls from imprisonment in the material world. Although Gnosticism arose independently of Christianity, by the second century CE there were many Christians who were blending the beliefs of Christianity with those of Gnosticism. The Gnostic Christianity that resulted was condemned as heretical by the leaders of the Christian church.

The author of the pastoral epistles appears to have been combating proto-Gnosticism, that is, an early—and thus not yet fully developed—form of Gnostic Christianity. For the pastoral epistles criticize two beliefs that some Christians had come to hold, both of which have a distinctly Gnostic ring to them. One was the belief that the resurrection of the dead had "already taken place" (2 Tim 2:18). On a Gnostic interpretation of Christianity, the resurrection promised by Christianity was not a miraculous transformation that would occur in the future, but rather a sort of spiritual illumination that could be attained in the present by acquisition of the secret knowledge that Gnostics claimed to possess. The other belief had to do with "speculations" about Jewish myths and genealogies (1 Tim 1:3–4; 4:7). Elaborate mythologies were a hallmark of Gnosticism; the secret knowledge that Gnostics claimed to possess almost always included stories about the origin and history of both divine and evil beings. In the face of such heterodoxy—that is, subscription to nonstandard beliefs—among his Christian audience, the author of the pastoral epistles stresses the importance of preserving and teaching "sound doctrine" (Titus 2:1), by which he meant the gospel as it was handed down from the apostles. He thus urges the letters' recipients to "give attention to the public reading of scripture, to exhorting, to teaching" (1 Tim 4:13).

Church Leadership

The pastoral epistles also discuss the qualifications for various positions of leadership within the church. In order to hold the office of *episkopos* (literally "overseer," but translated as "bishop"), one must be intellectually and morally "above reproach" (1 Tim 3:1–7; Titus 1:5–9). The office of *episkopos* was to be held by a *presbyteros* (elder), of which there were usually several in a given church community. The elders probably served as priests, and the *episkopos* was the recognized leader among the elders, to whose authority the others deferred. Finally, the office of *diakonos* (literally "servant," translated as "deacon") seems to have been a lower position; the deacons probably assisted the elders in their ministrations to the community (1 Tim 3:8–10). In the early church, the office of deacon seems to have been open to women as well as to men (1 Tim 3:11; see also Rom 16:1). This discussion of church offices in the pastoral epistles suggests a shift in the organization of the early church. Church leadership had at first been charismatic, that is, it had been based on the de facto authority of the apostles. By the time the pastoral epistles were written, however, the offices of church leadership were at least on their way to becoming institutionalized.

Finally, the author of the pastoral epistles stresses the importance of proper Christian conduct. Christians should treat their elders with respect, and Christian slaves should be good to their masters (1 Tim 5:1; 6:1). All Christians should be kindly, patient, and gentle toward others (2 Tim 2:24–26), and they should submit to the authority of their rulers (Titus 3:1–2).

Authenticity Debated

Scholars have traditionally regarded the pastoral epistles as Deuteropauline, for several reasons. First, the apostle Paul both spoke and wrote in vernacular *Koiné,* the common form of Greek (actually a mixture of various Greek dialects) that was in use throughout the Mediterranean world following the conquests of Alexander the Great. The pastoral epistles, on the other hand, were written in a more refined, literary form of Greek. Second, the vocabulary in the pastoral epistles is uncharacteristic of Paul; roughly one-third of the vocabulary used in the pastoral epistles is not found in any of the undisputedly Pauline texts. For example, the pastoral epistles contain five occurrences of the phrase *pistos ho logos,* "the saying is sure" (1 Tim 1:15; 3:1; 4:9; 2 Tim 2:11; Titus 3:8), a phrase that Paul never used in his other letters. Again, the pastoral epistles emphasize theological terms (such as piety, good conscience, and sound teaching) that do not appear anywhere in the undisputedly Pauline letters, whereas the theological terms that occur most frequently in the undisputedly Pauline letters (such as cross, freedom, and covenant) are absent in the pastoral epistles. Finally, the content of the pastoral epistles suggests that they were written at a time when church leadership had achieved a definite hierarchical structure, which most scholars believe was probably not the case until the subapostolic age—a generation after the apostle Paul's lifetime.

For reasons such as those cited above, most biblical scholars since the nineteenth century have doubted that Paul himself actually wrote the pastoral epistles. However, there is a minority of scholars who argue against this traditional view of the pastoral epistles. For instance, Luke Timothy Johnson has noted that, because each of the pastoral epistles—like every one of Paul's letters—was written in response to a distinct situation, it is unfair of scholars to lump them together as a single literary unit and then ask whether they are or are not the work of Paul himself. He argues that statistical studies of the vocabulary used in the pastoral epistles are misleading, for they fail to take into consideration (1) how small the sample size is, given the brevity of the pastoral epistles; (2) the fact that Paul's vocabulary also varies widely across the undisputedly Pauline letters; and (3) the specific subject matter that the pastoral epistles address. This last point is particularly significant. As Johnson observes, the stylistic elements of the pastoral epistles that strike many scholars as non-Pauline are clustered in precisely those parts of the letters that deal with issues unique to the pastoral epistles, issues that Paul never had the need to address in his other letters. Thus, it is not surprising that Paul should here use words and literary conventions that he does not use elsewhere.

Johnson also offers several reasons why the pastoral epistles' allusions to a hierarchical order of church leadership do not necessarily demonstrate that those epistles date to the subapostolic era. First, the offices of church leadership touched on in 1 Timothy and Titus—there is no mention of them in 2 Timothy—closely resemble the offices of leadership in the synagogues of first-century Diaspora Judaism. Second, Paul himself refers to the office of overseer at Philippians 1:1 and to the office of deacon at both Philippians 1:1 and Romans 16:1. Third, a general concern regarding the role of authority figures in local churches is a common aspect of the undisputedly Pauline letters (see Rom 12:8; 1 Cor 6:2–6; 12:28; 16:15–17; Gal 6:6; 1 Thess 5:12). Thus, according to Johnson, the elements of the pastoral epistles that some scholars take as evidence of Deuteropauline authorship do not, in fact, demonstrate that Paul was not the author of these letters. Instead, he believes that the pastoral epistles have the distinctive characteristics that they do at least in part because Paul was here addressing topics about which he had not had occasion to write elsewhere, and because the circumstances under which the pastoral epistles were written called for the use of literary conventions of which Paul's other letters had no need.

The issue of whether or not Paul himself wrote the disputed epistles (2 Thessalonians, Colossians, Ephesians, 1 and 2 Timothy, and Titus) will most likely never be resolved. Since there is both evidence for and evidence against Pauline authorship of these letters, scholars will continue to disagree about which pieces of evidence are most compelling. However, we should close this chapter by returning to an important point that we made at the outset: When scholars question the Pauline authorship of a given letter, they are not questioning the apostolic authority of that letter. Even if some of the letters attributed to Paul were in fact written by one or more of his associates, those letters are nonetheless Pauline in their inspiration, in their objective, and in the basic tenets of their theology. That the disputed letters bear the spirit of the apostle Paul is perhaps best demonstrated by the fact that those letters achieved canonical status, which means that the early church regarded them as being just as authoritative as those letters the Pauline authorship of which is not disputed.

14

Epistles and Revelation

Thus far, our examination of the New Testament has focused on the gospels, the Book of Acts, and the Pauline epistles. In this final chapter, we shall survey the remaining books of the New Testament. Eight of these books are considered epistles, and we shall consider them under three headings: the Letter to the Hebrews, the catholic epistles, and the Johannine epistles. We shall end this chapter with an examination of the book that falls last in the New Testament canon: the Revelation to John.

I. HEBREWS

Although it is considered an epistle, the Book of Hebrews is really more of a theological treatise than it is a letter. A tradition dating to the second century CE has attributed Hebrews to Paul. Hebrews does contain elements of Pauline theology, and it may date to the same time period as the Pauline epistles, but few scholars regard it as the work of the apostle Paul. Like the pastoral epistles, Hebrews is written in a much more literary form of Greek than the *Koiné* in which Paul wrote. There is also internal evidence suggesting that Hebrews was written in the subapostolic age. The author and audience appear to be second-generation Christians who have received the gospel as it was passed down from the apostles (2:3). There is a reference to the memory of church leaders whose lives seem to have ended (13:7). Finally, while the author refers to a period of persecution, that period seems already to have passed (10:32–33).

Platonic Influence

Another reason why scholars doubt that Hebrews was written by Paul is that its author seems to be very well versed in Platonic philosophy, something that is not evidenced in the undisputedly Pauline texts. The Greek philosopher Plato (428–348 BCE) was a metaphysical dualist; he posited that the world was made up of two distinct realms, the visible and the intelligible. The visible realm, which we experience through our senses, is physical, changing, and imperfect. The intelligible realm, which can only be accessed by the soul's power of reason, is immaterial, unchanging, and perfect. All things in the visible realm (these books, those horses) are mere shadows or imitations of the ideal "forms" that exist in the intelligible realm (the ideal Book, the ideal Horse). While particular things in the visible realm undergo change (these books will deteriorate, those horses will age and die), the ideal forms are eternal (the definitions of Book and Horse cannot deteriorate or die).

In a number of passages, the author of Hebrews seems to have been influenced by Platonic dualism. He characterizes the Son as a reflection and imprint of God (1:3), just as Plato characterized things that exist in the visible realm as shadows or reflections of the forms that exist in the ideal realm. He asserts that the "true tent" of the Lord exists in heaven (the ideal realm), not on earth (the visible realm) (8:2). He distinguishes heavenly things from the "sketches" of them on earth (9:23–24). He asserts that the Jewish law "has only a *shadow* of the good things to come and not the *true form* of these realities" (10:1; emphasis added). Finally, he explains that visible created things are "made from things that are not visible" (11:3). This evidence of Platonic dualism in Hebrews has led some scholars to think that its author may have been associated with Alexandria, where the study of ancient Greek philosophy was actively pursued. Some have suggested that the author of Hebrews may have been Apollos, an Alexandrian Jewish convert to Christianity and a contemporary of Paul (see Acts 18:24–28; 1 Cor 16:12).[1]

Purpose

The audience for which Hebrews was written seems to have been a group of Jewish Christians who were on the verge of giving up their Christian faith and returning to traditional Judaism. In an effort to prevent this, the author of Hebrews tries to persuade his audience that Christianity is superior to Judaism. His thesis is that God has been better and more fully revealed through Jesus Christ than God was revealed through the Hebrew scriptures. Thus, he argues that Jesus is superior to the angels, for only Jesus received the name of Son (1:3b–14). He also argues that Jesus is superior to Moses in the same way that the son of a household is superior to a household servant (3:1–6). Finally, he argues that Jesus is superior to the high priests of Jerusalem. Although Jesus was a human being, he was unlike the Jewish high priests in that he was without sin (2:14–18; 4:14–15). While the Jewish high priests served limited terms of office, God has appointed Jesus as a priest forever (5:5–10; 7:11–17). Whereas the Jewish high priests regularly offered animal sacrifices in the Temple, Jesus offered the perfect, eternal sacrifice of himself (9:11–14, 24–26).

Melchizedek

Quoting Psalm 110, the author of Hebrews also characterizes Jesus as a priest "according to the order of Melchizedek" (5:6). Melchizedek was a mysterious character mentioned only once in the Torah; he was a king of Salem who had blessed Abraham, and to whom Abraham had paid a tithe (Gen 14:17–20). At 7:1–10, the author of Hebrews interprets the significance of Melchizedek. The name Melchizedek literally means "King of Righteousness," but he was also the "king of peace" (Salem = Hebrew *shalom* = "peace"). Noting the fact that neither Melchizedek's birth nor his death is recorded, the author of Hebrews infers that Melchizedek was a priest forever, "having neither beginning of days nor end of life." Finally, because he blessed Abraham and received a tithe from him, Melchizedek must have been superior even to the father of Judaism, for it is "beyond dispute that the inferior is blessed by the superior." By asserting that Jesus is a priest according to the order of Melchizedek and that Melchizedek is superior to Abraham, the author of Hebrews thus implies that Jesus is superior to Abraham.

When we read this passage, we must remember that Jesus was not born into a priestly family; Jesus (through Joseph) was a member of the tribe of Judah, whereas high priests traditionally came from the Zadokite line of the Levites. In an effort to establish Jesus as the ideal high priest, the author of Hebrews uses the story of Melchizedek not only to assert the superiority of Jesus to Abraham, but also to defeat a potential objection that the audience of Hebrews was likely to raise—namely, that Jesus was not qualified to be a high priest because he was not of priestly descent. The author of Hebrews thus presents Melchizedek as the founder of an eternal order of priesthood that is not based on descent, and makes Jesus a member of that order by applying to him the quote from Psalm 110.[2]

The author of Hebrews further attempts to dissuade his audience from abandoning their Christianity by stressing the values of Christian faith. He asserts that faith allows a person entry into the heavenly sanctuary that Jesus-as-high-priest has opened by means of his perfect sacrifice (10:19–23). He also gives a roll call of the faithful (11:2–40), citing the great faith of such figures as Abraham, Isaac, Jacob, and Moses. While he lauds the faith of the ancestors, the author points out that they died without receiving the land that they were promised—evidence, in the author's eyes, that the true reward for a faithful life lies not on earth, but in heaven (11:13–16, 39–40).

II. THE CATHOLIC EPISTLES

We now turn to epistles in the Petrine tradition (1 and 2 Pet) and the Family of Jesus tradition (James and Jude). The letters 1 and 2 Peter, James, and Jude are collectively referred to as the catholic epistles (or general epistles). The word *catholic* means "universal" or "widespread." It is applied to 1 and 2 Peter, James, and Jude because these letters are addressed, not to a particular church community, but to the entire Christian church.

A. 1 Peter

The earliest of the catholic epistles seems to be 1 Peter. The main purpose of this letter is to give hope and encouragement to Christians who are suffering persecution. The author assures his readers that, though they may be suffering now, their faith will secure the salvation of their souls (1:4–9). He reminds them that those who suffer for the truth are blessed (3:13–16), and he likens the persecution they are experiencing to the suffering that Christ endured (4:1–19). While this letter purports to have been written by the apostle Peter in the city of Rome (referred to by the code name Babylon at 5:13), scholarly opinion is divided as to its authorship. On the one hand, extrabiblical sources agree that Peter spent the last two years of his life in Rome, where he was martyred in 65 CE. Thus, Petrine authorship of 1 Peter is suggested by the facts that (1) Peter is known to have been in Rome in the mid-seventh decade, and (2) Nero is known to have been persecuting Christians at this time. On the other hand, Nero's persecution of Christians was confined to Rome, whereas the persecution that 1 Peter addresses seems to have been spread throughout the empire (4:12; 5:9). Again, the apostle Peter was a Hebrew whose knowledge of Greek would have been limited to the vernacular *Koiné*, but 1 Peter is written in highly literary Greek, and it quotes the Septuagint rather than the Hebrew scriptures. Thus, some scholars suspect that 1 Peter may have been the work of an anonymous Roman Christian who wrote under Peter's name sometime after the apostle's martyrdom.[3]

B. James and Jude

The letters James and Jude are both thought to have been written in the late first century CE. The Letter of James is primarily concerned to correct a misunderstanding of the teaching of the apostle Paul. In his Letter to the Romans, Paul had stressed that justification comes not through works—by which he meant obedience to the Jewish law—but through faith in Christ (3:28). Apparently, some Christians interpreted Paul's teaching to mean that it was sufficient to profess faith in Christ without adhering to the moral standards embodied in the gospel. In order to counter this misinterpretation, the author of the Letter of James admonishes Christians to "be doers of the word, and not merely hearers who deceive themselves" (1:22). He rebukes those who are Christians in name only, who "say [they] have faith but do not have works," and he warns them that "faith without works is...dead" (2:14–26). This letter has traditionally been attributed to James the brother of Jesus (see Mark 6:3; Gal 1:19). While some scholars find reason to accept this attribution as accurate, others point to the fact that James is thought to have been martyred in 62 CE. In 62 CE, the apostle Paul was still living and the Christian church was still a fairly small group of people, virtually all of whom were poor. Because the Letter of James addresses a serious distortion of the teachings of the apostle Paul, and because its attack on wealth (5:1–6) suggests that a fair number of wealthy persons had been converted to Christianity by the time it was written, many scholars think that a significant amount of time must have elapsed between the lives of the apostles and the writing of the Epistle of James. Thus, many scholars would date the Letter of James to the subapostolic era (70 CE or later).[4]

The author of the Letter of Jude, who identifies himself as "a servant of Jesus Christ and brother of James" (v. 1), has traditionally been identified with Judas, the brother of Jesus mentioned at Mark 6:3 (not to be confused with Judas Iscariot). Some scholars question whether this letter is the work of a brother of Jesus, based largely on internal evidence regarding when the letter was written. At verses 17–18, the author calls upon his readers to "remember the predictions of the apostles of our Lord Jesus Christ." This passage suggests both that the author of the letter does not count himself as an apostle (since he refers to them in the third person rather than the first) and that some time has passed since the apostles were alive and teaching (hence their predictions must now be remembered). Evidence regarding the date of the letter can also be gleaned from the letter's purpose, which is to attack false teachings. While the letter is not clear on the views of those whom it attacks, it does refer to "intruders...who pervert the grace of our God into licentiousness and deny our only Master and Lord, Jesus Christ" (v. 4). The false teachers here would appear to be practitioners of an early form of Gnosticism; they believed that their secret knowledge was the key to salvation (leading them to deny that the Christ was the means to salvation) and that their possession of that knowledge exempted them from the moral requirements of Christianity (leading to licentiousness). Since Gnosticism did not begin to pose a threat to Christian orthodoxy until the subapostolic era, and since the author of the Epistle of Jude seems not to have been of the same generation as the apostles, this letter is also dated to the subapostolic era.[5]

C. 2 Peter

Little is known about the author or the date of 2 Peter. Scholars are quite certain that it was not the work of the apostle Peter, for several reasons. First, supposing that the apostle Peter did write the letter known as 1 Peter, differences in vocabulary and literary style make clear that 2 Peter was not written by the same person who wrote 1 Peter. Moreover, 2 Peter was written at a time when Paul's letters had come to be regarded as scripture by Christians, and were being distorted in the interpretations of false teachers (3:15b–16); neither is likely to have been the case during the apostle Peter's lifetime. Finally, like the Letter of Jude, 2 Peter seems primarily concerned to argue against proto-Gnosticism. Indeed, most of the material in Jude verses 4–18 has been incorporated in 2 Peter 2:1–18 and 3:1–3. This dependence of 2 Peter on the Epistle of Jude indicates a date for 2 Peter sometime after the Epistle of Jude was written.[6]

III. THE JOHANNINE EPISTLES

The author of the epistles attributed to John does not name himself; 1 John does not even contain the standard opening or closing of a letter, and the author of 2 John and 3 John refers to himself simply as "the elder" (2 John 1; 3 John 1). Still, the vocabulary, literary style, and theology of these three epistles strongly suggest that they were written by the same individual or school who wrote the Gospel of John. Little is known about when these Johannine epistles were written, but they could conceivably have been separated by a number of years. For instance, some scholars would date 1 John to as early as 80 CE, 2 John to 95 or 96 CE, and 3 John to as late as 110 CE.

A. 1 and 2 John

The primary concern in the first two Johannine epistles is to combat the heretical movement of Docetism, which was a form of Gnostic Christianity. Docetists believed that human flesh—along with everything else in the physical world—is evil, something with which the divine would have no contact. On the basis of this view, the Docetists denied the Christian doctrine of the incarnation, that is, the belief that God had taken human form in the person of Jesus Christ. Instead, the Docetists argued that Christ was a purely divine, purely spiritual being who only *appeared* or *seemed* to be human. (Docetism's name derives from the Greek verb *dokein*, "to seem.")[7] In order to check the spread of this heresy, the author of the Johannine epistles stresses that the Christ was a flesh-and-blood human being. He tells his audience that "every spirit that confesses that Jesus Christ has come in the flesh is from God, and every spirit that does not confess Jesus is not from God" (1 John 4:2). He insists that Jesus Christ came "not with the water [of baptism] only but with the water and the blood" (1 John 5:6), and he characterizes those who deny that Jesus came in the flesh as deceivers and antichrists (1 John 2:18–22; 2 John 7). It has been suggested that, in their attacks on Docetism, the Johannine epistles were designed to balance the preexistence Christology of the Gospel of John. In his Gospel, the Johannine author had emphasized the divinity of Jesus; in the epistles, he emphasizes Jesus' humanity instead.

B. 3 John

The third of the Johannine epistles offers us a look into the internal conflicts of a church community. In a brief note to an individual named Gaius, the elder refers to a member of Gaius's community named "Diotrephes, who likes to put himself first [and] does not acknowledge [the elder's] authority" (v. 9). It seems this Diotrephes had been slandering the name of the elder in the latter's absence, had refused to provide room and board to representatives whom the elder had sent to the community, and had prohibited others in the community from taking in those representatives. Neither the standing of Diotrephes in the local church community nor that of Gaius is made clear; we are not told whether they hold church offices or not. However, the elder's authority over this community is made clear in his suggestion that he might deal personally with the problems caused by Diotrephes: "[I]f I come, I will call attention to what he is doing in spreading false charges against us" (v. 10). While the elder may very well have been planning a visit to the community in question, he seems to have regarded the mere suggestion of his coming—which he could expect Gaius to relay to Diotrephes—as sufficient to bring about the desired changes in Diotrephes's behavior.

IV. THE REVELATION TO JOHN

Authorship and Date

The Revelation to John is a Christian apocalyptic work. The author identifies himself by name as John and tells his audience that he has been exiled to the island of Patmos (in the Aegean Sea) for preaching the Christian gospel (1:4, 9). While some have tried to identify this author with John the apostle, son of Zebedee, no evidence internal to the Book of Revelation supports this identification.

The Book of Revelation was written for Christians in Asia Minor (1:10–11) who were suffering persecution (6:9–11; 17:6). While the date of its writing is difficult to specify, most scholars are inclined to place the writing of Revelation in the early 90s CE, during the reign of Emperor Domitian (81–96 CE). Domitian was the son of Vespasian and the younger brother of Titus. One reason for dating Revelation to the reign of Domitian is an ancient Christian

Western Asia Minor

tradition according to which Domitian was a brutal persecutor of
Christians. Unfortunately, historical evidence of such persecution
under Domitian is scanty and, at best, inconclusive.[8] Yet there is
another reason to believe that Revelation was written during
Domitian's reign, and it has to do with the Roman imperial cult.

The Imperial Cult

From the time of Julius Caesar, the Romans believed that their
emperors joined the gods after they died.[9] It was thus common for
altars and temples to be erected to deceased emperors and for sacrifices to be made in their honor. Thus began the imperial cult, the
Roman practice of worshiping emperors as divine beings. Although
the cult originated in the offering of divine honors to the *genius*
(spirit) of emperors who were deceased, this would soon change.
Emperor Augustus (Julius's adopted son and heir) did not claim to
be a god per se, but he did take the phrase *Divi Filius* (Son of God)
as part of his official title, inscribing it on coins and statues throughout the empire. Later, Emperor Gaius Caligula (37–41 CE) made
overt claims to divinity while he was alive, demanding and receiving
divine honors. Because many Romans found Gaius's claims to divinity distasteful—including, no doubt, the members of the praetorian
guard who assassinated him—his successor Claudius (41–54 CE)
tactfully denied his subjects permission to dedicate temples or
priesthoods to him while he lived. Still, Gaius had set a precedent;
it was possible for a Roman emperor to claim divine status during
his lifetime. According to the second-century Roman historian
Suetonius, Emperor Domitian acted upon this precedent; he
demanded divine honors and insisted on being addressed and
referred to as *Dominus et Deus Noster* (Our Lord and God). Thus, the
Book of Revelation may date to the reign of Domitian, for Christians
of his time may very well have regarded Domitian as having taken
the imperial cult to new heights of blasphemy.

The fact that the Book of Revelation is addressed to seven
churches in Asia Minor further suggests a date for that book near
the close of the first century. Historical evidence indicates that,
during Domitian's reign, an intense rivalry broke out between the
three largest cities of western Asia Minor: Ephesus, Pergamum,

and Smyrna—three cities that are also listed among those to which the Book of Revelation is addressed (1:11). The rivalry took the form of a competition in which each city strove to outdo the others in its support of the imperial cult. This meant trying to secure the emperor's permission to build the largest temple in the region, maintaining the largest imperial priesthood, claiming the largest number of honors and sacrifices paid to the emperor by the citizens, and so on. The winner of such a competition stood to earn the favor of the emperor and to gain economically—in the form of tax exemptions, for example. Christians who refused to participate in the imperial cult of such cities would have been subject to persecution by the local officials. Thus, even if Domitian himself was not the terrible persecutor that Christian tradition has made him out to be, the fact that Christians who lived in Asia Minor during his reign were unwillingly caught up in an "alms race" gives us further reason to believe that the Book of Revelation was written during Domitian's reign.

Consolation for the Persecuted

As we noted in our discussion of the Book of Daniel, scholars believe that apocalyptic literature is produced in times of persecution as a means of consoling those who are persecuted. The author of the Book of Revelation thus gives an apocalyptic interpretation of current events, offering his readers the hopeful message that the present world order—and thus their suffering—will soon come to an end, and that they will be vindicated by the Lord (1:1, 3; 22:10). The structure of the work is interesting in itself. It begins with a brief prologue (1:1-8) and an account of the author's commissioning by "one like the Son of Man" (1:9-20; compare Dan 7:13). Next come seven letters to seven churches in Asia Minor, dictated to the author by the Son of Man (2:1—3:22). The author then recounts a series of visions that were revealed to him. These include the breaking of the seven seals on a scroll (4:1—8:5); events following upon the sounding of seven trumpets (8:6—11:19); visions of a lamb and a beast (12:1—15:4); the pouring out of seven bowls of wrath (15:5—16:21); the fall of Babylon and the erection of a new Jerusalem (17:1—22:5). The work closes with an epilogue in which the author assures his audience that their redeemer is "coming soon" (22:6–21).

Why was the author of Revelation so fixated on the number seven? Scholars have suggested one intriguing possibility: Jewish Christians might have recognized the number seven as an allusion to the *menorah*, the seven-headed lampstand that the Israelites had been ordered by the Lord to construct for the tabernacle (Exod 25:31–40), and which had been incorporated in Solomon's Temple (1 Kgs 7:49). Recall that, in 164 BCE, the forces of Judas Maccabeus recaptured the Jerusalem Temple from the forces of the Seleucid Empire, removed the pagan elements that the Seleucids had introduced there, and rededicated the Temple to the worship of YHWH. Since that time, Jews have celebrated the purification of the Temple in the annual festival of *Hanukkah*, the main symbol of which is the *menorah*. Thus, to those Jewish Christians who could recognize it, the repetition of the number seven in the Book of Revelation may have been a powerful reminder of the chosen people's historic triumph over their pagan oppressors. If so, it would also have served as a symbol of the victory over their Roman persecutors that the Lord would soon bring to Christians.[10]

Historical Symbols in the Book of Revelation

Because the authors of apocalyptic works did their writing in times of persecution in order to bring a message of hope to the persecuted, they often disguised their message in symbolic terms; this was a means of protecting both themselves and their work, should that work fall into the wrong hands. Whereas some people are inclined to regard the heavy symbolism in the Book of Revelation as a literal description of events that are yet to occur, scholars regard many of the visions recounted in Revelation as references to events of the author's time, carefully disguised so that the author's intended audience could recognize them but Romans could not. For instance, on the blowing of the sixth trumpet, the author witnesses the release of four angels who had been "bound at the great river Euphrates" and who lead a cavalry force of two hundred million on a killing spree (9:13–19). Scholars regard this passage as a reference to the Parthian Empire, which bordered the Roman Empire at its easternmost edge along the Euphrates. Since the Parthian Empire was the only serious military threat to Rome at the time, it would have been natural for persecuted Christians to hope for some relief to come from that direction.

Similarly, scholars regard many of the symbols in Revelation 13 as veiled references to contemporary persons and events. The seven-headed beast (vv. 1–4) is taken to be a reference to Rome itself, which was traditionally thought to have been built on seven hills. The "haughty and blasphemous words" uttered by the beast (vv. 5–6) are thought to refer to the imperial cult—specifically, the Roman emperor's claims to be a divine being. The second beast, which "exercises all the authority of the first beast on its behalf, and makes the earth and its inhabitants worship the first beast" (vv. 11–15), stands for the Roman emperor's local representatives in Asia Minor, who were empowered to persecute those who refused to pay divine honors to the emperor.[11] The "mark…of the beast," without which a person could neither buy nor sell (vv. 16–17), is thought to refer to the image and divine title of the emperor that were imprinted on all coins minted by the empire.[12]

We are also told that the number of the beast, which is either 616 or 666 (it varied among ancient texts), "is the number of a person" (v. 18). This is clearly a coded message to Jewish Christians. In the Hebrew language, as in Latin, letters could also be used to stand for numbers. The author of Revelation has given the beast the number 616 because this is the numeric value of the name Nero Caesar when it is written in Hebrew characters. The larger number 666 is the numeric value of the Greek version of Nero's name, Neron Caesar, when it is written in Hebrew characters. Emperor Nero (64–68 CE) would have been a fitting symbol of evil to the audience of the Book of Revelation, both because he had been the first Roman emperor to target Christians for persecution—he blamed them for the great fire of Rome in 64 CE—and also because he was known for demanding divine honors during his lifetime. In fact, the author of Revelation may have intended his audience to identify "the beast" Nero with the current emperor, who was most likely Domitian. This is suggested by the passage at 13:3, in which we are told that one of the seven heads of the beast seemed to have received a mortal wound, but that the wound had healed. This probably alludes to the fact that, after Emperor Nero committed suicide, few people actually saw his corpse. Thus, rumors spread that Nero was still alive, and would one day return to reclaim his throne; later rumors claimed that Nero had died, but that he would come back from the dead to rule Rome once again. Thus, Christians suffering persecution during the reign of Domitian might well have thought that Nero had indeed returned.

Finally, the Book of Revelation suggests that, on "the great day of God the Almighty," a battle will take place between the forces of good and the forces of evil at "the place that in Hebrew is called Harmagedon" (16:14–16). This Harmagedon (also known as Armageddon) is actually *Har Megiddo* (Hill of Megiddo) in Hebrew; it was the name of a fortified city protecting a mountain pass that led from the Mediterranean coast into the central plains of Palestine. Because of its strategic value, Megiddo had been the site of a number of significant battles throughout ancient history. It had been fortified as early as 3500 BCE. It was captured by the Egyptians under Pharaoh Thutmose III in 1468 BCE. It was later controlled by Canaanites; the Song of Deborah mentions it as the site of a battle between the Canaanites and the Israelites (Judg 5:19). It was also the site of the battle between King Josiah of Judah and Pharaoh Neco of Egypt, in which battle King Josiah was slain (2 Kgs 23:29). To the readers of Revelation, then, the oft-bloodied Hill of Megiddo would have been a natural place to expect the cataclysmic battle of battles to take place.[13]

Thus, from the perspective of biblical scholars, the Book of Revelation is not simply a prediction of events that have yet to occur. Rather, it is a heavily symbolic account and interpretation of events that were occurring at the time when the work's author and his audience were living. This does not mean that scholars reject the view that the Book of Revelation has a transcendent origin and value. Instead, it means that biblical scholars find interesting and meaningful parallels between the content of the Book of Revelation and the historical facts of the time, and make the reasonable inference that those historical facts may have played a role in the book's production.

Conclusion

The purpose of this book has been to provide a literary and historical introduction to the Bible. As we noted at the beginning, scholars who study the Bible from the academic standpoint strive to achieve a sort of scientific detachment from their subject, in order that their judgments about the available data will not be unduly biased by their personal beliefs. Thus, when biblical scholars apply the empirical historical method and engage in the various forms of literary criticism that are the tools of their trade, their goal is to try to select, interpret, and evaluate evidence as objectively as a biologist or a physicist would try to do. Once the literary and historical data about the Bible have been analyzed objectively, the results of such an analysis may then be incorporated into the more personal, subjective approach to the scriptures that is commonly taken by persons of faith.

As we have seen, the detached and objective research of biblical scholars has yielded some intriguing results. Literary analysis of the books that constitute the Bible suggests that the Bible is the culmination of the work of many different human beings, some of whom passed stories on orally, some of whom wrote stories down, and some of whom edited the various oral and written traditions into their current form. In considering such theories as the Documentary Hypothesis and the Four Source Hypothesis, we have seen how scholars attempt to reconstruct the process by which biblical works were produced. Finally, we have seen how the findings of archaeology, history, anthropology, and sociology can shed light on such biblical subjects as the Hebrews' Exodus from Egypt, the life of Jesus of Nazareth, and the context in which the Book of Revelation was written. While the available empirical data on such subjects often reveal parallels between the events recounted in the Bible and those of recorded history, that data does not always corroborate the biblical narrative, and sometimes even contradicts it.

To persons for whom this book has truly been a first introduction to scholarly theories about the Bible, some of these findings may be shocking. What, then, is a reader to conclude, especially one who is used to approaching the Bible from the devotional standpoint? If the scholars' theories are correct, what are the implications of those theories for persons of faith? As we bring our discussion of the Bible to a close, I would like to help the reader begin to formulate an answer to these questions.

One might draw the following conclusion: "If the biblical scholars are correct, then the Bible is just a book produced by human beings, and thus possesses no transcendent meaning or value." A person who draws this conclusion takes the findings of biblical scholars as reason to doubt her biblically based faith. I would suggest to the reader that this is the wrong conclusion to draw, because it confuses the academic approach to the Bible with the deflationary approach. As we noted in the first chapter, scholars who raise critical questions about the Bible are not interested in undermining the Bible's value. Rather, they are concerned to understand as much about the Bible as possible. We also noted that most biblical scholars are devoutly religious persons, which means that they are persons who are capable of taking *both* the academic *and* the devotional approach to the Bible. Thus, if we conclude that one can regard the scholarly theories as plausible only if one ceases to entertain the possibility that the Bible has a transcendent origin and value, then we have missed the point of the academic approach.

Of course, one might go to the opposite extreme instead: "Because I believe that the Bible is the inspired word of God, I must regard any scholarly theory that challenges the historical accuracy of the Bible as wholly false." This, I think, is also the wrong conclusion to draw. There is no good reason to assume that one's beliefs about the origin and value of the Bible cannot be reconciled with the sort of evidence that biblical scholars consider. Of course, if one believes that every statement in the Bible is true in the sense of being an objective account of historical events, then one will have a difficult time reconciling that belief with the conclusions of mainline biblical scholars, since the two are often incompatible. But to decide that one will simply reject any theory that conflicts with one's personal beliefs, regardless of the method used to produce that theory or the evidence offered in support of it, is to resolve not to use one's power of reason. For rational beings like ourselves to make such a resolution is unnatural, and probably unhealthy as well.

Is there a conclusion to be drawn that finds a middle ground between these two extremes? There must be, since most biblical scholars themselves find it possible to accept *both* the tenets of their faiths *and* the results of their critical inquiries. I would leave the reader with the suggestion that, if biblical scholarship poses a challenge to the person of faith, it is the challenge of reconciling one's faith with one's reason. This might require one to rethink what it means to say that the Bible was *inspired* or *revealed* by the Deity, but it certainly does not require one to give up one's belief that the Bible has both a transcendent origin and a transcendent value. On the contrary, when a person endeavors to reconcile that which she believes on faith with that which she accepts on the basis of reason, she grapples directly with what theologians rightly call the *mystery* of the divine.

Notes

CHAPTER 1. THE BIBLE AS
LITERATURE AND AS HISTORY

1. The values of the academic approach enumerated here are drawn from Raymond E. Brown, SS, and Sandra M. Schneiders, IHM, "Hermeneutics," in *New Jerome Biblical Commentary*, ed. Raymond E. Brown, SS, Joseph A. Fitzmyer, SJ, and Roland E. Murphy, OCarm (Englewood Cliffs, NJ: Prentice Hall, 1990), 1150; Robert Morgan and John Barton, *Biblical Interpretation* (Oxford: Oxford University Press, 1988), 35–41.

2. On synchronic and diachronic perspectives, see Christian E. Hauer and William A. Young, *An Introduction to the Bible: A Journey into Three Worlds*, 5th ed. (Upper Saddle River, NJ: Prentice Hall, 2001), 2; Richard N. Soulen and R. Kendall Soulen, *Handbook of Biblical Criticism*, 3rd ed. (Louisville, KY: Westminster John Knox Press, 2001), 47.

3. Raymond E. Brown, SS, and Raymond F. Collins, "Canonicity," in *New Jerome Biblical Commentary*, ed. Raymond E. Brown, SS, Joseph A. Fitzmyer, SJ, and Roland E. Murphy, OCarm (Englewood Cliffs, NJ: Prentice Hall, 1990), 1037–50.

4. My characterization of the various types of literary and historical criticism in which biblical scholars engage is based on Hauer and Young, *Introduction to the Bible*, 36–54; Soulen and Soulen, *Handbook of Biblical Criticism*, 61–64, 119–20, 159–60, 164–65, 178–79, 198.

CHAPTER 2. A BRIEF HISTORY OF BIBLICAL INTERPRETATION

1. My survey of early Jewish biblical interpretation is based on the work of Philip S. Alexander in *Oxford Companion to the Bible*, ed. Bruce M. Metzger and Michael D. Coogan (Oxford: Oxford University Press, 1993), 305–10; Louis Jacobs, *A Concise Companion to the Jewish Religion* (Oxford: Oxford University Press, 1999), 154–57, 178–79, 260–64; Raymond E. Brown, SS, Pheme Perkins, and Anthony J. Saldarini, "Apocrypha; Dead Sea Scrolls; Other Jewish Literature," in *New Jerome Biblical Commentary*, ed. Raymond E. Brown, SS, Joseph A. Fitzmyer, SJ, and Roland E. Murphy, OCarm (Englewood Cliffs, NJ: Prentice Hall, 1990), 1055–82; Raymond E. Brown, SS, and Sandra M. Schneiders, IHM, "Hermeneutics," in *New Jerome Biblical Commentary*, 1146–65.

2. My account of early Christian biblical interpretation is based on the work of William Baird, *History of New Testament Research, Volume One: From Deism to Tübingen* (Minneapolis: Fortress Press, 1992), xv–xvii; Brown and Schneiders, "Hermeneutics," 1146–65; Karlfried Froehlich in *Oxford Companion to the Bible*, 311–17; John Kselman, SS, and Ronald D. Witherup, SS, "Modern New Testament Criticism," in *New Jerome Biblical Commentary*, ed. Raymond E. Brown, SS, Joseph A. Fitzmyer, SJ, and Roland E. Murphy, OCarm (Englewood Cliffs, NJ: Prentice Hall, 1990), 1130–45.

3. My survey of medieval and Reformation biblical interpretation is based on the work of Philip S. Alexander in *Oxford Companion to the Bible*, 305–10; Baird, *History of New Testament Research*, xv–xvii; James Barr in *Oxford Companion to the Bible*, 318–24; Jerry H. Bentley in *Oxford Companion to the Bible*, 315–18; Brown and Schneiders, "Hermeneutics," 1146–65; Antony Flew, *Dictionary of Philosophy*, 2nd ed. (New York: St. Martin's Press, 1984), 217–18; Jacobs, *Concise Companion to the Jewish Religion*, 142–43.

4. My survey of modern biblical interpretation is based on the work of Baird, *History of New Testament Research*, 301–7; Kselman and Witherup, "Modern New Testament Criticism,"

1130–45; Robert Morgan and John Barton, *Biblical Interpretation* (Oxford: Oxford University Press, 1988), 47–82; Katherine Doob Sakenfeld in *Oxford Companion to the Bible*, 228–31; Alexa Suelzer, SP, and John Kselman, SS, "Modern Old Testament Criticism," in *New Jerome Biblical Commentary*, ed. Raymond E. Brown, SS, Joseph A. Fitzmyer, SJ, and Roland E. Murphy, OCarm (Englewood Cliffs, NJ: Prentice Hall, 1990), 1113–29.

5. Morgan and Barton, *Biblical Interpretation*, 56.

CHAPTER 3. PREHISTORY: CREATION AND ANCESTRAL LEGENDS

1. B. S. J. Isserlin, *The Israelites* (Minneapolis: Fortress Press, 2001), 206–7.

2. For a fuller treatment of the recurrence of this pattern in Genesis 3—11, see Christian E. Hauer and William A. Young, *An Introduction to the Bible: A Journey into Three Worlds*, 5th ed. (Upper Saddle River, NJ: Prentice Hall, 2001), 67–71.

3. Lawrence Boadt, *Reading the Old Testament: An Introduction* (New York/Mahwah, NJ: Paulist Press, 1984), 116–18; Michael D. Coogan, "In the Beginning: The Earliest History," in *Oxford History of the Biblical World*, ed. Michael D. Coogan (New York: Oxford University Press, 1998), 27–30; Isserlin, *The Israelites*, 232; Victor H. Matthews and Don C. Benjamin, *Old Testament Parallels: Laws and Stories from the Ancient Near East*, 2nd ed. (New York/Mahwah, NJ: Paulist Press, 1997), 9–18, 25–28.

4. I here summarize an argument offered by Wayne T. Pitard. See his essay, "Before Israel: Syria-Palestine in the Bronze Age," in *Oxford History of the Biblical World*, ed. Michael D. Coogan (New York: Oxford University Press, 1998), 36–37.

5. Boadt, *Reading the Old Testament*, 134–35.

6. Pitard, "Before Israel," 37.

7. Ibid., 37–38.

8. Ibid., 37, 73.

CHAPTER 4. THE EXODUS TRADITION

1. Carol A. Redmount, "Bitter Lives: Israel in and out of Egypt," in *Oxford History of the Biblical World*, ed. Michael D. Coogan (New York: Oxford University Press, 1998), 87–88, 96.

2. Ibid., 98–101. See also Wayne T. Pitard, "Before Israel: Syria-Palestine in the Bronze Age," in *Oxford History of the Biblical World*, ed. Michael D. Coogan (New York: Oxford University Press, 1998), 57.

3. B. S. J. Isserlin, *The Israelites* (Minneapolis: Fortress Press, 2001), 62–63.

4. Redmount, "Bitter Lives," 95.

5. Isserlin, *The Israelites*, 52, 232; Victor H. Matthews and Don C. Benjamin, *Old Testament Parallels: Laws and Stories from the Ancient Near East*, 2nd ed. (New York/Mahwah, NJ: Paulist Press, 1997), 85.

6. Redmount, "Bitter Lives," 88–89; Ogden Goelet, "Moses' Egyptian Name," *Bible Review* 19:3 (2003): 14–17.

7. Lawrence Boadt, *Reading the Old Testament: An Introduction* (New York/Mahwah, NJ: Paulist Press, 1984), 166–67.

8. Redmount, "Bitter Lives," 106.

9. Ibid., 105–6.

10. Boadt, *Reading the Old Testament*, 162–63.

11. Redmount, "Bitter Lives," 97, 106. See also Lawrence E. Stager, "Forging an Identity: The Emergence of Ancient Israel," in *Oxford History of the Biblical World*, ed. Michael D. Coogan (New York: Oxford University Press, 1998), 124–25.

12. Redmount, "Bitter Lives," 91.

13. Ibid., 85.

14. I here develop an argument offered by Boadt, *Reading the Old Testament*, 176–81.

15. On apodictic and casuistic laws, see Boadt, *Reading the Old Testament*, 185–86; Christian E. Hauer and William A. Young, *An Introduction to the Bible: A Journey into Three Worlds*, 5th ed. (Upper Saddle River, NJ: Prentice Hall, 2001), 93–95; Richard N. Soulen and R. Kendall Soulen, *Handbook of Biblical Criticism*, 3rd ed. (Louisville, KY: Westminster John Knox Press, 2001), 12, 31.

16. E. P. Sanders, *The Historical Figure of Jesus* (New York: Penguin, 1993), 36. See also Paula Fredriksen, *Jesus of Nazareth, King of the Jews* (New York: Vintage Books, 1999), 197–207.

17. Boadt, *Reading the Old Testament,* 184.

18. Ibid., 191–93.

CHAPTER 5. CONQUEST AND MONARCHY

1. Lawrence Boadt, *Reading the Old Testament: An Introduction* (New York/Mahwah, NJ: Paulist Press, 1984), 374–75.

2. Ibid., 207–9.

3. John J. McDermott, *What Are They Saying About the Formation of Israel?* (New York/Mahwah, NJ: Paulist Press, 1998), 1–2; Lawrence E. Stager, "Forging an Identity: The Emergence of Ancient Israel," in *Oxford History of the Biblical World,* ed. Michael D. Coogan (New York: Oxford University Press, 1998), 127.

4. Jo Ann Hackett, "'There Was No King In Israel': The Era of the Judges," in *Oxford History of the Biblical World,* ed. Michael D. Coogan (New York: Oxford University Press, 1998), 178–79.

5. See Madeleine S. Miller and J. Lane Miller, *Harper's Bible Dictionary,* 7th ed. (New York: Harper & Brothers, 1961), 642–43.

6. My explanation of the three hypotheses regarding Israel's occupation of Canaan is a summary of those presented in McDermott, *Formation of Israel,* 36–45; Stager, "Forging an Identity," 128–40.

7. B. S. J. Isserlin, *The Israelites* (Minneapolis: Fortress Press, 2001), 57.

8. Hackett, "There Was No King In Israel," 202–3.

9. Ibid., 200. See also Stager, "Forging an Identity," 152–54.

10. Stephen L. McKenzie, *King David: A Biography* (New York: Oxford University Press, 2000), 11–16.

11. Ibid., 32–35, 122, 178–79.

12. Carol Meyers, "Kinship and Kingship: The Early Monarchy," in *Oxford History of the Biblical World,* ed. Michael D. Coogan (New York: Oxford University Press, 1998), 253.

13. Boadt, *Reading the Old Testament,* 236–37; Miller and Miller, *Harper's Bible Dictionary,* 692–94.

14. Meyers, "Kinship and Kingship," 261.

15. Boadt, *Reading the Old Testament,* 238.

16. Ibid., 294–96; Miller and Miller, *Harper's Bible Dictionary,* 369–70.

17. Isserlin, *The Israelites,* 82.

18. Edward F. Campbell Jr., "A Land Divided: Judah and Israel from the Death of Solomon to the Fall of Samaria," in *Oxford History of the Biblical World,* ed. Michael D. Coogan (New York: Oxford University Press, 1998), 288.

19. Boadt, *Reading the Old Testament,* 296.

20. Campbell, "A Land Divided," 316–17; K. Lawson Younger Jr., "Israelites in Exile," *Biblical Archaeology Review* 29:6 (2003): 37–42.

CHAPTER 6. THE PROPHETS

1. My account of Jehu's usurpation and its aftermath is a summary of that given by Edward F. Campbell Jr. See his essay, "A Land Divided: Judah and Israel from the Death of Solomon to the Fall of Samaria," in *Oxford History of the Biblical World,* ed. Michael D. Coogan (New York: Oxford University Press, 1998), 300–302.

2. Ibid., 314–16.

3. Mordechai Cogan, "Into Exile: From the Assyrian Conquest of Israel to the Fall of Babylon," in *Oxford History of the Biblical World,* ed. Michael D. Coogan (New York: Oxford University Press, 1998), 329–35; B. S. J. Isserlin, *The Israelites* (Minneapolis: Fortress Press, 2001), 88–89.

4. Cogan, "Into Exile," 346–47.

5. Ibid., 348–56.

6. Ibid., 356–60.

7. Mary Joan Winn Leith, "Israel Among the Nations: The Persian Period," in *Oxford History of the Biblical World,* ed. Michael D. Coogan (New York: Oxford University Press, 1998), 375.

8. Ibid., 375–78.

9. Aelred Cody, OSB, "Haggai, Zechariah, Malachi," in *New*

Jerome Biblical Commentary, ed. Raymond E. Brown, SS, Joseph A. Fitzmyer, SJ, and Roland E. Murphy, OCarm (Englewood Cliffs, NJ: Prentice Hall, 1990), 349–61; Leith, "Israel Among the Nations," 392–93; Madeleine S. Miller and J. Lane Miller, *Harper's Bible Dictionary,* 7th ed. (New York: Harper & Brothers, 1961), 241, 836–37.

10. Cody, "Haggai, Zechariah, Malachi," 349–61; Miller and Miller, *Harper's Bible Dictionary,* 413.

11. Cogan, "Into Exile," 355.

12. Miller and Miller, *Harper's Bible Dictionary,* 473.

CHAPTER 7. SONGS AND WISDOM LITERATURE

1. B. S. J. Isserlin, *The Israelites* (Minneapolis: Fortress Press, 2001), 205–6.

2. Stephen L. McKenzie, *King David: A Biography* (New York: Oxford University Press, 2000), 38–39.

3. Madeleine S. Miller and J. Lane Miller, *Harper's Bible Dictionary,* 7th ed. (New York: Harper & Brothers, 1961), 589–91.

4. My explanation of the different types of psalms is based largely on that of Christian E. Hauer and William A. Young, *An Introduction to the Bible: A Journey into Three Worlds,* 5th ed. (Upper Saddle River, NJ: Prentice Hall, 2001), 161–63.

5. Ibid., 172.

6. Miller and Miller, *Harper's Bible Dictionary,* 694–95.

7. Hauer and Young, *Introduction to the Bible,* 172.

8. Ibid., 173.

9. Miller and Miller, *Harper's Bible Dictionary,* 378–79. See also Hauer and Young, *Introduction to the Bible,* 173–75.

10. Lawrence Boadt, *Reading the Old Testament: An Introduction* (New York/Mahwah, NJ: Paulist Press, 1984), 472–75.

11. Miller and Miller, *Harper's Bible Dictionary,* 587–88.

12. My table is based, in part, on Boadt, *Reading the Old Testament,* 475; Victor H. Matthews and Don C. Benjamin, *Old*

Testament Parallels: Laws and Stories from the Ancient Near East, 2nd ed. (New York/Mahwah, NJ: Paulist Press, 1997), 274–82.

13. Miller and Miller, *Harper's Bible Dictionary,* 337–39.

CHAPTER 8. POSTEXILIC WRITINGS

1. The material in this section on the Persian Empire is drawn primarily from Lawrence Boadt, *Reading the Old Testament: An Introduction* (New York/Mahwah, NJ: Paulist Press, 1984), 431–32; Mary Joan Winn Leith, "Israel Among the Nations: The Persian Period," in *Oxford History of the Biblical World,* ed. Michael D. Coogan (New York: Oxford University Press, 1998), 375–79, 388–89. I am also greatly indebted to Lenore Erickson for helping me to understand Zoroastrianism.

2. See *Funk and Wagnalls New Standard Bible Dictionary,* 3rd ed., ed. Malancthon W. Jacobus, DD, Elbert C. Lane, DD, and Andrew C. Zenos, DD, LLD (Philadelphia: Blakiston, 1936), 46–48.

3. Madeleine S. Miller and J. Lane Miller, *Harper's Bible Dictionary,* 7th ed. (New York: Harper & Brothers, 1961), 99–100.

4. Leith, "Israel Among the Nations," 387–88.

5. Ibid., 391–93; Miller and Miller, *Harper's Bible Dictionary,* 839.

6. See *Funk and Wagnalls,* 252–55.

7. Leith, "Israel Among the Nations," 368.

8. Shaye J. D. Cohen, *From the Maccabees to the Mishnah,* Library of Early Christianity 7, ed. Wayne A. Meeks (Philadelphia: Westminster Press, 1987), 21–24.

9. Miller and Miller, *Harper's Bible Dictionary,* 630.

10. My account of the nature and purpose of the Book of Esther, in this paragraph and the next, is based on that offered in Miller and Miller, *Harper's Bible Dictionary,* 174.

11. The material on Alexander the Great, in this paragraph and the next, is drawn from Boadt, *Reading the Old Testament,* 492–96; Peter Green, *Alexander of Macedon, 356–323 B.C.: A Historical Biography* (Berkeley: University of California Press, 1991).

12. My account of the Ptolemies and Seleucids, in this paragraph and the three that follow, is a summary of that given by Leonard J. Greenspoon. See his essay, "Between Alexandria and Antioch: Jews and Judaism in the Hellenistic Period," in *Oxford History of the Biblical World*, ed. Michael D. Coogan (New York: Oxford University Press, 1998), 424–39.

13. On apocalyptic literature in general, and on the Book of Daniel in particular, see Boadt, *Reading the Old Testament*, 506–15; Louis F. Hartman, CSSR, and Alexander A. Di Lella, OFM, "Daniel," in *New Jerome Biblical Commentary*, ed. Raymond E. Brown, SS, Joseph A. Fitzmyer, SJ, and Roland E. Murphy, OCarm (Englewood Cliffs, NJ: Prentice Hall, 1990), 406–20.

14. Hartman and Di Lella, "Daniel," 408; Miller and Miller, *Harper's Bible Dictionary*, 126–27.

CHAPTER 9. LATE SECOND TEMPLE JUDAISM

1. Material on the Hasmonaeans, in this paragraph and the next, is a summary of that given by Leonard J. Greenspoon. See his essay, "Between Alexandria and Antioch: Jews and Judaism in the Hellenistic Period," in *Oxford History of the Biblical World*, ed. Michael D. Coogan (New York: Oxford University Press, 1998), 439–50. See also Lawrence Boadt, *Reading the Old Testament: An Introduction* (New York/Mahwah, NJ: Paulist Press, 1984), 504–5; Madeleine S. Miller and J. Lane Miller, *Harper's Bible Dictionary*, 7th ed. (New York: Harper & Brothers, 1961), 406–8; James VanderKam, *The Dead Sea Scrolls Today* (Grand Rapids, MI: Eerdmans, 1994), 101–3; Geza Vermes, *The Complete Dead Sea Scrolls in English* (New York: Penguin, 1997), 50–53.

2. Amy-Jill Levine, "Visions of Kingdoms: From Pompey to the First Jewish Revolt," in *Oxford History of the Biblical World*, ed. Michael D. Coogan (New York: Oxford University Press, 1998), 467–70.

3. My survey of the Roman Empire and the Hasmonaean Dynasty, in this paragraph and the six that follow, is a summary of Levine, "Visions of Kingdoms," 467–72. See also Marcel Le

Glay, Jean-Louis Voisin, and Yann Le Bohec, *A History of Rome* (Oxford: Blackwell, 1996), 125–259.

4. Levine, "Visions of Kingdoms," 498.

5. Pheme Perkins, *Reading the New Testament,* 2nd ed. (New York/Mahwah, NJ: Paulist Press, 1988), 29.

6. Levine, "Visions of Kingdoms," 472–74.

7. Ibid., 477–78; Vermes, *The Complete Dead Sea Scrolls,* 53.

8. Levine, "Visions of Kingdoms," 503–6.

9. The material that follows—on the various Jewish sects of the Second Temple period—is an amalgam of material borrowed from a number of sources: Boadt, *Reading the Old Testament,* 521–27; Shaye J. D. Cohen, *From the Maccabees to the Mishnah,* Library of Early Christianity 7, ed. Wayne A. Meeks (Philadelphia: Westminster Press, 1987), 130–65; Greenspoon, "Between Alexandria and Antioch," 455–59; Levine, "Visions of Kingdoms," 484–89; Perkins, *Reading the New Testament,* 32–49; Lawrence Schiffman, *Reclaiming the Dead Sea Scrolls,* Anchor Bible Reference Library (New York: Doubleday, 1995), 65–81; VanderKam, *The Dead Sea Scrolls Today,* 72–149; James VanderKam and Peter Flint, *The Meaning of the Dead Sea Scrolls* (San Francisco: Harper Collins, 2002), 239–51; Vermes, *The Complete Dead Sea Scrolls,* 18–78.

10. Cohen, *From the Maccabees to the Mishnah,* 154–59, 219.

11. Ibid., 159–61.

12. VanderKam, *The Dead Sea Scrolls Today,* 79–81.

13. Schiffman's translation, *Reclaiming the Dead Sea Scrolls,* 85.

14. Ibid., 83–95.

15. VanderKam, *The Dead Sea Scrolls Today,* 94–97.

16. Levine, "Visions of Kingdoms," 503–4. The quotation of Josephus is from *The Jewish War,* ii, 427.

17. See Yigael Yadin, *Masada: Herod's Fortress and the Zealots' Last Stand* (New York: Welcome Rain, 1998), 193–201.

CHAPTER 10. JESUS OF NAZARETH

1. Dermot A. Lane, *The Reality of Jesus: An Essay in Christology* (New York/Mahwah, NJ: Paulist Press, 1975), 10–12.

2. Luke Timothy Johnson, *The Real Jesus* (San Francisco: Harper Collins, 1996), 134.

3. Ibid., 82.

4. E. P. Sanders, *The Historical Figure of Jesus* (New York: Penguin, 1993), 97.

5. Johnson, *The Real Jesus,* 142–43.

6. Thomas P. Rausch, SJ, *Who Is Jesus? An Introduction to Christology* (Collegeville, MN: Michael Glazier/Liturgical Press, 2003), 5–6, 12.

7. My treatment of references to Jesus in the work of Josephus, including the quotations from the *Antiquities,* is drawn from John P. Meier, *A Marginal Jew: Rethinking the Historical Jesus,* vol. 1, Anchor Bible Reference Library (New York: Doubleday, 1991), 56–88.

8. Quoted in F. F. Bruce, *New Testament History* (Garden City, NY: Doubleday & Company, 1980), 164.

9. Ibid., 165.

10. Lane, *The Reality of Jesus,* 23–25.

11. My list of authenticating criteria is a composite of those found in Daniel J. Harrington, SJ, *Interpreting the New Testament: A Practical Guide,* New Testament Message, vol. 1 (Wilmington, DE: Michael Glazier, 1979), 88–89; Lane, *The Reality of Jesus,* 29; Rausch, *Who Is Jesus?,* 36–38.

12. Sanders, *The Historical Figure of Jesus,* 263.

13. Johnson, *The Real Jesus,* 117.

14. Sanders, *The Historical Figure of Jesus,* 218–23.

15. My sketch of the life of the historical Jesus incorporates material from Bruce, *New Testament History;* Lane, *The Reality of Jesus;* John P. Meier, "Jesus," in *New Jerome Biblical Commentary,* ed. Raymond E. Brown, SS, Joseph A. Fitzmyer, SJ, and Roland E. Murphy, OCarm (Englewood Cliffs, NJ: Prentice Hall, 1990), 1316–28; Meier, *A Marginal Jew;* Pheme Perkins, *Reading the New Testament,* 2nd ed. (New York/Mahwah, NJ: Paulist Press, 1988); Rausch, *Who Is Jesus?;* Sanders, *The Historical Figure of Jesus.*

16. Rausch, *Who Is Jesus?*, 71–72.

17. Johnson, *The Real Jesus*, 158; see also Sanders, *The Historical Figure of Jesus*, 202–3, 231–33.

18. Rausch, *Who Is Jesus?*, 67–68.

19. Johnson, *The Real Jesus*, 124; Rausch, *Who Is Jesus?*, 97–98; Sanders, *The Historical Figure of Jesus*, 67–68, 257–62.

20. My discussion of the title *mashiah* is based on those found in Bruce, *New Testament History*, 121–31; Madeleine S. Miller and J. Lane Miller, *Harper's Bible Dictionary*, 7th ed. (New York: Harper & Brothers, 1961), 439–41; Perkins, *Reading the New Testament*, 101–3.

21. My discussion of the title Son of God is adapted from Sanders, *The Historical Figure of Jesus*, 161–62, 244.

22. My discussion of the title Son of Man is based on those found in Bruce, *New Testament History*, 131–34, 173–77; Miller and Miller, *Harper's Bible Dictionary*, 697; Perkins, *Reading the New Testament*, 103–5; Sanders, *The Historical Figure of Jesus*, 246–47.

CHAPTER 11. THE GOSPELS

1. Christian E. Hauer and William A. Young, *An Introduction to the Bible: A Journey into Three Worlds*, 5th ed. (Upper Saddle River, NJ: Prentice Hall, 2001), 265.

2. The material presented here on the Synoptic problem and the Four Source Hypothesis is drawn from Hauer and Young, *Introduction to the Bible*, 265–67; Madeleine S. Miller and J. Lane Miller, *Harper's Bible Dictionary*, 7th ed. (New York: Harper & Brothers, 1961), 232–34, 343; Pheme Perkins, *Reading the New Testament*, 2nd ed. (New York/Mahwah, NJ: Paulist Press, 1988), 62–65.

3. Material on the Gospel of Mark is drawn from Daniel J. Harrington, SJ, "The Gospel According to Mark," in *New Jerome Biblical Commentary*, ed. Raymond E. Brown, SS, Joseph A. Fitzmyer, SJ, and Roland E. Murphy, OCarm (Englewood Cliffs, NJ: Prentice Hall, 1990), 596–629; Hauer and Young, *Introduction to the Bible*, 268–72, 285–86; Miller and Miller, *Harper's Bible Dictionary*, 418–21; Perkins, *Reading the New Testament*, 203–12.

4. Material on the Gospel of Matthew is drawn from Hauer and Young, *Introduction to the Bible*, 272–76, 286–87; Miller and Miller, *Harper's Bible Dictionary*, 427–29; Perkins, *Reading the New Testament*, 214–28; Benedict T. Viviano, OP, "The Gospel According to Matthew," in *New Jerome Biblical Commentary*, ed. Raymond E. Brown, SS, Joseph A. Fitzmyer, SJ, and Roland E. Murphy, OCarm (Englewood Cliffs, NJ: Prentice Hall, 1990), 630–74.

5. Material on the Gospel of Luke is drawn from Hauer and Young, *Introduction to the Bible*, 276–79, 287; Robert J. Karris, OFM, "The Gospel According to Luke," in *New Jerome Biblical Commentary*, ed. Raymond E. Brown, SS, Joseph A. Fitzmyer, SJ, and Roland E. Murphy, OCarm (Englewood Cliffs, NJ: Prentice Hall, 1990), 675–721; Miller and Miller, *Harper's Bible Dictionary*, 403–5; Perkins, *Reading the New Testament*, 229–40.

6. Material on the Gospel of John is drawn from Hauer and Young, *Introduction to the Bible*, 279–85; Miller and Miller, *Harper's Bible Dictionary*, 342–45; Pheme Perkins, "The Gospel According to John," in *New Jerome Biblical Commentary*, ed. Raymond E. Brown, SS, Joseph A. Fitzmyer, SJ, and Roland E. Murphy, OCarm (Englewood Cliffs, NJ: Prentice Hall, 1990), 942–85; Perkins, *Reading the New Testament*, 242–53; Thomas P. Rausch, SJ, *Who Is Jesus? An Introduction to Christology* (Collegeville, MN: Michael Glazier/Liturgical Press, 2003), 137–46.

7. Rausch, *Who Is Jesus?*, 143.

8. Dermot A. Lane, *The Reality of Jesus: An Essay in Christology* (New York/Mahwah, NJ: Paulist Press, 1975), 54–56.

CHAPTER 12. ACTS OF THE APOSTLES

1. Madeleine S. Miller and J. Lane Miller, *Harper's Bible Dictionary*, 7th ed. (New York: Harper & Brothers, 1961), 6.

2. Ibid., 6.

3. Material on kerygmatic and apologetic speeches is drawn from Miller and Miller, *Harper's Bible Dictionary*, 6; Pheme Perkins, *Reading the New Testament*, 2nd ed. (New York/Mahwah, NJ: Paulist Press, 1988), 259–60.

4. Christian E. Hauer and William A. Young, *An Introduction to the Bible: A Journey into Three Worlds*, 5th ed. (Upper Saddle River, NJ: Prentice Hall, 2001), 304–5; Perkins, *Reading the New Testament*, 68–70; E. P. Sanders, *The Historical Figure of Jesus* (New York: Penguin, 1993), 277.

5. F. F. Bruce, *New Testament History* (Garden City, NY: Doubleday & Company, 1980), 213, 231–32.

6. Material in this paragraph and the two following—on the Hellenists and Hebrews, and on the first persecution of Christians in Jerusalem—is drawn from Bruce, *New Testament History*, 217–33.

7. Material on the Jerusalem Conference, in this paragraph and the two following, is drawn from Bruce, *New Testament History*, 279–90.

CHAPTER 13. THE PAULINE EPISTLES

1. F. F. Bruce, *New Testament History* (Garden City, NY: Doubleday & Company, 1980), 235–36.

2. Ibid., 236–38.

3. See Christian E. Hauer and William A. Young, *An Introduction to the Bible: A Journey into Three Worlds*, 5th ed. (Upper Saddle River, NJ: Prentice Hall, 2001), 318–20; Pheme Perkins, *Reading the New Testament*, 2nd ed. (New York/Mahwah, NJ: Paulist Press, 1988), 142–47.

4. E. P. Sanders, *The Historical Figure of Jesus* (New York: Penguin, 1993), 94–95.

5. The reconstruction presented here is that defended by Victor Paul Furnish in his book *II Corinthians*, Anchor Bible 32A (New York: Doubleday, 1984), 22–57, 152–69, 371–83.

6. Madeleine S. Miller and J. Lane Miller, *Harper's Bible Dictionary*, 7th ed. (New York: Harper & Brothers, 1961), 549–50.

7. Ibid., 550.

8. The material on Philemon presented here is drawn primarily from Joseph A. Fitzmyer, SJ, *The Letter to Philemon*, Anchor Bible 34C (New York: Doubleday, 2000), 7–24.

9. Bruce, *New Testament History*, 297–99; Daniel N. Schowalter, "Churches in Context: The Jesus Movement in the

Roman World," in *Oxford History of the Biblical World*, ed. Michael D. Coogan (New York: Oxford University Press, 1998), 531–34. The passage from Suetonius is quoted in Bruce, *New Testament History*, 297.

10. See Hauer and Young, *Introduction to the Bible*, 333–34; Miller and Miller, *Harper's Bible Dictionary*, 166–67.

11. Most of the material in this paragraph is borrowed from Maurya P. Horgan, "The Letter to the Colossians," in *New Jerome Biblical Commentary*, ed. Raymond E. Brown, SS, Joseph A. Fitzmyer, SJ, and Roland E. Murphy, OCarm (Englewood Cliffs, NJ: Prentice Hall, 1990), 876–77.

12. Material on the pastoral epistles is drawn primarily from Luke Timothy Johnson, *Letters to Paul's Delegates: 1 Timothy, 2 Timothy, Titus*, The New Testament in Context (Valley Forge, PA: Trinity Press, 1996), 1–36, 141–49; Perkins, *Reading the New Testament*, 281–91; Robert A. Wild, SJ, "The Pastoral Letters," in *New Jerome Biblical Commentary*, ed. Raymond E. Brown, SS, Joseph A. Fitzmyer, SJ, and Roland E. Murphy, OCarm (Englewood Cliffs, NJ: Prentice Hall, 1990), 891–93.

CHAPTER 14. EPISTLES AND REVELATION

1. Pheme Perkins, *Reading the New Testament*, 2nd ed. (New York/Mahwah, NJ: Paulist Press, 1988), 272–74.

2. Myles M. Bourke, "The Epistle to the Hebrews," in *New Jerome Biblical Commentary*, ed. Raymond E. Brown, SS, Joseph A. Fitzmyer, SJ, and Roland E. Murphy, OCarm (Englewood Cliffs, NJ: Prentice Hall, 1990), 931–32.

3. Madeleine S. Miller and J. Lane Miller, *Harper's Bible Dictionary*, 7th ed. (New York: Harper & Brothers, 1961), 543.

4. Thomas W. Leahy, SJ, "The Epistle of James," in *New Jerome Biblical Commentary*, ed. Raymond E. Brown, SS, Joseph A. Fitzmyer, SJ, and Roland E. Murphy, OCarm (Englewood Cliffs, NJ: Prentice Hall, 1990), 909–10; Miller and Miller, *Harper's Bible Dictionary*, 301–2.

5. Miller and Miller, *Harper's Bible Dictionary*, 358–59.

6. Ibid., 543–44; Perkins, *Reading the New Testament*, 299–302.

7. F. F. Bruce, *New Testament History* (Garden City, NY: Doubleday & Company, 1980), 416.

8. Ibid., 412.

9. Material on the imperial cult and its relevance to the Book of Revelation, in this paragraph and the one that follows, is drawn from Daniel N. Schowalter, "Churches in Context: The Jesus Movement in the Roman World," in *Oxford History of the Biblical World*, ed. Michael D. Coogan (New York: Oxford University Press, 1998), 522–49.

10. Christian E. Hauer and William A. Young, *An Introduction to the Bible: A Journey into Three Worlds*, 5th ed. (Upper Saddle River, NJ: Prentice Hall, 2001), 355–56.

11. Schowalter, "Churches in Context," 547.

12. Perkins, *Reading the New Testament*, 324–25.

13. See Miller and Miller, *Harper's Bible Dictionary*, 434–35.

Bibliography

Baird, William. *History of New Testament Research, Volume One: From Deism to Tübingen.* Minneapolis: Fortress Press, 1992.

Boadt, Lawrence. *Reading the Old Testament: An Introduction.* New York/Mahwah, NJ: Paulist Press, 1984.

Bourke, Myles M. "The Epistle to the Hebrews." In *New Jerome Biblical Commentary,* edited by Raymond E. Brown, SS, Joseph A. Fitzmyer, SJ, and Roland E. Murphy, OCarm, 920–41. Englewood Cliffs, NJ: Prentice Hall, 1990.

Brown, Raymond E., SS, and Raymond F. Collins. "Canonicity." In *New Jerome Biblical Commentary,* edited by Raymond E. Brown, SS, Joseph A. Fitzmyer, SJ, and Roland E. Murphy, OCarm, 1034–54. Englewood Cliffs, NJ: Prentice Hall, 1990.

Brown, Raymond E., SS, Pheme Perkins, and Anthony J. Saldarini. "Apocrypha; Dead Sea Scrolls; Other Jewish Literature." In *New Jerome Biblical Commentary,* edited by Raymond E. Brown, SS, Joseph A. Fitzmyer, SJ, and Roland E. Murphy, OCarm, 1055–82. Englewood Cliffs, NJ: Prentice Hall, 1990.

Brown, Raymond E., SS, and Sandra M. Schneiders, IHM. "Hermeneutics." In *New Jerome Biblical Commentary,* edited by Raymond E. Brown, SS, Joseph A. Fitzmyer, SJ, and Roland E. Murphy, OCarm, 1146–65. Englewood Cliffs, NJ: Prentice Hall, 1990.

Bruce, F. F. *New Testament History.* Garden City, NY: Doubleday & Company, 1980.

Burn, A. R. *The Penguin History of Greece.* London: Penguin Books, 1990.

Campbell, Edward F., Jr. "A Land Divided: Judah and Israel from the Death of Solomon to the Fall of Samaria." In *Oxford*

History of the Biblical World, edited by Michael D. Coogan, 273–320. New York: Oxford University Press, 1998.

Charlesworth, James H., ed. *Old Testament Pseudepigrapha.* 2 vols. New York: Doubleday, 1983.

Cody, Aelred. "Haggai, Zechariah, Malachi." In *New Jerome Biblical Commentary,* edited by Raymond E. Brown, SS, Joseph A. Fitzmyer, SJ, and Roland E. Murphy, OCarm, 349–61. Englewood Cliffs, NJ: Prentice Hall, 1990.

Cogan, Mordechai. "Into Exile: From the Assyrian Conquest of Israel to the Fall of Babylon." In *Oxford History of the Biblical World,* edited by Michael D. Coogan, 321–66. New York: Oxford University Press, 1998.

Cohen, Shaye J. D. *From the Maccabees to the Mishnah.* Library of Early Christianity 7. Edited by Wayne A. Meeks. Philadelphia: Westminster Press, 1987.

Coogan, Michael D. "In the Beginning: The Earliest History." In *Oxford History of the Biblical World,* edited by Michael D. Coogan, 3–32. New York: Oxford University Press, 1998.

Fitzmyer, Joseph A., SJ. *The Letter to Philemon.* Anchor Bible 34C. New York: Doubleday, 2000.

Flew, Antony. *Dictionary of Philosophy.* 2nd ed. New York: St. Martin's Press, 1984.

Fredriksen, Paula. *Jesus of Nazareth, King of the Jews.* New York: Vintage Books, 1999.

Funk and Wagnalls New Standard Bible Dictionary. 3rd ed. Edited by Malancthon W. Jacobus, DD, Elbert C. Lane, DD, and Andrew C. Zenos, DD, LLD. Philadelphia: Blakiston, 1936.

Furnish, Victor Paul. *II Corinthians.* Anchor Bible 32A. New York: Doubleday, 1984.

Goelet, Ogden. "Moses' Egyptian Name." *Bible Review* 19:3 (2003): 12–17, 50–51.

Green, Peter. *Alexander of Macedon, 356–323 B.C.: A Historical Biography.* Berkeley: University of California Press, 1991.

Greenspoon, Leonard J. "Between Alexandria and Antioch: Jews and Judaism in the Hellenistic Period." In *Oxford History of the Biblical World,* edited by Michael D. Coogan, 421–66. New York: Oxford University Press, 1998.

Hackett, Jo Ann. "'There Was No King In Israel': The Era of the

Judges." In *Oxford History of the Biblical World,* edited by Michael D. Coogan, 177–220. New York: Oxford University Press, 1998.

Harrington, Daniel J., SJ. "The Gospel According to Mark." In *New Jerome Biblical Commentary,* edited by Raymond E. Brown, SS, Joseph A. Fitzmyer, SJ, and Roland E. Murphy, OCarm, 596–629. Englewood Cliffs, NJ: Prentice Hall, 1990.

———. *Interpreting the New Testament: A Practical Guide.* New Testament Message, vol. 1. Wilmington, DE: Michael Glazier, 1979.

Hartman, Louis F., CSSR, and Alexander A. Di Lella, OFM. "Daniel." In *New Jerome Biblical Commentary,* edited by Raymond E. Brown, SS, Joseph A. Fitzmyer, SJ, and Roland E. Murphy, OCarm, 406–20. Englewood Cliffs, NJ: Prentice Hall, 1990.

Hauer, Christian E., and William A. Young. *An Introduction to the Bible: A Journey into Three Worlds.* 5th ed. Upper Saddle River, NJ: Prentice Hall, 2001.

Horgan, Maurya P. "The Letter to the Colossians." In *New Jerome Biblical Commentary,* edited by Raymond E. Brown, SS, Joseph A. Fitzmyer, SJ, and Roland E. Murphy, OCarm, 876–82. Englewood Cliffs, NJ: Prentice Hall, 1990.

Isserlin, B. S. J. *The Israelites.* Minneapolis: Fortress Press, 2001.

Jacobs, Louis. *A Concise Companion to the Jewish Religion.* Oxford: Oxford University Press, 1999.

Johnson, Luke Timothy. *Letters to Paul's Delegates: 1 Timothy, 2 Timothy, Titus.* The New Testament in Context. Valley Forge, PA: Trinity Press, 1996.

———. *The Real Jesus.* San Francisco: Harper Collins, 1996.

Josephus, Flavius. *Complete Works.* Translated by William Whiston. Grand Rapids, MI: Kregel, 1973.

Karris, Robert J., OFM. "The Gospel According to Luke." In *New Jerome Biblical Commentary,* edited by Raymond E. Brown, SS, Joseph A. Fitzmyer, SJ, and Roland E. Murphy, OCarm, 675–721. Englewood Cliffs, NJ: Prentice Hall, 1990.

Kselman, John S., SS, and Ronald D. Witherup, SS. "Modern New Testament Criticism." In *New Jerome Biblical Commentary,* edited by Raymond E. Brown, SS, Joseph A. Fitzmyer, SJ, and

Roland E. Murphy, OCarm, 1130–45. Englewood Cliffs, NJ: Prentice Hall, 1990.

Lane, Dermot A. *The Reality of Jesus: An Essay in Christology*. New York/Mahwah, NJ: Paulist Press, 1975.

Le Glay, Marcel, Jean-Louis Voisin, and Yann Le Bohec. *A History of Rome*. Oxford: Blackwell, 1996.

Leahy, Thomas W., SJ. "The Epistle of James." In *New Jerome Biblical Commentary*, edited by Raymond E. Brown, SS, Joseph A. Fitzmyer, SJ, and Roland E. Murphy, OCarm, 909–16. Englewood Cliffs, NJ: Prentice Hall, 1990.

Leith, Mary Joan Winn. "Israel among the Nations: The Persian Period." In *Oxford History of the Biblical World*, edited by Michael D. Coogan, 367–420. New York: Oxford University Press, 1998.

Levine, Amy-Jill. "Visions of Kingdoms: From Pompey to the First Jewish Revolt." In *Oxford History of the Biblical World*, edited by Michael D. Coogan, 467–516. New York: Oxford University Press, 1998.

Matthews, Victor H., and Don C. Benjamin. *Old Testament Parallels: Laws and Stories from the Ancient Near East*. 2nd ed. New York/Mahwah, NJ: Paulist Press, 1997.

May, Herbert G., ed. *Oxford Bible Atlas*. 3rd ed. New York: Oxford University Press, 1984.

McDermott, John J. *What Are They Saying About the Formation of Israel?* New York/Mahwah, NJ: Paulist Press, 1998.

McKenzie, Steven L. *King David: A Biography*. New York: Oxford University Press, 2000.

Meier, John P. "Jesus." In *New Jerome Biblical Commentary*, edited by Raymond E. Brown, SS, Joseph A. Fitzmyer, SJ, and Roland E. Murphy, OCarm, 1316–28. Englewood Cliffs, NJ: Prentice Hall, 1990.

———. *A Marginal Jew: Rethinking the Historical Jesus*. 3 vols. Anchor Bible Reference Library. New York: Doubleday, 1991.

Metzger, Bruce M., and Michael D. Coogan, ed. *Oxford Companion to the Bible*. Oxford: Oxford University Press, 1993.

Meyers, Carol. "Kinship and Kingship: The Early Monarchy." In *Oxford History of the Biblical World*, edited by Michael D. Coogan, 221–72. New York: Oxford University Press, 1998.

Miller, Madeleine S., and J. Lane Miller. *Harper's Bible Dictionary.* 7th ed. New York: Harper & Brothers, 1961.

Morgan, Robert, and John Barton. *Biblical Interpretation.* Oxford: Oxford University Press, 1988.

New Oxford Annotated Bible with the Apocrypha, Revised Standard Version. New York: Oxford University Press, 1977.

New Revised Standard Version Bible. New York: Oxford University Press, 1989.

Oates, Joan. *Babylon.* Revised edition. Ancient Peoples and Places. New York: Thames and Hudson, 1986.

Perkins, Pheme. "The Gospel According to John." In *New Jerome Biblical Commentary,* edited by Raymond E. Brown, SS, Joseph A. Fitzmyer, SJ, and Roland E. Murphy, OCarm, 942–85. Englewood Cliffs, NJ: Prentice Hall, 1990.

———. *Reading the New Testament.* 2nd ed. New York/Mahwah, NJ: Paulist Press, 1988.

Pitard, Wayne T. "Before Israel: Syria-Palestine in the Bronze Age." In *Oxford History of the Biblical World,* edited by Michael D. Coogan, 33–78. New York: Oxford University Press, 1998.

Rahner, Karl, and Herbert Vorgrimler. *Dictionary of Theology.* 2nd ed. New York: Crossroad Press, 1988.

Rausch, Thomas P., SJ. *Who Is Jesus? An Introduction to Christology.* Collegeville, MN: Michael Glazier/Liturgical Press, 2003.

Redmount, Carol A. "Bitter Lives: Israel in and out of Egypt." In *Oxford History of the Biblical World,* edited by Michael D. Coogan, 79–122. New York: Oxford University Press, 1998.

Sanders, E. P. *The Historical Figure of Jesus.* New York: Penguin, 1993.

Schiffman, Lawrence. *Reclaiming the Dead Sea Scrolls.* Anchor Bible Reference Library. New York: Doubleday, 1995.

Schowalter, Daniel N. "Churches in Context: The Jesus Movement in the Roman World." In *Oxford History of the Biblical World,* edited by Michael D. Coogan, 517–60. New York: Oxford University Press, 1998.

Soulen, Richard N., and R. Kendall Soulen. *Handbook of Biblical Criticism.* 3rd ed. Louisville, KY: Westminster John Knox Press, 2001.

Stager, Lawrence E. "Forging an Identity: The Emergence of Ancient Israel." In *Oxford History of the Biblical World,* edited by Michael D. Coogan, 123–76. New York: Oxford University Press, 1998.

Suelzer, Alexa, SP, and John Kselman, SS. "Modern Old Testament Criticism." In *New Jerome Biblical Commentary*, edited by Raymond E. Brown, SS, Joseph A. Fitzmyer, SJ, and Roland E. Murphy, OCarm, 1113–29. Englewood Cliffs, NJ: Prentice Hall, 1990.

VanderKam, James. *The Dead Sea Scrolls Today.* Grand Rapids, MI: Eerdmans, 1994.

VanderKam, James, and Peter Flint. *The Meaning of the Dead Sea Scrolls.* San Francisco: Harper Collins, 2002.

Vermes, Geza. *The Complete Dead Sea Scrolls in English.* New York: Penguin, 1997.

Viviano, Benedict T., OP. "The Gospel According to Matthew." In *New Jerome Biblical Commentary*, edited by Raymond E. Brown, SS, Joseph A. Fitzmyer, SJ, and Roland E. Murphy, OCarm, 630–74. Englewood Cliffs, NJ: Prentice Hall, 1990.

Wild, Robert. A., SJ. "The Pastoral Letters." In *New Jerome Biblical Commentary*, edited by Raymond E. Brown, SS, Joseph A. Fitzmyer, SJ, and Roland E. Murphy, OCarm, 891–902. Englewood Cliffs, NJ: Prentice Hall, 1990.

Yadin, Yigael. *Masada: Herod's Fortress and the Zealots' Last Stand.* New York: Welcome Rain, 1998.

Younger, K. Lawson, Jr. "Israelites in Exile." *Biblical Archaeology Review* 29:6 (2003): 36–45, 65–66.

Index